THE VOYAGE OF *BARAKA A*

Mary Stephenson

MINERVA PRESS
MONTREUX LONDON WASHINGTON

THE VOYAGE OF *BARAKA A*

ISBN 1 86106 038 6

First published 1997 by
MINERVA PRESS
195 Knightsbridge
London SW7 1RE

Printed in Great Britain by
Antony Rowe Ltd, Chippenham, Wiltshire

THE VOYAGE OF *BARAKA A*

Dedicated to the memory of my daughter Karen
Always, my shining star.

When I wake up in the morning
And I see a new day dawning
And I see the sky above me
And I know somebody loves me
And I want to stand and shout
Tell the whole wide world about it
It's a wonderful thing to be me!

Karen – 1978

Acknowledgements

I would like to thank my 'research assistants', Matthew and Peter Mark Verwoerd, students at the Continental School in Jeddah, who photocopied copious amounts of material from the school library for me.

Also my husband Jim who made sure all my nautical terminology was correct.

And finally, Jameel and Sherry who shared their story with me

About the Author

Mary Stephenson lives in northern California with her husband Jim. During their thirty-five years of marriage they have travelled extensively and lived overseas numerous times.

The Voyage of Baraka A was written while they were on a two year assignment in Jeddah, Saudi Arabia.

Ms Stephenson's first book, *My Child is a Mother*, was published in America by Corona Press in 1990. She is currently working on a story about her experiences while living in the Peruvian Andes.

Foreword

After sailing around the world we settled back in Jeddah where Jameel opened a diving shop and recreation business while I sold artefacts from our home. We hoped to put our story down on paper but it turned out to be an impossible task to find a talented writer who also knew something about sailing and life at sea. Seven years passed and then one day, either by luck or destiny, we met Mary Stephenson. Jameel had agreed to be the featured speaker at the monthly meeting of the British Women's Club. Mary was in the audience. We learned that Mary and her husband Jim were avid and experienced sailors and owned a sloop which they had sailed around San Francisco Bay for the last twenty-five years. Our partnership was born.

Thanks to Mary, our unique and memorable voyage came to life over the next eighteen months. Writing this book helped us to relive our two years at sea. The power and beauty of nature, our determination to survive and the appreciation of simple things that life at sea offers are memories we will cherish for ever.

So many people helped us achieve our dream of being the first Arabs to circumnavigate the world. The professionals at Camper Nicholson in Gosport England who built our boat with so much care and precision, especially Jeremy Lines whose love and dedication to his work gave us a great feeling of confidence that *Baraka A* was being built for a long demanding voyage which would take us around the world and bring us back alive.

We will never forget Roy Mullender. Camper Nicholson, at Jameel's request, found an experienced skipper to help us learn how to manage the boat. Roy was an excellent teacher – patient, encouraging, charming and knowledgeable. He soon became our good friend. During one of my low points I remember him saying,

'Sherry, I've met a lot of women on boats before and you're good. You will make an excellent first mate. Of that I have no doubts. You just have to get used to it.' His confidence helped me take a second look at my capabilities of coping with life at sea.

The memories of the boats we met along the way will remain in our hearts for ever. *Mr John IV*, *Moline*, *Canada Goose*, *Socorro*, *Pasha*, *Couscous*, *Svanhild*, *Rosita*, *Crossbow*, and so many more. We all had the dream of discovering the world, and searching for its beauty. Saying farewell to our friends as we left an anchorage to set out across the ocean always made our hearts ache. We wished each other well and prayed we would survive to meet again at another anchorage.

I have always believed in God. My faith was fortified after this voyage. I still thank God for making this impossible task one of my greatest experiences in life so far. The memories are worth a lifetime. Like they say, 'an old day is a good day'. If I'm still alive when I'm eighty I will still have so many wonderful memories of our adventure in my mind.

I continue to thank God for our safe return. Although we did our best, there was such a thin line between life and death at all times. I know someone was watching over us. Thank you...

Chahrazad H. Zaky
September 15, 1995

'One crowded hour of glorious life is worth an age without a name.'

This is one of Sherry's favourite quotations which she uses many times throughout her journal. Whether she composed these words herself or they are the work of another author is not clear. In either case, it encapsulates Sherry's feelings both during and after the voyage.

Jameel parallels this with one of his well-used sayings:

> But do not hurry the journey at all. Better that it should last many years. Be quite old when you anchor at the island, rich with all you have gained on the way.
>
> by Ithaca Cavafy
> translated by John Mavrogordate

Contents

A Love Story

The winds caress the sails
With a soft kiss
Lovingly, tenderly,
A portent of things to be

The sails fill
Enclosing the wind
In a soft embrace
Of billowing whiteness

The helmsman grasps the tiller
Scanning the sky and horizon
Contemplates, appreciates
The ballet of wind and sail

Uninvited to participate
He acquiesces
Only the destination
Can be his decision

Mary Stephenson 1982

Chapter One

I stood in the cockpit of *Baraka A* and took a final look around Plymouth harbour which had been my home for more than a week. Overhead a watery moon poked through a leaden sky, bathing the jetty in a ghostly light. The pounding, unrelenting rain had degenerated into an intermittent drizzle. Even dressed in the prescribed layers of woollen sweaters, topped by a waterproof jacket, I still shivered. I was accustomed to the hot, sandy, desert climate of Saudi Arabia, not the rain and biting cold of autumn in southern England.

My wife Chahrazad, whom everyone calls Sherry, and my friend and mentor, Roy Mullender, stood on the jetty.

"It's bad luck you can't wait till morning," said Roy.

"The tide and the wind direction are as good as I'm going to get so I have to leave now. It might be days before I get another chance," I replied.

'Besides,' I thought, 'I don't want to linger around these cold, storm-plagued waters a moment longer than necessary, not with the warm south Atlantic breezes beckoning me.'

Sherry's voice broke into my thoughts.

"Please Jameel, don't go. I am frightened. It is so far to Casablanca."

I knew Sherry was terrified about my setting off alone and, if the truth be known, the thought of sailing single-handed to Casablanca, Morocco, was causing my gut to cramp with fear. I guessed that was a normal reaction since this would be my first attempt at sailing the boat alone – all alone with no Roy on board to help me figure out what to do. But, I kept reminding myself, a little healthy fear was good. It would keep me alert and focused on the job ahead unlike the unhealthy kind which would immobilize me.

My apprehensions had a special twist. It was the fear that I might *fail* which haunted me. Physical challenges and the mental ones too would test my confidence and spirit. How would I cope? "By staying on top of things and keeping a cool head," was the stock answer I gave to anyone who asked. It was only when I talked to myself that I found that too familiar phrase, 'easier said than done', creeping into my thoughts. Maybe so, I reasoned, but if a circumnavigation were 'easy', then I wouldn't be attempting it.

Sherry tugged at my sleeve dragging me back to the present.

"Please Jameel, don't forget these," she said, handing me a paper sack. "I bought you some special treats for the trip."

I smiled, hoping that I would find raisins, nuts and dates and perhaps a chocolate bar or two inside. Sherry knew all my weaknesses, especially the sweets I so enjoyed at home in the evening while watching TV or reading. Now my evening hours would be devoted to watching the horizon for freighters and searching out the constellations.

I grasped the tiller in my right hand and felt *Baraka A* straining against her mooring lines. Like a horse at the starting gate, she was eager to go. And so was I. Casablanca, the jumping-off point for the sail around the world was, according to my calculations, an eight day sail away. Sherry would meet me there and I hoped she would change her mind so that 'my trip' would again become 'our trip'.

What had happened to our carefully conceived plans? When Roy and Sherry and I sat down to plot our course for the maiden voyage of *Baraka A*, it had made so much sense. The natural starting point was Gosport on the south coast of England. That was where *Baraka A* had been built, commissioned and launched, at the Camper Nicholson boat yard. Our destination was Falmouth which lies at the south-western tip of England, the bit that juts out into the Atlantic Ocean like a dog's hind leg. A logical place, we thought, to start the next part of our voyage which would take us to Casablanca, Morocco and the true beginning of the circumnavigation. There Roy would leave us and return home. Sherry and I would head off alone to the Canaries, then cross the Atlantic to the Caribbean.

Again Sherry's voice sliced through the thoughts churning around in my head.

"I'm really sorry I can't go with you, Jameel. I'm just too scared. If the trip to Falmouth had gone like we expected, if..." Her voice faltered as she scuffed her shoe across the rough planks of the jetty.

"It's okay, Sherry, I understand. We'll talk about it again in Casablanca."

We'd had variations of this same conversation during the long week in Plymouth harbour. And we always came back to the same thing. Sherry's questions were perfectly reasonable. Why, she wondered, had we ever left Gosport knowing that a low pressure system was moving in? Hadn't the angry dark clouds banked along the horizon like slate shingles on a roof been evidence enough?

To begin with, Roy and I had to admit that we hadn't paid enough attention to the clouds or the weather reports. Overhead the sky seemed clear enough, just a few trailing wisps which decorated the overcast sky like a child's scribblings on a sheet of grey construction paper.

And there were good, even compelling reasons for us to leave when we did. In the first place, how could we *not* leave with throngs of people on the jetty wishing us good luck and waving goodbye? People like our friends from Camper Nicholson, most especially Jeremy and Claire Lines. Jeremy was a marine architect by profession and wore many hats as 'the man in charge' at the boatyard. He and Claire had extended the hand of friendship to us while the boat was being built, even making arrangements for us to live in the chairman's house so that we could be close to the boatyard. And they had found Roy Mullender to teach me all the things I didn't know about sailing, which was a task bigger than anyone imagined.

Even our son Essam had managed to take a few days off from boarding school to come and wish us farewell. Accompanying him were Ghada Alireza (who is the wife of my cousin Fahad Zahid) and her mother and grandmother. But of the immediate family, only my son. Being there to say goodbye would indicate the stamp of approval, something my family was not prepared to give.

Jock was there too, the man who had become our personal chauffeur, friend and confidante during our six months in Gosport. His taxi had become a familiar sight as he came to fetch us in the morning and bring us home after our daily shopping expeditions. Our long lists of things to do and things to buy seemed endless, as was Jock's patience as he transported us from one place to the next: the marine supply stores, the supermarket and the Southampton Boat Show.

On our departure day, he'd presented Sherry with a bon voyage present, a picture of a schooner under sail which we hung in the cabin.

Two reporters from the local newspapers were there to record our departure. Now if we *didn't* leave as scheduled, that would make really interesting reading. Not likely but, even so, I could imagine the lead headline 'Arab Couple Chickens Out of Circumnavigation in Face of Possible Low Pressure System'.

Sherry had insisted that these reasons were nothing more than flimsy excuses.

"You're right," I'd admitted. "I guess that it all comes back to me and Roy. We were eager and very determined to get going. A few clouds weren't going to stop us."

Another factor was time, the enemy of all sailors, which was snapping at my heels. There is an order to the seasons at sea which sets the timetables only rarely left to the whim of the man at the helm, but dictated by the weather seasons which sweep the globe with a schedule as predictable as the tides. We were precariously close to 'gale season' in the English Channel and the North Atlantic, which was definitely not prime time. We had to reach Antigua by the beginning of the New Year so that the rest of our voyage would fall into place, allowing us to miss the typhoons in the Pacific and the monsoons in the Indian Ocean. The sooner we got away the better.

Also, Roy's schedule did not permit him much leeway. We had counted on a three day sail from Gosport to Falmouth. Then we estimated that the voyage from Falmouth to Casablanca should take seven or eight days. There Roy would catch a plane back to England to teach a course in celestial navigation. So, even though the weather forecasters had predicted an approaching weather front, we thought that we could beat it by leaving promptly.

It had almost come down to leaving now or waiting till spring, a plan I was not prepared to accept. And so we had set sail with chase boats from Camper Nicholson following close enough behind us to get some good footage on video. There was, however, no video footage of the next three days at sea. Roy and I were too busy to take pictures; Sherry was too scared.

As we sailed out of Gosport on October 18 we had been optimistic in spite of the pessimistic weather forecast. Even with the grey skies looming above us, the sea seemed in a friendly mood as we sailed out of the Solent, past the Isle of Wight, heading for Needles' Point. When we cleared the point, about mid-afternoon, the seas had started to kick up a little; nothing serious, we thought as we ate the lunch that Sherry had prepared. By nightfall the seas were definitely lumpy. With the wind behind us and sullen swells chasing our stern. Roy and I fought the tiller to keep the boat on course. Falling off and rounding up in a seemingly never-ending cycle slowed our forward progress so that the projected three day voyage to Falmouth was sure to take four or five.

By the morning of Saturday October 19, we knew that we were in for it as the winds picked up to Force 7, approaching gale force. Neither Roy nor I were as alert as the weather conditions demanded, having spent most of the night together on watch. Looking down into the cabin, all I could see were flying objects: pans, books, papers – anything that was not tied down was airborne. Somehow Sherry managed to fix us sandwiches and coffee and down her seasick pills before crawling back into her bunk.

"I better check on Sherry," I told Roy. "She hasn't done much sailing and..." My voice trailed off. I hadn't done much sailing either and if Sherry was feeling what I was feeling, then I knew she was scared. The boat heeled sharply as I started down the companionway. By grabbing on to the hand rails I was able to make it safely to her bunk on the port side.

Sherry lifted her head at my approach.

"I'm staying right here. If we sink, at least I'll be warm in my sleeping bag until the last possible moment," she muttered.

I gave her shoulder a squeeze.

"Don't worry. This storm will blow over and everything will be fine."

Sherry groaned and pulled the sleeping bag over her head. No string of soothing words was going to convince my wife that sailing was anything but a nightmare.

As the weather conditions deteriorated, I began to think about finding a safe harbour even though I realised that this rough weather sailing could give me some invaluable experience. But on the other side of the scale was Sherry who was frightened and miserable. Sherry's comfort came first.

Where should we put in? Was it a stroke of bad luck or bad planning that neither Roy nor I had purchased charts for harbours other than our destination, Falmouth?

"I know Plymouth harbour well enough to find my way without charts," said Roy.

After changing course, we put another reef in the main. Even with the reduced sail area and a slower speed, *Baraka A* pitched and rolled and slammed into the waves making for another miserable night at sea. Sherry did not even try to fix us a meal. In the end we ate from tins with a spoon: cold unappetising fare which did little to lift our spirits.

By Sunday it had become clear that my promises to Sherry about the storm blowing over would not materialise. This storm was not going to go away. In fact it was getting steadily worse, with gale force winds screaming through the rigging.

"Force 8, I'm guessing," said Roy as he stood in his oilskins in the cockpit. A wave of cold salt water crashed over the bow, hitting him full in the face. "Might get worse, according to the weather reports."

There was nothing to do but hang on and head for Plymouth. Why hadn't I purchased charts for Dover coast? With the proper charts, we would have run for cover earlier and would now be snug in some harbour. 'Why buy charts I will never need?' I had reasoned as we set off from Gosport. Was my monetary restraint about to have repercussions I didn't even want to think about? I made a firm resolve never to pinch pennies in that department again. Sailors simply must have contingency charts for contingency plans. When you sail from A to B sometimes you end up at D and you better be prepared.

Roy stood in the cockpit, his face haggard as he clutched the tiller.

"There's a part of me that hates to admit we're giving up," I said. "If we were in the middle of the ocean we'd have to ride this out."

Roy nodded.

"In the middle of the ocean you have no choice as you will no doubt discover. Here we do. You've made the right decision, especially for Sherry. In the teeth of a gale, a smart sailor heads for port. Too bad Plymouth is still a way off."

I could only nod in agreement.

It wasn't until 6 p.m. on October 20 that we finally pulled into Sutton Marina, only to be told that there was no space for us. At nearby Mayflower Marina the reception was warm and friendly. Even before we had finished securing the lines, Sherry was out of the cockpit and on to the jetty.

"I need a hot shower, a meal that doesn't come out of a tin and a warm bed which stays level," she announced. "And I don't want to go sailing ever again!"

Sherry and I checked into the Grant Hotel, overlooking the harbour, while Roy bunked down on *Baraka A*, where he said he was beautifully cosy thanks to the butane heater. We would wait for the weather to clear. Then Roy and I would set out for Casablanca and Sherry would fly back to Cairo.

I really could not blame Sherry for jumping ship. Our maiden voyage from Gosport had left us shell-shocked and dispirited. I had pictured moonlit nights and gently rolling seas with my arm resting gently on the tiller. We would search the skies for familiar constellations while sipping small cups of strong Turkish coffee.

Instead we had endured three days of pitching seas, howling winds and the cold, cold sea surging over the bow, sending gallons of icy water into the cockpit.

Day after day we waited patiently in Plymouth harbour looking for some sign of a break in the weather. Instead the pelting rain and gusty winds continued unabated, buffeting both the boat and our spirits. The weather in Plymouth was, the locals told us, the worst in years.

We began each day with a call to the Mountbatten Weather Station for the latest scoop, only to receive the same gloomy news. The weather, if anything, worsened as one front followed another in a relentless relay race across the Dover Coast. The sky remained a gun metal grey, spewing rain down upon us which made working on deck miserable. Inside we found the leak over the port bunk on the first try, which I assumed was beginner's luck. As any sailor knows, most leaks are of the mystery variety whose source is never found! Then we inventoried the equipment and the stores and dismantled the table which had served no other purpose than to be in the way on our sail from Gosport. Too many times Sherry had careened across the cabin, crashing against a table edge while *Baraka A* pitched and yawed in the violent seas. Now the purple blotches which decorated her legs and thighs were fading to yellow. Not fading, however, were the memories of how those bruises came to be.

The sea crashed against the quay in frantic slaps, churning the waves into an angry froth. Like egg whites being whipped by a giant mixing machine was how Sherry described it. How typical that Sherry chose to compare our terrible weather to something in the culinary department. Sherry is a first-class chef who can create delicious meals from anything at all but I still love to tease her about the early days of our marriage when our diet consisted solely of spaghetti, which was the only dish she knew how to prepare. In preparation for our voyage, Sherry had spent hours poring over cook books designed for sailors, learning the right way to store and preserve foods, how to create gourmet dinners from tinned provisions, how to plan the galley so that all the necessary tools fit into a very small space. Roy had been impressed, calling her 'a first-class quartermaster and as well-organised as you can ever hope to be'.

As we sat on the boat or in the Grant Hotel listening to the dull thud of rain, I realised more and more how much I was going to miss Sherry.

Over coffee in the evening in the hotel lounge, I would talk about the upcoming voyage as if she were still a part of it. I really couldn't blame Sherry for saying no more. The storm in the English Channel had scared her very badly. And, I was willing to admit, rattled my confidence and enthusiasm. But never seriously. Although the task ahead was enormous, there was no way I was going to give up. Giving up was not in my nature. I would not cry enough after just a few days of bad weather. Wouldn't the media have a time with that? And wouldn't all our detractors say, 'told you so!'

Ever so slowly I began to coax Sherry to rethink her position. I desperately wanted her to share my dream. We had planned so long and worked so hard to make *Baraka A* perfect for us. After a few days on terra firma, when the worst memories of our trip through the English Channel had softened at the edges, she began to listen.

"We've been through the worst and the boat will take it. I learned so much in the storm. Now I have a lot more confidence. I know we can make it around the world. Go home to Cairo and then join me in Casablanca. The weather will be warm, the sun shining. It will be beautiful, I promise."

Under the barrage of my honeyed words, Sherry began to relent as I knew she would.

"Okay," she agreed. "I will think about it."

By the end of the week, Roy had run out of time and, as hard as I tried, I could not persuade him to cancel or delay his teaching assignment and sail with me to Casablanca.

"It's not that I don't want to go, you understand. But this continuing bad weather has chewed up all my free days. Right now I should be on a flight home from Morocco." He paused. "I've never had any doubts about your sailing ability since the sea trials. And you certainly proved yourself on the trip from Gosport. You can take it and the boat can take it."

Sherry tried to persuade me to look around for someone to take Roy's place. But I knew that was an insurmountable task. When you've sailed with the best in the business it's impossible to tolerate a runner-up.

A cool wind whipped around Plymouth harbour, dragging me back to the present and the job at hand. A formidable job since our original threesome was down to one man: me, a neophyte in every sense of the word with only fifteen hours of sailing experience under my belt. All our carefully made plans had gone down the drain because of the one thing over which we had no control – the weather.

I leaned over and pressed the starter and heard the diesel engine roar to life, then settle down to a gentle steady throb. My departure time was set for 9 p.m. A glance at my watch told me that already the minute hand was at the twenty past mark.

Sherry and Roy began to untie the docklines. As I watched Sherry's eyes growing glassy with tears, I suspected that mine would soon follow suit. Again, an icy fear gripped me. How easy it would be to jump out of the boat back on to the pier and just say, "Okay, everybody, you're right. This is a crazy idea and I've decided not to go anywhere." No one would blame me. Some might even praise me for showing good sense. I swallowed hard and put on my jaunty sailor's smile and threw the engine into reverse. What crazy thoughts. I could no more jump out of the boat than jump out of my dream. Did anyone, even Sherry, realise that my commitment to the circumnavigation was total and absolute? There would be and could be no compromises. I *would* sail around the world!

As I headed out of the harbour, I looked back and waved once again at Sherry and Roy standing on the pier, the two of them almost a blur in the gloom. They seemed to be shouting and pointing at the bow. Or were they just waving? I looked again. No, pointing for sure. I scrambled forward along the deck to check the lines. Everything appeared to be in order although it was hard to see in the dark. Behind me another boat was fighting for space to manoeuvre so I quickly returned to the helm. I looked back at Sherry and Roy and shrugged my shoulders. They continued their frantic waving and pointing. Must be a problem with the rigging. I'd sort it out once I was safely in the Channel.

A feeling of despair washed over me. What was I doing heading out to sea on my own without Sherry to make me laugh, without Roy to help me iron out the kinks? That there were still plenty of kinks, I had no doubt. It was lonely in the cockpit. Any sailor who takes it in his head to circumnavigate the globe knows that there will be many moments, hours, even days of solitude. But solitude and loneliness are as different as sugar and salt. Solitude is like a good book, something to savour. Loneliness is like having no books at all, just endless stretches of time with nothing to do but wish you weren't alone.

Being alone had not been part of the plan. Sherry should have been with me now, busy down in the cabin preparing some hot coffee to ward off the evening chill. Roy should have been here too, standing beside me in the cockpit consulting the charts and checking the barometric pressure.

I had promised myself not to dwell on the past. But I could not free myself of the memories of those three days in the English Channel, memories which were etched into my brain like engraving on a pewter mug.

And then I heard Roy's voice, almost as if he were standing right there beside me. He was repeating those same words he'd uttered again and again while we waited in Plymouth for the weather to clear.

'You can do it and you will do it. You are the most determined man I have ever met. Determined and stubborn too. Nothing will stop you.'

'Well, I hope Roy's belief in me is sound,' I thought as Plymouth disappeared from view. My dream of circumnavigating the world in a small boat was about to begin. The trip to Casablanca would be long and lonely. But, looking on the bright side, I would have lots of time to find the right words to persuade Sherry to sign on again as first mate.

Sherry's Journal, Plymouth Harbour

I feel sorry for Jameel and at the same time I admire his guts and courage. Jameel is the kind of person who would never let himself be ruled by the fear of what might happen or not happen. I hate to admit this weakness in myself. I couldn't do it for the world: take off alone at night, knowing what was waiting for me out in the Channel. I tried to convince him to take someone with him but he refused. So I guess it's best just to do some praying and leave it in God's hands. It was hard to keep from crying when we said goodbye. I felt so helpless. I ran to the hotel and up to our room where I watched him sail away. I could see his mast light for a long, long time and I could tell from the motion of the light that the seas were rough. Gradually he became just a dot on the horizon and then he was gone.

Chapter Two

About three hours after I ceased being a dot on the horizon, I heard an ominous whooshing sound coming from the vicinity of the engine. 'Now what?' I wondered as I peered over the stern into water as dark as pitch. Had something fouled the propeller? Seaweed or other flotsam? I got my flashlight and took another look. Nothing. Could it be a clogged fuel line? Unlikely but… Nothing to do but restart the engine and hope. Instead of a reassuring whirr, all I heard was a dull thud as the engine stalled again. Oh brother, what was I supposed to do now? But I knew the answer – raise the sails, turn around and head back to Plymouth harbour and find out what was wrong with my brand new engine, which should be purring like a kitten. Proceeding on to Casablanca, sailing single-handedly on the ocean for the first time, without an engine would be a step beyond foolhardy to just plain stupid.

I went forward and uncleated the main halyard and be an to raise the mainsail, no easy task in a rolling sea. The sail began to inch forward up the slot in the mast and then, suddenly, when it was almost two-thirds there, it stopped. I wrapped the halyard around my wrist and gave it a sharp vicious tug but the sail was stuck fast. A cursory inspection told me that the main halyard had become entangled with the ensign lanyard, which had never happened before so why now? 'Not an auspicious beginning for a round-the-world voyage,' I thought as I yanked at the lanyard with zero results. I hurried back to the cockpit. Untangling the lines would not be a huge problem but it was one I didn't have time to fiddle with as the wind had picked up and was methodically blowing me back on to Ediston Rocks.

Next I tried dropping the main but it would not budge, either up or down. I knew that I needed to get control of the boat and quickly so I left the main, which was cracking like a whip in the wind, hurried below, consulted the charts and then advised the coastguard of my predicament and estimated position. Although my nautical knowledge was embryonic, I had the radio protocol down pat (or so I hoped), thanks to a course Sherry and I had taken during our months in Gosport. I knew that my situation was not a 'Mayday' (really serious, boat heading for the bottom), or 'Pan Pan' (boat in danger, maybe with people on board), but the less urgent 'Securite' (no disaster yet but advice and help definitely needed).

To their offer of help, I replied that I thought I could make it back to Plymouth harbour under genoa. "I would be so grateful," I continued, "if you would call my wife. She's at the Grant Hotel."

"Affirmative. And we'll keep track of you on our radar and call you back. Also we'll keep an emergency channel open in case you need to call us."

Again I thanked them. I remembered what Roy had told me:

"You can do it Jameel," and I felt a surge of confidence course through my body. Besides, how humiliating to barely disappear over the horizon, to be just a few short miles from shore and then find it necessary to call for help.

Back on deck I quickly raised the genoa then pushed the tiller over hard, bringing the boat around, then winched in the sheet and cleated it. When I had the boat sailing on what I presumed was the right course, I tackled the next problem – the mainsail. Should I leave it up and consider it a reefed sail or try immobilising it? I had to run the choices through my mind but once to know the answer. The sail had to be tied down so that the genoa could do its job. I scrambled down into the cabin and luckily was able to lay my hands on some lengths of line without a frantic search. Back in the cockpit, I pulled the mainsheet tight to stop the boom from flying across the cockpit. Then I inched forward to the mast, grateful that I'd had the foresight to install those six additional handholds. I wondered how I'd accomplish the next bit: keeping my balance while I tried to grab the sail, haul it in and tie it down. I remembered Roy's words to Sherry during one of our sea trials:

"At sea two pairs of hands are always better than one. The same goes for eyes and ears."

I could forget the eyes and ears but, oh, how I needed an extra pair of hands. Holding the lines in my teeth, I wrapped one arm around the mast which left my hand free. With the other I caught the sail (not on the first attempt) and was able to bunch some of it up against the mast and around the boom and tie it down. A couple more 'grab and tie' manoeuvres and the job was done. Not tidily or nautically but I didn't care. I suspected that I was being pulled by the tide and the currents so my plan to duck back into the cabin for a quick check of the charts had to be abandoned. All my attention was focused on keeping the boat on what I hoped was the right heading.

When the coastguard called an hour later, as promised, I explained the situation.

"We have your *exact* position," a crisp voice informed me. "You are presently between Ediston Rocks and the coast."

'That does it,' I thought. 'The wind and the sea were about to dash me on to the rocky Cornwall coast. And that would be the end of *Baraka A* and the end of my dream and very possibly, the end of me.'

I quickly consented to their renewed offer of help.

Then I waited with my stomach tied in half hitches for what seemed like an eternity, but in fact the rescue motor launch from the Royal National Lifeboat Institute arrived in less than an hour. Soon I was under tow back to the Mayflower Marina, thankful that both the boat and I had survived the night.

I arrived back at the marina a little after 5 a.m. Just eight hours earlier I had jumped on board *Baraka A*, full of confidence, and waved goodbye to Plymouth harbour for, what I thought, was the last time. And here I was, back again, having completed my circumnavigation, not of the world but of Ediston Rocks!

The crew from the rescue launch helped me tie the boat to the pier.

"What's this then?" one of them remarked, pointing to a line that ran from the starboard bow cleat to the stern. He held out his hand. "Didn't get a chance out there to introduce myself," he continued with a grin. "Name's Graeme and these fellows in the boat are Alistair and Jason."

"I'm Jameel Adnan and all I can say right now is thank you for all your help. If you hadn't come along, my boat would be a heap of splinters."

"Blimey. This will be one to tell the missus. Aren't you that Arab fellow who's sailing around the world with his wife? Read all about you in the paper." He craned his neck to get a look into the cabin. "Haven't seen your wife. Is she all right?"

"She's not on board. She's still here in Plymouth at the Grant Hotel. After the trip from Gosport, she was too frightened to face the English Channel again."

Graeme nodded.

"Weather's been pretty dicey lately."

"Mmm," I murmured, only half-listening to the conversation. My eyes were glued to a blue and white line which lay as taut as a guitar string against the hull. I gave it a tug wondering if this was my unlucky day for lines being in the wrong place – first the lanyard, halyard tangle and now this.

"I reckon this is how you came to grief," said Graeme, reaching over to give the line a twang. "Bet this is wound around your propeller tighter than the best seaman's knot."

I nodded, almost afraid to speak. On the one hand, I hoped that my problem was indeed as simple as a line around a propeller, which meant that the repair bill might not be out of sight and I could be underway again soon. On the other hand, I felt so foolish. Sherry and Roy had seen it: I now knew the reason for all the pointing and waving. And I had paid so little attention!

Beside me, I heard Graeme clearing his throat.

"I know you feel the fool, but don't worry about it, mate. There's not a sailor alive who hasn't done the same thing – forgotten a line in the water with the same unfortunate results. Look on the bright side. Most folks learn this lesson once and never forget it. You'll become a fanatic about having all lines aboard and secured before casting off. Experience is the best teacher, they say."

I smiled wanly and shrugged. I didn't trust myself to speak. How many other lessons were there to learn, I wanted to ask. If something as simple as a misplaced bow line had almost caused my circumnavigation to end in disaster, what did the future hold? That I would make other mistakes was a certainty, but what about the consequences? Maybe my dream of sailing around the world should remain that, just a dream.

I felt a friendly hand on my shoulder.

"Things will look brighter after a bite of breakfast and forty winks. You did everything right, mate – called the coastguard, asked for help when you needed it. A fellow can't do more than that."

"Thanks for your help and encouragement." I jumped back on board *Baraka A* and retrieved the bag of snacks from the sink. I handed them to Graeme, "You might as well have these. I don't know how long it will take the boat to get fixed."

"You'll be back in the water and on your way before you know it, mate." He hefted the bag of snacks. "Anyway, thanks for these and good luck." He began walking across the pier to the launch but then he paused and turned around. "Hope you'll not think me rude for asking, but, you see, I've never really met an Arab before. At least not an Arab sailor. I thought you folks preferred sand and camels."

"Most of us don't ride camels and you're right - most of us don't go sailing. I'm hoping that this trip of mine will show other Arabs the magic of an ocean voyage."

Graeme smiled.

"I'd like to shake your hand again and wish you a safe journey. If you're ever back in this part of the world, let us know."

I hardly trusted myself to speak. People in England had been so nice to us. Instead I waved as Graeme joined the others in the launch and watched until it disappeared from view.

"No doubt off on another rescue mission," I murmured as I hunched my shoulders against the wind and pulled the collar of my jacket up around my ears. As I walked back to the Grant Hotel I looked at the sky and then at my watch. Almost 6 a.m. How could it be morning and still as dark as midnight? Back home in Jeddah, the day had begun close to 5 a.m. with the muezzin calling the faithful to the first prayer of the day: the Fajr prayer which occurs about an hour before sunrise. Sunrise. I let the word roll around in my head. How many times had I envisioned sunrise at sea on board *Baraka A*. I would be checking the rigging and Sherry would be below making breakfast. I smiled as I imagined her retort to my romantic visions of life at sea.

'Jameel, you fix the coffee this morning. I'm going to sleep in.'

I quickened my pace. Sherry was waiting for me, worrying and wondering if I were safe.

It came as no surprise to find Sherry pacing the lobby, looking anxiously out of the windows.

"Jameel," she said her voice catching in her throat, "I am so thankful you are back here, safe with me. The coastguard called and I have cancelled my flight to Cairo."

I smiled for the first time in hours. With Sherry beside me, I could sort everything out. But first a cup of very strong, hot coffee.

As we sat together in the hotel breakfast room sipping the scalding brew, I told Sherry about my misadventures on the high seas. Suddenly I was weary beyond belief. Those 'forty winks' that Graeme had suggested were definitely the next item on the day's agenda. As we walked to the elevator, I glanced out the window. Was it my imagination or did the horizon seem less grey? Was it possible that the sun was actually planning on making an appearance?

I woke from a deep sleep around mid-morning and immediately called Roy and told him that I was back in Plymouth.

"Now I know why you were pointing at me as I sailed out of the harbour," I said. "There's probably a line snagged around the propeller."

"You're probably right and I've been thinking that it's mostly my fault," he replied. "Do you remember when I used your spare genoa sheet as a spring line to keep the boat from crashing against the pier during that last storm? When you were leaving, I decided to be helpful so I untied it and threw it on the bow. But I missed and it fell into the water. Before I could tell you what had happened, you had the boat in reverse and then you were gone. I could kick myself for not mentioning the spring line."

"And I should have checked more carefully that all lines were safely on board. A fellow from the RNLI said that I'd never forget to do that again. Anyway, now I can figure out what happened. You know how I have all the lines on the boat colour-coded so I can find what I need in a hurry?"

"Well, I always thought that was a first-rate idea," said Roy.

"When I saw you and Sherry jumping up and down on the dock I went forward to check and all I saw was a blue and white line. I knew that blue and white meant genoa sheet. I didn't realise that the spare one, that blasted spring line, was trailing in the water."

"Hindsight's a wonderful thing, Jameel. But what's important is that you made it back safely," said Roy. "I suppose you won't know the extent of the damage until you haul the boat."

"I hope that happens tomorrow. I'm going down to the marina after breakfast."

"Righty-ho. Let me know how it all goes. I'll be in touch."

After what the British call a proper English breakfast - of eggs and fried tomatoes and baked beans and sausage - Sherry and I put on our jackets and headed for the marina. If I had to give up my career as a circumnavigator, I might find a job as a weather forecaster. My predictions of a sunny day had proved to be true. The marina manager said that they would haul *Baraka A* the next morning and he hoped the weather would hold.

Not to be. The next morning Plymouth harbour was shrouded in mist - a damp, grey, penetrating presence which enveloped us like a damp cloak. As we approached the harbour we could hear the frantic slapping of halyards against the masts and the roar of the surf as it hit the shore. Force 10, the forecast said, possibly escalating to hurricane velocity. Sherry squeezed my hand tight and told me again how happy she was that I was safe in the harbour and not out on the ocean in this weather. I thought of the two other sailors who had followed me out of the marina on October 29. I wondered where they were and how they were doing, especially the fellow who was single-handling it to Australia. I gave Sherry's hand an answering squeeze. Only a fool would not be grateful to be safe in the harbour instead of out there battling the waves and wind. But I said nothing. Barring horrendous, time-consuming, expensive repairs, I would soon be back out there myself, heading for Casablanca. At least that's what I kept telling myself. But if the truth be known, my spirits were in the cellar. Maybe I was crazy to think I could sail around the world. One, two, three strikes and you're out at the old ball game - and I'd already used up two in this foolish game of mine. To say that I'd been ill-prepared to tackle the English Channel was an understatement. I should have spent a few pounds on some coastal charts. That responsibility was mine, as skipper, not Roy's. Nor had I been ready for the weather, as we battled our way to the safety of Plymouth harbour - cold rain and colder sea water drenching me, gale force winds slamming *Baraka A*. And then the fouled prop. In hindsight such a stupid mistake. All mine even though Roy wanted to share it.

Sherry, I knew, wanted me to tell her that everything would be okay. I would sail to Casablanca under sunny skies. She would meet me there and we would cast off our lines and sail away with a gentle wind at our backs. Beautiful picture but was it realistic? How could I reassure Sherry when I could not even reassure myself?

'Stop wallowing in self pity,' I told myself. 'Did you think this circumnavigation was going to be like a dinghy race on a pond? Not for a moment. So you've had a few bad days but you've survived. There'll be other bad days ahead but good ones too.'

Baraka A was hauled out in spite of the weather and, sure enough, snarled around the propeller was a blue and white line, twelve metres long which had pulled the shaft out of the engine. Luckily the shaft was not bent. The marine mechanic said it would be an easy job to reset the propeller and pack it. Resetting I understood but I was a little hazy on 'packing' although I'd heard the term before. Later on in the voyage I would learn first-hand what packing was all about!

A few hours later the boat was back in the water. With a touch of the throttle, the engine once more roared to life.

That evening, while we were eating dinner, Sherry remarked that so far we hadn't seen any of the good part of sailing.

"It's only been hardship," she commented.

Just the opening I needed.

"The good part lies ahead of us," I said. "Remember how you promised to think about our trip while you're home in Cairo? When you come to meet me in Casablanca we'll discover all the nice things about sailing. Like some sun."

I shivered as I looked out of the window at the rain streaming in sheets from the slate roofs of the cottages which lined the street.

"A promise is a promise," said Sherry. "I will think about it."

Sherry's Journal, October 31

Today was my departure day. We had breakfast in the morning, both of us were very quiet. I could tell that Jameel was thinking hard about what's ahead. We have always been together since the day we got married. This time I was leaving him with a big task ahead. I felt guilty but I was so scared. I knew I couldn't do it, not in that kind of weather. Now we knew that the English Channel was as bad as everybody had said it was. This morning the weather was still miserable. I dropped Jameel at the marina and we said goodbye again and then I went to the airport. I was so unhappy that I could barely speak, like my throat was stuffed with cotton wool. I felt like crying again.

All the way on the plane to Cairo I thought about what Jameel must be doing. He said he would call me to tell me his departure date. Everyone was very happy to see me back home, especially my family who had been very worried. But my mind was somewhere else. I knew what Jameel was facing and wondered how he would do it. When I left him, he looked exhausted. My morale was down. Everyone seemed to want me to stop 'this crazy idea'. 'One lesson is enough,' they said. But I remembered my promise to Jameel. Yes, I would think about it.

After Sherry left for the airport I placed a call to Roy Mullender in Gosport. After assuring him that the boat was back in the water and ready to set sail for Casablanca, I took a deep breath and put it to him straight.

"Look, Roy, I want you on board with me. I know if I spend some hours with you, I will be better prepared to continue on around the world as I planned. I need you to show me how to put all the theory into practice."

When I paused to take a breath, Roy jumped in.

"I've been thinking about you a lot, Jameel," he said. "Maybe the reason you came back to Plymouth harbour was to pick me up. I've been with you and Sherry for so many weeks now that I feel that *Baraka A* is almost my boat too."

"You're coming?" I asked, in disbelief. "What about that course you're supposed to teach?"

"Found I could change the dates. Thing is," Roy continued, "I can only give you seven days."

"When are you leaving Gosport?"

"As soon as I hang up the phone and throw some things into a bag. You get the boat stocked, the fuel tanks filled. You know the drill."

A few hours later I called Sherry with the good news. I could tell that she felt less nervous about my tackling the English Channel again with Roy along as first mate. The weather forecast looked good too with five days of clear weather and moderate seas forecast.

When Roy arrived, we modified my original sail plan. Most books I had read suggested sailing a westerly course out into the Atlantic for about two hundred miles before changing tack and heading for the Madeira Islands. The object is to avoid sailing across the Bay of Biscay where many a sailing ship has come to grief in a storm, especially a westerly one, which might result in *Baraka A* being pushed dangerously close to the French coast. Had I been alone, I probably would not have even considered Roy's suggestion to sail across the mouth of the Bay of Biscay. But there really was no other choice. Father Time was squeezing, and squeezing us hard. We agreed that we should try to make Vilamoura, Portugal. Looking back, I realise that Roy's suggestion was clearly an ultimatum: do it my way or I can't do it at all.

As soon as we got the 'all clear' from the weather station we readied the boat for departure. The low pressure systems that had plagued the English coastline for weeks had finally lifted. Where does bad weather go anyway? Does it suddenly just disappear like a puff of smoke or does it travel on to some new place to wreak havoc and make everyone miserable? I didn't have time to ponder too long on the ins and outs of weather systems. There was a couple of 'must do's, at the top of which was 'check all lines', underlined in black ink. Next was to call Sherry and Essam and tell them goodbye. Sherry seemed to be in good spirits when she wished me good luck. We paid the marina bill, cleared customs and at 2 p.m. sailed out of Plymouth harbour under mottled skies, which was just a step above overcast. Things were looking up. At least it wasn't raining and I had Roy Mullender on board.

Chapter Three

Our first night at sea the skies were clear. I sat on the bow of *Baraka A* gazing at the carpet of stars and thinking of the sailors in years gone by who had plotted their course across the seas by looking at the heavens. Sherry and I had taken courses in celestial navigation and felt confident that we could pinpoint our position with a sextant if the SatNav broke down. Or if we ever had to leave *Baraka A* and take to the life-raft. I shoved this possibility to the back of my mind and told it to stay there. I had always believed that sailors should make use of every navigational tool at their disposal, including the five senses. What good was a SatNav if it broke down? How could you use a sextant if the skies were covered with clouds? Every sailor must know how to sail by 'deduced' or 'dead reckoning', which translates into DR in sailor's shorthand. Know your compass bearing, speed and elapsed time and you should be able to figure out where you're headed. On the other side of the coin, there were sailors who shunned modern electronic navigation by satellite, preferring to do it 'the old way', relying on their wits and knowledge to cross vast expanses of open water. But not me. If we lived in the modern world we should make use of modern things. With the simple flick of a switch the SatNav would give me an exact position every three to four hours.

Roy checked the barometer and told me that the glass seemed to be rising. Good news for us. Already the seas were less lumpy. I would wait to call Sherry until after we had left the English Channel, which held so many terrifying memories for her. And for me, if I wanted to be completely honest. The English Channel could be a nasty stretch of water. I thought back to my history lessons. During the Second World War that 'nasty stretch' had protected England from a German invasion. But, on one special night, the seas had been like glass, which had allowed the British to rescue their troops from the beaches at Dunkirk. I hadn't expected 'smooth as glass' when we set of from Gosport. A gentle chop would have been quite acceptable. Then Sherry would have stayed on board. But all that was past tense. When I talked to her in a day or two, I hoped I would be speaking the truth... 'It's fabulous out here, just like we imagined.'

Another item of equipment which took top billing with the SatNav was our SSB (single side band) radio and VHF telephone. I had actually bought the equipment in the States and brought it to England where we wisely signed up with an instructor named Michael Gale. By the end of the course we not only had our radio licenses but new friends too, Michael and his wife. The four of us spent many happy hours together exploring Gosport and the surrounding villages. Funny about people you meet along the way. With some there is an instant rapport, some sort of magic glue that bonds you together and you know the friendship will always be there even if you're on opposite sides of the globe. Other friendships are more transitory: nice while they last but easy to leave behind.

I glanced over my shoulder at Roy, who was taking his turn at the tiller. He, more than anyone, fell into the first category. I wondered again what stroke of fate or good luck had brought this man into our lives. I knew the official reason. Camper Nicholson Yachts, at my request, had agreed to find an experienced sailor to accompany me on a few shakedown cruises, to fill in the blanks in my nautical know-how and to sail with us from Gosport on our maiden voyage. There were probably dozens of competent sailors who could have done the job. But not too many with Roy's credentials. Here was a man who had spent most of his life either sailing or teaching others to sail. The Royal Navy's Small Boat Sailing programme had Roy's stamp on it. I once asked Roy the size of boat he used in this programme and was surprised at his reply: 'About fifty feet, I'd guess.' This was no 'small boat' in my experience but, as Roy hastened to explain, compared to a huge navy frigate, a fifty foot sailboat was just a speck.

I felt a mixture of admiration and envy when he described his participation in the 1973 Whitbread Race, the Sydney to Portsmouth leg, which had taken him around Cape Horn, one of the most treacherous pieces of water known to mankind but one which holds a fascination for sailors. 'Rounding the Horn' was a nautical achievement that I hoped lay in my future. But there was more to Roy than his ability to sail a boat. I hoped he knew how much I liked him as a person. His gentle unassuming manner counterbalanced my feisty nature, which could be either a source of strength or my worst enemy.

Roy and I had decided to stand four hour watches. A glance at my watch told me that the hour had arrived to relieve him. Sailing under genoa and mainsail, *Baraka A* was slicing through the waves at a good clip. Roy informed me that in twelve hours we had come 73 nautical miles.

***Baraka A* Log – November 2**

We are still making good time. It's almost as if *Baraka A* is feeling the freedom of the open seas. She responds to the lightest touch of the helm and is prancing through the waves like a horse that's been locked in the barn too long. We're anxious to get across the mouth of the Bay of Biscay while the weather holds. Roy and I take turns checking that we are holding the boat on the right course. I keep thinking about the rocky French coast to the east of us, which is something we must avoid.

The following day the winds piped up to Force 7. Hoping to make the best time possible we decided not to shorten sail. The weather remained clear and I hoped we would again enjoy a starry night. We had a wonderful dinner of steak and potatoes which I'd purchased in Plymouth. Roy and I had very differing opinions about food. He loved such things as steak and kidney puddings which Sherry and I found to be soggy and heavy, just bits of pastry folded around some slivers of meat. I preferred lighter, more natural food.

"You can't stand watch with only a handful of raisins in your stomach," Roy had told me during the sea trials.

"Raisins are the perfect snack while on watch," I had countered. "And I *never* eat them for dinner. I like beans and rice and dried salami. But never that heavy pudding. It gives me a stomach ache."

After dinner I noticed that the mainsheet shackle was loose. After tightening the screws, I continued around the boat checking the rigging. How many disasters at sea can be blamed on the skipper not being on top of things? I didn't need to look farther than my own experience - disabled in the English Channel with a line around my prop. I was learning that a sailboat was unlike any other vessel which called water home. I had practically memorised a passage from *Single Handed Cruising and Sailing* by Frank Mulville:

> As an inviolable routine the sailor must inspect the deck at least three times a day, once at nightfall, once at dawn and once at midday. He must walk slowly around his tiny domain and check every rope, every shackle, every block and every lashing to make certain that the constant movement of the yacht has not brought on chafe or wear or looseness.

I told Roy a funny story about Frank Mulville which I'd read in one of my sailing magazines. Apparently he left his boat at anchor in some harbour, went ashore and when he returned the boat was gone. Probably the anchor dragged and the boat just drifted away and was never seen again.

"Even the experts make mistakes," replied Roy.

***Baraka A* Log - November 4**

I am beginning to find out what sailing is all about! We are racing along under main and a winged genoa. Will have to jibe soon. The main is the easy one. Resetting the whisker pole for a port tack is hard work. I called Sherry today and told her that all was going as planned. I hope she heard the enthusiasm in my voice. I am really gaining confidence in my ability to handle the boat. Again, I have been watching Roy and learning more and more how and why things are done. I feel like a conductor who knows how to play all the instruments in the orchestra but is unsure of how it all goes together. So I keep asking questions. If Roy thinks they're foolish he never lets on.

I realised today that there are many empty hours at sea. When there are things to do like raising sails or reefing them or performing manoeuvres like tacking and jibing, the focus must be on the job. When Roy and I found ourselves 'off duty' and just sitting around the cockpit or the cabin, we passed the hours talking. I knew more about his culture than he did mine because I'd spent many years living in 'The West' (which is how people from the Arab world describe Europe and English speaking countries on both sides of the Atlantic). My time abroad had been spent in Miami and in the San Francisco Bay area where I attended university at Menlo College. Roy had never been to Egypt or Saudi Arabia.

"There are many people from my country who think taking this trip around the world is a crazy idea," I said. "But I'm doing it to prove a point - if I can. Let's rekindle that spirit of adventure which used to be part of our culture. We need to tackle new frontiers. Why can't we encourage our citizens to follow the example of people like Prince Sultan bin Salman bin Abdulaziz, who was the first Arab and the first Muslim in space?

"It saddens me that Arab sailors used to be renowned for their daring exploits," I continued. "Arabs were great shipbuilders and master navigators. But all that happened about twelve hundred years ago. I find that incredible. Did you know that when Captain Cook sailed across the Pacific some of his crew were Omani Arabs? I keep thinking I'm the first Arab ever to attempt a circumnavigation, ever! I hope my trip will encourage others to take up this sport, which is part of their history."

"No doubt your trip will have an impact," Roy replied.

"There's another reason for this trip," I replied. "So many people have a picture of us which is not true. I know there have been some terrorist acts committed by Arabs but most of us are peace-loving."

"Arab countries are not unique on that score. There is not a nation on earth that has not spawned terrorism. I take people as I find them and avoid stereotyping," said Roy.

"That is kind of you to say, but there are still many who have a different picture of us. Even official people. Sherry can tell you about our problems getting a visa for Tahiti, which we quickly learned is really French Polynesia, and the paperwork had to be done through the French embassy in London. Lucky for us that Sherry could speak almost flawless French so we didn't have a language barrier to crack. But, even so, it took the authorities many weeks to check us out. We were different. Were we really Arab circumnavigators or terrorists in disguise and part of the group responsible for those bombings in Paris? We used to joke that the political storms on land were worse than anything we'd find at sea. But the joke wore thin after a while. Don't know how many times we visited the embassy. Finally we took the news articles about our trip and showed them to the visa people. We had almost given up hope when the visas came through."

"And if they hadn't..." Roy paused. "I know the answer to that one better than my own name. You'd be sitting on the embassy steps right now instead of being out here with me. There's no way you can cross the Pacific without passing through French Polynesia – if not Tahiti itself, then one of the atolls."

"Well, I suppose we could have headed straight for Australia but the point of the trip was to visit the South Pacific. We would have felt very cheated if we had to miss Polynesia. I'm just grateful that we finally got that visa. Exploring those tropical south sea islands is one of the main reasons we're making this trip."

Baraka A Log – November 6

The winds remain vigorous and have swung around to the north-west so we have a following sea which has increased our speed by a knot or two. What a thrill to feel _Baraka A_ being picked up and carried along by the waves. If this is surfing, I like it. Roy is calling this a 'boisterous sail'. English has some very descriptive words. I say the boat is heeling, pitching and lurching. I can hardly remember the dark days in Plymouth when my confidence was at a very low ebb. But even then I knew that I would not give up my dream. I am not a quitter. I learned that during my years as an amateur boxer. When you're knocked down you get up and go on. Tonight the stars are out again and we are reeling off the miles. The Bay of Biscay is no longer visible off the port rail.

Roy hit the nail square on when he called this a boisterous sail. Boisterous and exhilarating. It was a full time job to keep the boat on course and avoid a broach, which is a nasty complication if you are sailing downwind with a heavy following sea. According to

Chapman's book *Piloting and Small Boat Handling*, which I had read and reread many times, a broach occurs when the stern gets thrown around by overtaking waves and the boat is thrown sideways into the trough. The danger of a capsize is very real. Again I realised that most of my knowledge came from books and that my experience with the 'real thing' was very limited. As if to correct this oversight, the sea decided to give me a 'hands on' lesson that afternoon in the form of a huge wave that came out of nowhere knocking us broadside. The boat rolled so far over that the cockpit filled with water. I held tight to the tiller and the boat rounded up to meet the next wave head on. Roy said there was nothing like a soaking with cold salt water to wake a man up. But there were other consequences of the broach that I did not discover till I climbed into my bunk. I called it 'The Case of the Flying Milk Container'. How did a milk carton leap from the sink, fly across the cabin and land in my bunk, spilling milk everywhere? A mystery at sea! I concluded that the milk carton was frightened and decided the safest place to be was the bunk. Just like Sherry on the trip from Gosport. How happy I was that my sense of humour had cranked up into high gear again.

Last night after a meal of tinned meat and baked beans which Roy pronounced delicious (for me the beans were okay but the meat was not good at all), Roy and I got talking about how we got into sailing. His story was the more traditional. He began sailing when he was young and turned a sport he loved into a vocation. He'd been racing and teaching sailing all his adult life. For a time he had worked for Camper Nicholson delivering boats.

My interest in sailing began in my early years. Someone snapped a photo of me in a sailor suit when I was just a toddler. My father told me that when we used to go to the beach I loved to draw pictures of sailboats in the sand with a stick.

"But when did you really get into it?" asked Roy as he sipped his after dinner coffee.

"I've always known that I was going to sail around the world. When I was a teenager I got hooked on that TV programme, *Adventures in Paradise*, and I wanted to be just like the main character, Adam Troy. Every week he would sail his boat, *Tiki*, to a new exotic place. I watched every episode and decided that some day that could be me. No, *would* be me! I didn't know when or how but I knew it would happen with a certainty that I can't explain."

"One thing I've been curious about but didn't want to pry. You said you'd lived in coastal cities on both sides of America but you never learned how to sail."

"Not exactly true. I spent one summer at the Chapman Sailing School in Florida and then Sherry and I took some lessons in navigation on San Francisco Bay. Once we took lessons on a catamaran, which was actually a cruise from Long Island Sound to Boston. We seemed to motor most of the time. Didn't really get the feel of the boat but, even so, I wasn't ready to abandon thoughts of a multi-hull. I contacted the editor of *Multi-Hull Magazine* who seemed like a friendly honest guy. He said that, for my type of voyage, a mono-hull would be more forgiving. And I knew that they beat to windward better."

"Smart thinking," said Roy. "On a long voyage forgiving and manageable are key words."

"While lying in my bunk that evening, I thought again about this dream of mine to sail around the world. My father could never understand why I would even contemplate doing such a dangerous thing.

There was no easy answer. I had known from the time I was a kid that I was going to sail around the world. Why? Because the challenge intrigued and fascinated me. When? I had no timetable other than 'some day' but I felt sure that, when the right time arrived, I would know it. Many times my dream had been put on hold while I got involved with something like studying for my university degree. But still it was always with me, like a pebble in my shoe. Sailing a dinghy across a lake could never provide the adventure I craved.

No doubt I had provided Roy with a good portion of adventure and challenge. I wondered if he'd known how inexperienced I really was when he signed on to help me.

Did he know, for instance, that the day the winches and lines and cleats were to be installed that I had just disappeared from the boatyard. Me, who hardly missed a day in six months, just suddenly wasn't there? I didn't want anyone to know about my lack of knowledge regarding rigging, which just looked like a plate of spaghetti to me. That evening, after most everyone had left, I went back to the boatyard and figured it out, which was the best way for me to learn.

The next morning, after breakfast, I shared this story with Roy and we both laughed and agreed that figuring something out for yourself really is the best way to learn.

"I must say," said Roy, " that I have never known a man to just buy a boat, then jump into it and sail around the world. Neither has Jeremy Lines. But, on the other hand, aside from practical experience, neither of us has ever met a person so knowledgeable about the technical details. Jeremy tells a story about you arriving at the Camper Nicholson boatyard and saying something like, 'I believe the CN 31 is the right boat for me.' It was obvious after just a few questions that you'd researched the boat market extensively and knew which was the perfect boat for your journey. Very impressed was Jeremy."

"Speaking of Jeremy," I said. "Did you know that he never told me I should not attempt the circumnavigation? I remember his exact words – 'You know what you're supposed to do. You just haven't done much of it yet.'"

"Is anyone ever ready for a circumnavigation?" Roy asked. "Jeremy and I used to say that you can never be ready – not until you've done it. Then maybe you're ready to do it again.

"So in that sense," Roy continued, "you're probably as ready as anyone. It's obvious that you've researched every detail. Like with the outfitting of your boat. You did your homework on what was the best equipment to buy. The self-steering gear you ordered from Australia is top-notch. You did not make the mistake of skimping on the important things."

"You're forgetting the charts for Plymouth which I didn't buy just to save a few cents."

"Well, neither did I," said Roy. "That's a mistake neither of us is likely to repeat. You're a quick learner. I watch you watching me do things and the next time you do it, it's right as rain with no mistakes. I guess what I'm trying to say is that you shouldn't sell yourself short. I wouldn't advise the average bloke to do what you're doing but I think you'll be just fine. This is a grand little vessel you have here. She can take you anywhere."

"I hope that I can persuade Sherry to come with me. There is something I can't get out of my head. One day in Gosport we were listening to a playback of one of our radio interviews, which I found interesting and exciting, but Sherry didn't say one word. Then she told me how she hated lying to the news people.

'How have you been lying?' I asked her.

'Well,' she replied, 'when anyone asks me if I'm scared I just say, 'a little bit' or 'I'm looking forward to the adventure'. I never say what I really feel: that I am more scared than anyone could imagine. If I tell people the truth, they're going to ask me why I'm going and I'm not sure I know the answer to that myself.'"

"She's not had a good day on the boat, Jameel, except during the trials. The cold north Atlantic in late October is an awful time and place for someone who has always lived in the sunshine. Sailing really can be blue water and flying-fish."

I nodded.

"I know. How am I going to get her back on board? I've even thought about kidnap in Casablanca. I'll tell her that we're just going for a little sail and then take off."

The way Roy looked at me I knew that he was trying to figure out if I were joking or serious. The truth is I didn't know myself

"Why not break the trip up into smaller parts?" he suggested. "Then Sherry doesn't have to say yes to 'around the world'. Start with Tenerife. You should have no trouble persuading her to go that far. And, once she completes that passage, I'm betting that she carries on. During the sea trials, I got the idea that Sherry was every bit as excited about this journey as you. And then we ran into that unfortunate weather on our first leg out of Gosport."

I smiled. How like a Brit to describe three days of gale force winds and thundering seas as 'unfortunate'.

***Baraka A* Log – November 6**

We are somewhere off the north coast of Spain, that part which wraps itself around northern Portugal.

Today was the best yet, lovely and balmy, and the water was, for the first time, warm enough to take a bath. The winds have really moderated so that we are now motoring with just a light breeze filling the sails, helping to push us ahead. Our speed is almost 5 knots. Tonight the stars are out again and the sea is calm.

***Baraka A* Log – November 7**

We made good time today. At 21.00 the lights of Lisbon are dropping out of sight. Again the night is clear with excellent visibility. Still sailing with main and genoa with an assist from the motor to get maximum speed. Fuel is getting low so we have reduced engine speed and we are proceeding mostly under sail.

By early morning we had run out of fuel so we made the decision to put in at Sines. Unfortunately the wind shifted from NW to SE so we were faced with a beat. We ended up being towed into the harbour. Sines will stick in my mind as cheerful chaos, with fishing boats, seagulls and bird droppings everywhere. And people shouting. We left at 12.00 with 25 gallons of fuel which cost too much ($40) but it was worth it because we are approaching Cape de São Vincente at the bottom tip of Portugal. If we run out of wind, we need the motor to keep us clear. Roy says that Cape de São Vincente is the last hurdle on this leg.

We rounded Cape de São Vincente at 22.00. Very peaceful; a clear moonlit night. There is the beautiful scent of juniper wafting across the water to *Baraka A*. What a welcome. We have sailed 1000 miles in 7 days, 18 hours.

We reached Vilamoura in the late afternoon on November 7. I decided to watch Roy and learn how to dock the boat rather than attempting it myself. In truth I was itching to do it but a wise voice inside my head said, 'Watch and learn. You have to do it alone in Casablanca.' We checked in with customs then set off to explore the town. I felt exhilarated and confident in both myself and the boat. We had sailed from England to Portugal with no mishaps and in good enough time for Roy to stay over an extra day before flying back to England. Together we plotted the safest course for me: due south making sure to keep well clear of the Strait of Gibraltar. A couple of days should do it. I called Sherry and told her to start packing her bags.

The night before Roy left we met up with a group of British Royal Navy types. Some of them knew Roy and a few had even participated in his small boat sailing classes in their formative years. Then the stories started to fly around the room. Roy was not only an ocean racer and a sailing instructor but also a deep sea diver. I thought we had probably missed some lively discussions because I also held a diving licence. My diving was mostly of the pleasure variety and I spent many happy hours exploring the extensive coral reefs in the Red Sea which lie just offshore in Jeddah. Some say it is as spectacular as the Great Barrier Reef in Australia. Roy's diving was of a more serious variety. For years he had been a member of a volunteer rescue squad. These are the fellows who answer maritime distress calls (mainly in the English Channel) via helicopter. While it hovered a few feet above the water, Roy used to jump in and pluck survivors from the sea. Now I understood why Roy had been almost philosophical about the gale force winds in the English Channel.

The following morning, Roy and I waited in front of the hotel for the taxi which was to take him to the airport. I tried to find the right words to convoy my appreciation for his help and encouragement and in the end only managed a simple 'Thank you'.

Over the past weeks Roy had become as close to me as any family member and had proved to be a person I admired and respected. But mostly I felt a sense of appreciation towards Roy for believing in me and never once wavering.

"You can do it, Jameel," he told me more than once. Amazing how a few simple words could make such a difference.

My own father, a man I also admired and respected, could not muster any enthusiasm for my 'crazy idea' of sailing around the world. Arabs, but most especially the Saudis, are bound by conservative traditions. To my father, as head of the family, fell the awesome task of safeguarding the well-being of all family members. In his eyes, he had not fulfilled his obligations *vis-à-vis* me and sailing around the world. So convinced was he that I would perish that he refused to give me any financial help and convinced other family members to follow suit: 'If you give him a nickel you are sending him to death,' he used to say. I had never been a model son, doing all the things that were expected of me. Adulthood did not change my intractable make-up. I rarely turned my back on a challenge. And when I made up my mind to do something, I usually succeeded.

While I had every confidence that I would sail around the world and arrive back in Jeddah intact, my father did not. Surely I would founder and end up in a watery grave at the bottom of the sea. Then how would he answer those who asked, "Why did you let Jameel go?" as if it were proper that the blame for my leaving should fall at his door. He used every ploy to discourage me. But he must have known that ploys would not work with me; they would only make me more determined. If, by some miracle, I succeeded, I knew how proud he would be of my accomplishments.

I was the first to acknowledge that my father and I shared a special relationship. Although I promised other family members that I would phone home often and talk to them, it was a promise I could not make to my father who is deaf. He can speak and read lips both in Arabic and Turkish with an agility that amazes all who know him. While I was off sailing around the world he would have to content himself with receiving news of me second-hand. We would both miss the unique father/son bond we had cultivated and nourished over the years, especially since I was his only son.

When the taxi arrived, I threw Roy's bag into the back seat. There was a lump in my throat as I shook his hand.

"You made all the impossible tasks seem possible," I said. "You helped me untangle the mess of spaghetti. I am going to miss your company very much."

"And I yours," he answered. "But this is your trip, not mine. The time has arrived for me to go home and you to get on with it. You're ready."

"Sherry and I will think of you often and try to remember all the things you taught us."

"Please send me a postcard from your ports of call. And when you come to England, call me. I will want to hear all your adventures first-hand."

That afternoon I prepared for my departure from Vilamoura. This would be my second attempt at single-handling. Was I up to the challenge? If I could believe Roy, the answer was yes. I promised myself that this time there would be no mishaps. I provisioned the boat for the two day sail, called Sherry then cleared customs.

I decided not to check with the weather station. What if I got bad news. Then I would be caught in Vilamoura with a very thin wallet. But perhaps even more important, with a heavy heart. It was so unlike me to be depressed. I felt half there, as if a part of me had climbed on the plane with Roy that morning. I couldn't bear to hang around Vilamoura for one extra moment and think about how much I was going to miss his company and counsel and guidance.

What I needed was some fresh ocean breezes to bolster my confidence and self-reliance.

I looked at the sky. It was the colour of stone-washed denim with feathers of clouds along the horizon. The sun was shining and a gentle breeze rippled the surface of the water. Everything would be fine.

My last task before I turned on the engine and left the harbour was to check that all the lines were on board and secured tight!

Chapter Four

I slipped quietly from the harbour at Vilamoura, Portugal under motor in the middle of the afternoon on November 10. This time there were no crowds to bid me farewell – no Roy or Sherry or my son Essam waving frantically from the jetty. If I got into trouble would there be the Portuguese equivalent of Graeme and his mates from the RNLI to bail me out? Somehow I doubted it. For the first time I felt truly on my own as I headed out into open water on my way to Casablanca.

The Egyptian and Saudi flags flew proudly from the lanyard. Since *Baraka A* had been built and registered in England, the Union Jack alone flew from the official place on the stern staff. How I wished that it could have been otherwise. I still had moments of regret that we had not been able to begin and end our voyage in our home port of Jeddah, Saudi Arabia. Although I was a determined man, I was also a pragmatic one. I knew that my father would have pulled every possible string to prevent my leaving which in his mind was synonymous with my certain demise. I feared that he might even try to have the boat confiscated. I could not take the chance that his string-pulling would accomplish its purpose.

Also I could not face the tangle of paperwork and bureaucratic red tape which was sure to ensnare me if I had tried to depart from Jeddah. I was a 'first' and consequently there was no protocol on how to proceed. The Saudi Government always moves cautiously into new territory. A million details would have to be ironed out while I waited and waited for the boat to be registered and permission granted for me to leave. For many reasons, it just made sense to register the boat in England and be done with it.

But because we were *Arab* circumnavigators, it had become a matter of pride to begin and end our journey at an *Arab* port of call. Casablanca was ideal. Located in northern Africa, it was close to the Mediterranean and the last leg of our journey. It was also just a short hop from the Canaries and would give us a chance to test our sea legs before heading off across the Atlantic.

Why was I still thinking 'we'? Sherry had made no promises but she hadn't said 'no' either. I would continue to think positively.

The trip down the Portuguese coast had been close to perfect. Surely the weather would remain fine for a few more days. Hadn't I earned it? As soon as I cleared the two moles which guard the entrance to Vilamoura harbour, I shut off the engine and raised the main and genoa, then set the self-steering. I shucked off my shirt and lay back in the cockpit with my face to the sun. 'This is more like it,' I thought.

Back in Cairo, Sherry would be getting ready to join me in Casablanca. What was she packing? Just a few changes of clothes to see her through a couple of days in Morocco? Or a more substantial suitcase full of cruising gear?

Sherry knew I had very little experience sailing a boat and like everyone else called me 'crazy'. But to my mind (and Sherry's too) there were two kinds of crazy. One was synonymous with exuberance, a sense of adventure and an eagerness to tackle the elusive. But foolhardy, the other side of the coin, never! Did I take chances? Yes, as anyone who knew me could attest. But the other question – 'Did I usually know what I was doing?' – Also deserved the 'yes' answer. I admit I enjoyed telling people that I bought a sailboat and after fifteen hours experience, just jumped on board and decided to sail around the world. A good story that always got the expected reaction – but not the whole story. I had taken several courses in sailing and navigation which I understood and passed. And I had read everything I could lay my hands on from news-stand yachting magazines to technical books on how to sail. But the ones that consumed my interest above all others were the circumnavigation stories, like *Around the World Alone* by Alan Colas, *The Gypsy Moth* by Sir Francis Chichester and *Great Voyages in Small Boats* co-authored by Guzwell, Dumas and Slocum.

There was another question that popped up with predictable regularity from family and friends and even the folks at Camper Nicholson: 'Why now?' 'What finally moved you to take action and do what you have been talking of doing for years?'

Was it Sherry telling me to 'put up or shut up'. She'd been listening to me drone on about my dream for all the years of our marriage. I'm sure her fingers were crossed that I'd choose the latter and put the dream away. Or was it because there is an order to the way things happen. Sherry said 'decide' and suddenly I just knew in my heart that the time had arrived. Was it the 'right time'? Most circumnavigators ask themselves this question and most come up with the same answer. There is no magic formula. A sailor must make his decision, choose *his own time* and trust that everything will fall into place.

I took a leave of absence from school, relinquished the lease on our house in California and tied up all the loose ends after our five year stint there. What was Sherry thinking? I hated to guess but I supposed that she was less than enthusiastic about leaving her lovely California home - and going where? She had always listened politely when I talked about my dream but had never once suggested that this was her dream too or that she had any intention of jumping aboard a sailboat and sailing around the world. But once Sherry realised that I was not all talk and no action, that I was committed, determined and full of enthusiasm, she didn't exactly say 'whither thou goest' but something close enough, so I got the picture. If she wanted to be with me, she had no choice but to sign on as first mate. The fat was in the fire.

Knowing Sherry's level of interest in my dream, I had always planned on a single-handed voyage. But then Sherry told me that this worried her more than she had ever been able to admit. Even though she was the first to give me top marks in the physical fitness department, she could not imagine what toll a single-handed voyage would exact from both my body and my spirit. And so she jumped into the fire with me.

"If you're going then I'm going too," she announced with a mixture of reluctance and enthusiasm, which meant that I had to begin thinking about a larger vessel. But bigger boats cost a lot more money and I had only a limited supply of that commodity.

When Sherry said, "Let me help. I have some funds put aside which will let us buy the kind of boat we need," I knew that enthusiasm had beaten reluctance around the first mark.

Once Sherry had made the commitment to come with me, she knew that she had to get herself into high gear and learn all she could about sailing and sailboats. She read her way through my library and then began mastering the practical stuff, like how to use a sextant and provision a galley and operate the radio. Boat handling she'd learn on the way. We felt reasonably well prepared. How could we go wrong with all the latest and best electronic navigational equipment on board our vessel and a captain and first mate who knew how to operate it?

The sun lulled me into an uneasy doze. Every book I had ever read on single-handed sailing warned against sleeping at night. That's when freighters prowl the oceans catching small boats unawares. And I was sailing across the Strait of Gibraltar, one of the busiest shipping lanes in the world. Jeremy Lines told me that, in his opinion, sailing single-handed was a very dangerous undertaking. There was simply no time when you could fall into a deep refreshing sleep. Two days wasn't for ever. I would make it.

The thought of freighters looming on the horizon kept me awake most of the night so I remained topside, 'on duty', only dashing below to grab a piece of bread and some fruit when my stomach began to grumble. Now if Roy were here, we would be on four hour watches. Sherry had been right. Sailing alone was proving to be a lot of work. I couldn't imagine going around the world like this.

***Baraka A* Log - November 11**

Around midnight I noticed the wind velocity increasing to Force 8. A quick check confirmed my worst fears. The barometer was falling fast and the wind had shifted direction so that I was sailing into the teeth of it and making very little progress. When dawn arrived I realised that there would be little chance of a catnap during the day. I am approaching 24 hours without sleep. The weather continues to worsen.

Wouldn't you know it! Every time I set off alone, something unforeseen happens. While double-reefing the main, I noticed that the gooseneck which holds the boom to the mast seemed to be loose. How could this be? I had done my 'Frank Mulville Inspection' before leaving Portugal and had walked around my tiny kingdom as he advised, inspecting every line and fitting. Had I missed something?

With the boat pitching and rolling, I decided that the weather was too fierce to attempt repairs. I would leave it and hope it held until the weather moderated a little. Bad decision. I was inside the cabin foraging for some food when I heard a crash. Leaping back into the cockpit, I discovered that the boom and mast had parted company. The foot of the sail was flailing wildly in the wind with the boom still attached. Luckily the luff had not come out of its slot but that might happen at any moment, especially if I made the mistake of sheeting in the main. Also the weight of the boom was sure to tear the mainsail unless I got everything back on deck and quickly.

'You've done this before,' I reminded myself as I grabbed some tiedowns and crawled forward to the mast. 'Remember your adventure near Ediston Rocks? Right, but that was just a simple sail. Now there's a boom attached which might knock you on the head.'

To this day I do not know how I found the strength to get control of the boom and sail. I guess I knew the job had to be done so I did it. Next I dropped the main and wrapped it around the boom, then stowed it behind the shrouds where I lashed the whole mess down with a spare length of anchor chain. By the time I was finished, my heart was beating like a bongo drum and my mouth was chalk dry. I staggered back into the cabin and collapsed on a bunk, exhausted and worried but also proud of myself for facing the crisis and resolving it.

Later, when I checked the boom, I found that a nut had worked itself loose – not the double-locking variety or a cotter pin, which you would expect on a sloop rigged for ocean cruising, but a simple nut. With the constant friction, I was surprised that it hadn't given way sooner. But, as annoyed as I was with Camper Nicholson, I refused to let myself off the hook that easily by saying, 'it was their fault'. Yes, it was. But it was mine too. The boat was my responsibility and I needed to know that every part of it, however small, was in top-notch working order. Later, it gave me some comfort to hear that Jeremy Lines was even more annoyed than I when he heard about the nut.

"Not part of the standard rigging on a Nick 31. Someone was taking short cuts."

Someone's short cut would never again put me in jeopardy. I promised myself to be even more vigilant. So far both of my misadventures at sea had been caused by little things, not big things like a whale or a freighter ramming into me.

***Baraka A* Log – November 11**

This will be a voyage to remember! If anything can go wrong it has. The last time I checked the SatNav, I was somewhere in the Mediterranean, which is hundreds of miles to the east of me! Maybe I can tighten a gooseneck nut when the weather eases up but I can't fix this piece of equipment. That will have to wait till Casablanca.

I have never seen waves like I'm experiencing now, only read about them in books. Giant breakers are cascading over the bow, sending foaming white water everywhere. *Baraka A* must look like a plastic toy in this monstrous sea. The waves keep getting bigger and now seem to be as tall as my mast which is 12 metres. Sometimes the boat actually climbs to the crest of the wave, then slips down into the trough. It's almost like a roller-coaster ride but I'm too tired to enjoy it. With the mainsail out of commission, I am sailing on a reefed jib and staysail with an assist from the motor. The scales in the head show that I've lost 2 kilos since I left England.

This leg had turned into a trip from hell. But I took comfort in the fact that, so far, I was okay. I knew that Sherry was waiting by the phone in Cairo. I decided not to call her. I knew she would hear the fatigue and apprehension in my voice, not to mention the background noises – wind screaming through the rigging and the sea crashing around the boat.

Also, I knew that if I called Sherry I might be tempted to tell her about an unfortunate incident, this time a near fatal one. We had always been honest with one another. She would sense it if I were keeping something back.

I didn't need to read a book to know that the wise sailor wears a harness in rough weather. Some say a single-handed sailor should always wear one. As I stood in the cockpit trying to unclog one of the scuppers, a monster wave hit the boat broadside, causing a near broach. All of a sudden I seemed to be suspended in mid-air, looking down into the trough of a wave. Luckily the boat rolled back before I dropped into the sea. Instead I crashed to the floor of the cockpit, grabbing a handrail for assistance on my way down. I had always thought that a person fell overboard by slipping on the deck. I had never imagined that the boat could suddenly just disappear from under me. When I'm out here on deck in the future, you won't find me without my safety harness.

A very unexpected event happened this evening. I went below to get out of the weather and decided to rest, just for a few moments on my bunk. I sat ramrod straight so that I would not be tempted to lie down and fall asleep. But I did fall asleep and what wakened me were lights flashing around the boat and a foghorn blaring. I leapt to my feet and raced into the cockpit, my heart thudding in my chest. There, almost on top of me, was a huge freighter. The crew were standing by the rail beaming spotlights at *Baraka A*. They yelled down to me in some language I could not understand so I gave them the thumbs up sign, which I assumed reassured them that I was okay because soon they were underway with waves and cheers in my direction. I wondered if I would ever know who they were or where they were headed. They'd probably thought *Baraka A* was an abandoned vessel, just bobbing around like a cork in a laundry tub, so they stopped to take a look. After the freighter disappeared over the horizon, I gave my head a good shake as though I was clearing a clogged pipe. Had the freighter been a dream or had it really been there beside me, dangerously close beside me? This was my first experience with a freighter but not my last. Next time I hoped to be better prepared.

***Baraka A* Log – November 11**

Earlier today I was sitting on the floor of the cockpit trying to capture the fury of this storm on videotape. Good thing I had the foresight to buy a waterproof camera. Almost impossible to keep a written log, the way the boat is heeling then rounding up into the wind as it careens through the waves. I have been staying topside so I can see the waves coming and brace myself. The creaking and groaning of the rigging, the shrieking of the wind and the sound of the hull slamming into the waves seem like some badly out of tune orchestra. Poor *Baraka A* is taking a beating but she will survive. I take comfort that the hull is doubly reinforced

with fibreglass. Boats of this design have been known to beat a collision with an iceberg. Hope I never have to put it to that test. I keep thinking of Roy's words...

'This is a grand little boat. She will take you anywhere.' Please, don't take me anywhere. Just to Casablanca and Sherry.

Out of the last two days' sailing, I could only chalk up one afternoon and one evening on the pleasure side of the chart. I reckoned that Casablanca could not be that far away unless I had been blown way off course. With the SatNav out of commission, I could get no quick fix on my position. With no sun the sextant was useless so I proceeded by 'deduced reckoning' which involved watching my bearing and lapsed time and estimating my speed. By my calculations, I was headed in the right direction.

Also, I hadn't eaten a real meal since November 10, which was the least of my worries. Today I had two accidents. While sitting at the chart table I leaned over to pick up my cigarettes which had fallen on the floor. Suddenly the boat lurched and I took off like one of those circus clowns who gets blown out of a cannon and makes everyone laugh. Except that this was no joke. My shoulder collided with the dodger stanchion, then I followed suit, crashing on to the floor of the cockpit. The force of the impact broke the stanchion but luckily my shoulder seemed okay. The second incident was more serious. I was sitting in the same place, the chart table, and, remembering the earlier incident, was just about to strap myself in with a safety harness. I heard a crash, then the boat heeled sharply, going over so far that I wondered if she would recover. While the boat was righting herself, I again found myself flying across the cabin as though I'd been launched from a giant catapult, this time headed on a downward glide path instead of outside to the cockpit. I heard a crack as my thigh made contact with the oven door. The pain took my breath away. Lying slumped on the cabin floor, I gingerly explored my leg. Could anything which hurt so much not be serious? Broken? Please God, not a broken leg. How could I continue my voyage with my leg in a cast? How could I persuade Sherry that sailing was really lots of fun and not at all dangerous if I met her in Casablanca on crutches? I crawled back to the chart table and pulled myself to my feet. Gingerly, I put some weight on my injured leg.

Pain travelled up and down my leg, then settled into a vicious throb. I didn't think it was broken. For sure I'd have some purple bruises, maybe even a match for the ones Sherry had collected on our maiden voyage from Gosport to Plymouth.

Sherry's Journal

Jameel kept in regular phone contact with me during the sail to Portugal. He said that he and Roy were having a very good time and that he was learning new things about the boat every day. I was very glad that Roy had decided to go with Jameel. Roy has been such a good friend to both of us and he always gives us good advice. I decided to phone him from Cairo and ask him if I should go with Jameel. He knows how scared I was in the English Channel. Roy said he couldn't tell me what to do. But he did tell me to consider all the pluses. The boat is sturdy, heavy and reliable. Jameel is in top form physically and mentally and he has learned to handle the boat in very bad conditions. We will probably not see worse than the English Channel. He then gave me his 'two pairs of hands, two pairs of eyes and two pairs of ears' speech which Jameel and I have heard so many times we know it by heart. He told me that was the main reason to go. How can one person stand all the watches and do all the work and be ready to deal with the problems?

In my heart I knew that I was going to join Jameel even before I talked to Roy. I guess I needed some positive advice from a friend I trust. All the people in Cairo, my friends and my family, keep telling me that I am as crazy as Jameel. Maybe I am. I keep coming back to the same question. Why did I marry this man if I did not want to share his dreams? Of course I am still very frightened that we will be lost at sea. Should I sit in Cairo waiting for him to come back or ***not*** *come back? My family says yes. My heart says that if I do not take this trip with Jameel, he will be lost to me whatever happens. Because when he sails back he will be a different man from the one who sailed away. We will be oceans apart. So many experiences will be his alone.*

When I decided to share my life with Jameel, I meant my whole life, not just bits here and there. If my father were still alive, I don't know what I would do. I think that I could not have left with him so sick. I know the worry about me would have made him even sicker.

Jameel promised to phone on his way to Casablanca but he has not. I am very anxious. I hope the trip has gone as smoothly as he hoped. In just a few days I will see Jameel in Casablanca. Shall I tell him my decision right away or let him persuade me? Persuading can sometimes be a lot of fun.

On the afternoon of November 12, after just two days at sea, two days which seemed as long as a century, I sensed a change in the weather. The winds had subsided and the sea looked not calm, but manageable. At least the towering crests and troughs of yesterday had flattened out to a mere menacing roll. But the best news of all was that my leg appeared to be okay. Hurting less but still more than I cared to think about.

By my calculations I thought I should be sighting land sometime in the late afternoon. No one could imagine my euphoria when I saw the smudge on the horizon that must be Casablanca. I had done it – and without the help of the SatNav.

Suddenly the boat was surrounded by dolphins, leaping and cavorting and talking to me in their special language. I imagined they were saying, 'Well done, sailor and welcome to Morocco.' Joining the welcome party were dozens of seagulls swooping and diving across a sky which was showing the odd patch of blue. I felt I had earned a well-deserved pat on the back. But that would have to wait until I had safely negotiated the entrance to the harbour. I remembered some lines from a sailing book I'd read, lines which had been imprinted on my brain for years: 'Most often the most dangerous part of a voyage is not on the open sea but close to land.'

From my reading and from studying the charts, I knew that the harbour at Casablanca was notorious for its narrow channel and heavy swell. Miss by even a few feet and I'd be aground and at the mercy of the breaking rollers. The trick was to come with the waves and at the last possible moment duck into the channel, hopefully avoiding a broach. While proceeding cautiously to the channel entrance, I noticed a sloop tacking back and forth in the fading light.

"Can I help?" I shouted across the water.

"We've lost our engine and we need a tow," the man at the helm answered.

'Well, I know how that feels,' I thought, as I tossed them a line. Even though a sailboat is theoretically supposed to go from A to B under sail, if your motor conks out you're in a pickle. How did the sailors of old manage? The skeletons of sailing ships which litter the ocean bottom tell the story. Often they did not manage very well.

I secured the line to my stern cleat and proceeded into the channel. Just a couple of weeks before I had been the disabled vessel in need of help. 'This is what sailing's all about,' I thought. 'Someone helps me, then I help someone else.' Now I truly understood the meaning of the words 'sailing fraternity'. I was a member; I belonged.

I towed the other boat right to the customs dock. Luckily there were two spaces available, one behind the other. The skipper jumped on to the pier and shook my hand.

"Thanks, mate. There's been a hell of a storm," he said pointing to several other boats which were being towed into the harbour. "Look at them."

My eyes followed his finger.

"Torn sails, masts down," I said. "Must have been rough out there."

The furrows between his eyes grew deeper.

"You're saying that you don't know how bad it was when you were out there yourself? You're pulling my leg."

"Well, this is more or less my first voyage single-handed," I replied. "I don't know the difference between bad and really bad yet."

"Well, this one you can chalk up as being really bad. Heard there was a fleet of racing boats which took a real beating. And a fishing boat that went down with twenty-two on board." He doffed his cap. "Thanks again for the tow."

A few days later I came across a brief news article which made me realise that the man had spoken the truth. 'The 1986 running of the Single-handed Classic started off from the north-western French city of St Malo on November 9. In the first week three consecutive deep depressions swept the course with winds frequently exceeding fifty-five knots. The toll on the fleet was heavy.'

I never learned where the race was supposed to end or if there had been any casualties. But the important stuff was imprinted on my brain. Those depressions had chased me and caught me but they had not beaten me. I was proud and grateful that *Baraka A* had come through intact. I could hear Roy's voice:

'Give the skipper a little credit too.'

My good leg felt wobbly after two days on a rolling sea. The other one just hurt. I must have looked like an old sea dog as I hobbled up to the customs shed. After completing the paperwork, I called Sherry. Next on the agenda was to tie the boat to the anchor buoy, then get the dinghy ready, row back to the pier and locate the ablution block. Those chores accomplished, I took a taxi into town and treated myself to my first real meal in days.

Seated on the restaurant chair, I had trouble keeping my balance. The entire room seemed to be going up and down. Just as a sailor needs a few days to get his 'sea legs', it appeared that I would need some time to find my 'land legs'. Maybe tomorrow. My body was craving sleep, deep, delicious, uninterrupted slumber with no freighters or storms or booms flying in the wind to disrupt me. I took a taxi back to the harbour and then limped along the jetty to the dinghy. When I reached *Baraka A*, I discovered I had visitors: two plainclothes detectives from the Moroccan police force. One was short and very thin with a huge moustache; the other was just as thin but tall and angled like a pretzel.

"What is the problem?" I stammered. "I have only been in your country for a few hours and I have done nothing wrong."

"We would prefer to talk to you downtown," said the tall one.

"Downtown? What have I done? I have been to customs, filled out the forms. Did I miss something?"

"We would like to ask you some questions at headquarters," the tall one repeated.

I noticed that his hand was resting on his sidearm.

"But can't you give me a hint of what's happening? I just got here after two horrible days at sea. I am tired beyond belief."

"That would not be possible," said the short one with an edge to his voice. "Please, we will go now!"

"Okay, anything you say," I replied. "Just let me get a few things from the boat - my passport and papers."

I opened the hatch and descended into the gloom of the cabin. I picked up my portfolio of official documents and, almost as an afterthought, included the publicity pieces from the newspapers about Sherry and I being the first Arab couple to circumnavigate the globe.

I heard the officers whispering and shuffling their feet on the deck. "Hurry up," one of them barked while the other shot a furtive glance in my direction. I climbed back into the cockpit and locked the hatch. A hundred questions were racing through my mind. What was going on here anyway? The two detectives were not about to reveal any secrets. But I knew the answer. I was under arrest!

Chapter Five

I sat silent as a statue in the back of the police car as it made its way through the streets of Casablanca, deciding that I would not give the two police officers the satisfaction of again refusing to give me any information. I had done nothing wrong so this matter was sure to be cleared up quickly. But still nagging doubts nibbled at the corners of my mind. What if I were falsely accused of some misdeed or other then, unable to prove my innocence, disappeared into the dim recesses of some jail? No one would know where I was, especially Sherry, whom I knew would conjure up the worst case scenario if I failed to meet her at the airport.

When we arrived at the police station, I was ushered into a room with a wooden table and three wooden chairs and told to wait. An officer would be with me in a few moments. The room could have been a carbon copy of any interrogation room used on a movie or TV set - cracked brown linoleum, walls the colour of pond scum, a scarred rickety table and a small barred window, high up. I wondered if they would play 'good cop, bad cop' with me. They left me stewing for about fifteen minutes, which gave me ample time to work myself into a state of righteous indignation. 'Cool it,' I told myself. 'There is a time for anger and a time to co-operate. You know how to be charming so do it!'

I stood up and extended my hand when the two officers entered the room.

"I am more than willing to give you any assistance I can."

"It's your customs declaration," said Mr Thin and Tall.

"I went to customs as soon as I arrived and filled out the form. Did I miss something?"

"It seems that you declared a pistol, a Walther 9 mm," said the short thin one. "Customs alerted us and we are now going to ask you why you are carrying a weapon."

"I do not think I am doing anything illegal. I have a licence for the gun. As to the why," I shrugged my shoulders, "my wife and I are leaving here in a few days to circumnavigate the world. Because we will be visiting some ports where there may be bandits and other criminal elements, we were advised to have a gun on board."

I smiled and offered them another apologetic shrug.

"Just as a precaution. We have no wish to harm anyone."

"Have you or your wife connections with an underground organisation in Lebanon?"

"Lebanon? No we don't." I furrowed my eyebrows in puzzlement. "Why are you asking me these things?"

"Last week there were two bomb blasts in Paris and just last night we arrested three suspects with bombs and weapons."

"Yes, and... " I replied, the question implicit in my voice.

"Some members of this terrorist organisation are in jail in France. There are threats of more bombings and more violence if these men are not released," said the thin tall one. "The police in Europe and North Africa have been asked to co-operate with the French authorities," he continued.

"Do you think I am a terrorist?"

"We do not know," said the other officer. "We are questioning all people we think are suspicious, especially travellers from the Middle East."

"I ask you to believe me. I am not a terrorist."

I opened the document portfolio and pulled out the news clippings. "These will tell you who I am and what I'm doing. As you can see, I am telling you the truth." I pointed to a picture of Sherry and me taken in Gosport. "That's us, the Arab Circumnavigators, the first people from this part of the world to ever attempt such a thing."

I spread out the news clippings on the table. I would like to say that the two police officers immediately became absorbed in the news articles, made profuse apologies and let me go. That is what essentially happened if you leave out the 'immediately' part. Like a tennis ball the questions and answers went back and forth in a succession of perfect volleys.

"Are you a terrorist?"; "No, I am just a circumnavigator."

More than two hours after my arrival at the police station, I was removed from the lists of suspects and told I was free to go. All I could think about was crawling into my bunk aboard *Baraka A* and falling into a deep dreamless sleep. But the police officers, their official business done, were now in the mood to chat: what kind of boat did I have?; such a small vessel for such a large trip!; was I really going around the world?; my wife, was she accompanying me? How extraordinary. I nodded and smiled and willed my eyes to stay open and my leg to stop throbbing. It always pays to be polite to police officers. You never know when you might need them on your side.

It was after midnight when I finally got back to the boat. 'Here's one to tell Roy,' I thought as I opened the hatch. I remembered how surprised he'd been when I mentioned that some folks think all Arabs are terrorists. Sometimes even other Arabs, like the fellows at the police station! How frustrating it was to be stereotyped. If you're a young Arab male you must be a terrorist walking around with a hand grenade in your hip pocket.

I sagged on to my bunk, took off my shoes, then rolled myself up in a sleeping bag. That was all I could manage tonight. As I was drifting off to sleep I thought again about our voyage. Perhaps there was a deeper purpose to 'this crazy idea' than simply lolling around on South Sea island beaches. Maybe Sherry and I were meant to be goodwill ambassadors for all Arabs. But how could we go about doing that? Surely not by standing up and making speeches – 'We're not terrorists, just ordinary folks like yourselves, leading ordinary lives in search of peace and harmony and the freedom to follow our dreams. Of course there are some bad apples in our barrel, just as there are in any other barrel. But it is unfair to judge all of us by the wrongful acts of a few.'

I pulled the sleeping bag over my head to ward off the evening chill. I knew we would make no speeches. That was not our style. Instead we would extend our hands in friendship to those we met along the way. I guess that it came down to just being ourselves and hoping that actions really would speak louder than words.

I looked out through the hatch to a sky washed with stars. As I lay in my bunk, drinking in the night, I could hear Sherry's voice in my ear:

'Lovely sentiments, Jameel, except for one small point. No one is going to buy the story that we're just ordinary folks. Like it or not, we're unique. How many other Arab couples are attempting to go around the world in a 31 foot sailboat?'

"True enough," I replied turning over in the bunk and punching my pillow back into shape.

'But that's good,' I thought as sleep crept softly over me. 'People will hear about us, be anxious to meet us and then, once they get to know us, they will find out what Arabs are really like. It's hard to get your point across if you don't have an audience.'

The next afternoon Sherry arrived from Cairo. When I saw her walking into the arrival lounge, my heart caught in my throat. How lonely the days had been without her. Being apart was also not our style. During our years of marriage we had seldom been separated.

On the taxi ride back to the harbour I jabbered non-stop about the sail from Portugal. I made sure to put the emphasis on all the positive aspects of the journey, like how well the boat and I had come through a pretty substantial storm. I didn't leave out the dolphins. Dolphins make any story better.

When we arrived at the marina we were stopped at the gate by marina security, demanding to see our papers. I passed muster, Sherry did not. It appeared that although I had a permit to be on the premises and *Baraka A* had a permit to be tied to the buoy, Sherry had no permit. Neither persuasion nor bluster had any effect. The message came across loud and clear – no permit, no entry. Then, no worries, I told myself with a jaunty wave to the security officers. We would simply find a taxi and go into town to a hotel.

A few moments later my heart fell to my boots as the clerk behind the hotel desk reviewed my documents then eyed me suspiciously.

"Sir," he said in nasal tones, "this permit only allows you to stay on your boat at the harbour. I'm sorry but I cannot give you and your wife a room."

"Please help me to understand. My wife, whom I have not seen in many days, has just arrived from Cairo today. Apparently she cannot stay with me on the boat because she does not have a permit. Now it seems that I cannot stay here with her because my permit is for the boat only. Why not just issue me a hotel permit?"

"We cannot do that, sir. The police must issue a special permit."

"Ah, the police," I said, grabbing Sherry's hand and heading for the door. "I was there last night so I know the way."

"Jameel, what are you not telling me?" asked Sherry as we climbed into a taxi.

"I have a couple of friends at the police station. Everything will be all right, I promise."

My two friends of the previous evening were not on duty but it appeared that they had told their fellow officers all about us and our plans to sail around the world. Soon we were surrounded by police officers jabbering and chattering and asking questions.

"Please," I said, holding up my hand like a cop directing traffic. "Help us cut through this red tape; then we can talk."

"Most certainly, sir," came the prompt reply and, with the flourish of a pen, the deed was done. Once that piece of paper and another giving Sherry permission to stay in the harbour were safe in my pocket, we began edging towards the door, fielding questions, smiling as we pleaded fatigue, inviting one and all to drop by and see us at the marina. Eventually we escaped on to the street, flagged a taxi and headed back to the hotel. We were convulsed with laughter during that ride as I recounted my two visits to the police station on two consecutive nights.

"There must be a reason for the way things happen," I said. "If I hadn't been arrested last night, hadn't made friends with those two officers, then tonight's outcome might have been very different - me at the marina and you here in town. Not a good plan. We need to be together in the same place. How else can I convince you to come with me to the Canaries."

I hardly noticed that Sherry said nothing.

Sherry's Journal

When Jameel met me at the airport, at first I didn't recognise him. He looked extremely tired and had lost a lot of weight in such a small period of time. We talked on the way from the airport about his trip, the bad weather he faced alone and the boom that came loose and almost flew away taking the sails with it. He was able to hoist it back and he felt confident in himself and in the boat after what it went through.

What a treat it was to sleep in a real bed. And sleep and sleep and sleep until my body felt like its old self. What luxury to order room service and read the newspaper and laugh with Sherry over the comic strips. From our hotel room, the streets of Casablanca spread out below us like a spider's web. Just barely visible was the marina where *Baraka A* bobbed at her mooring, her mast just one of the dozens of matchsticks lined up along the horizon. Poor old *Baraka A* – she needed these few days off as much as her master.

Sherry wanted to know every detail of my trip from Portugal which threw me into a quandary. How could I depict that leg as anything but a horrendous experience which was apt to frighten Sherry so thoroughly that she might refuse to sign on for the trip to Tenerife? But what story could I tell her except the truth? Keeping secrets from one another topped the list of things which were not our style.

"I never want to go through a storm like that again," I said. "But, if I do, I know that the boat can handle it and so can I. This boat is so sturdy, Sherry, so strong. You should have seen the other boats being towed into the harbour, with masts down and sails torn. I even towed one in myself. I bet those skippers had much more experience than me. But I've been thinking that maybe experience isn't the key. So what if you've been sailing for years and years? If your boat won't stand up to the wind and the waves then you're in trouble for sure. What's important is to have a good boat. You would have been so proud of *Baraka A*, Sherry. Even without a boom and mainsail, she made it safely to harbour. And so did I, only slightly the worse for wear."

"What if you had been really injured?" asked Sherry as she examined my leg. "Nice bruises, Jameel, but I think the ones I got on the trip from Gosport were much more colourful."

"Every time something bad happens, I learn another lesson," I replied. "Sitting at the chart table, even with a safety harness, while the boat is rolling and pitching may be a bad idea. I should have chosen my bunk. But after this accident, I know that we must be prepared for anything, whether it is an accident or illness. There are no doctors in the middle of the ocean."

Sherry nodded in agreement. "I will check our medical supplies to make sure that we have everything we need."

The next day we moved back to the marina. Our too brief sojourn at the hotel had been worth every penny, for during that time, Sherry agreed to put on her first mate's cap once again, at least as far as the Canaries. There was a new strength in Sherry. She seemed confident and determined and less apprehensive than when I had left her in Plymouth. She also was determined to not get into another verbal sparring match with her family in Cairo over her decision. She would call and tell them where she was and what she was doing once we were safely out at sea. Then the arguments and persuasive words would be too late.

Sherry's Journal

Everybody we have met in the marina is very nice. Rafted up right next to us are some French sailboats. Fortunately I speak French so we have had many good conversations. They want to know everything about us and then they go and tell other people about us. So we spend a lot of time talking and explaining while we are loading provisions. One man said that he had never before seen Arabs living on a sailboat. One day the local newspaper sent a reporter asking the same questions we have answered many times: where were we going and what did we hope to accomplish? The marine officers and personnel here, those people who have lived around boats and salt water, understand the lure of the sea and don't need to ask the usual questions. Still they are amazed that we are attempting such a long trip in such a small boat. They wished us luck and promised that when we returned there would be a big celebration. We don't know when we are leaving yet. We cannot find a marine weather forecast so we are relying on our eyes and what we hear from the locals. They are saying that the waves 'out there' are 10 feet high. Too high for me, as Jameel knows. Meanwhile we continue our preparations while enjoying the sunshine. It is so much warmer than England. This alone makes a difference in our morale.

The sun felt good on my back as I loaded supplies on board the boat this afternoon. I have read many books on provisioning a vessel but this is the first time I am doing it for an offshore voyage. Every book emphasised that it was better to over provide than skimp. For a two week voyage, you should take supplies to last a month. You need that margin of error so you don't run out. The goal is to have everything you will need which makes life on board pleasant and comfortable. Yesterday we visited the produce market and bought green unripe fruits which I washed, dried thoroughly and then wrapped in aluminium foil. Hard fruits last longer than soft ones so I concentrated on green mangoes, oranges, grapefruit and lots of lemons. Forget bananas because they go soft or all ripen at the same time. Carrots and potatoes and onions will keep a long time so I bought a good supply. I don't know what foods will be available in Tenerife so I am really stocking up here. I am writing this as if leaving Tenerife is really on my agenda. No commitments yet. Jameel hates meat from tins but we need some meat on board so I bought a few tins anyway. He doesn't mind canned fruit, vegetables and beans. Our favourite is foul medames beans which we can eat with rice. I also bought many cans of tomato sauce which I will use to make macaroni and spaghetti dishes. Another favourite is beef salami and beef jerky which doesn't need refrigeration and will keep very well. I wonder if we made a mistake in choosing an icebox rather than refrigeration. Jameel says that once the ice melts, the icebox is nothing but a bin. The French sailors think a refrigerator uses too much battery power. We'll know a lot more in a few days. Maybe someday I'll write my own book about provisioning a boat.

While Sherry loaded and sorted the provisions I took care of the broken and malfunctioning gear, which proved to be easier than I anticipated. Replacing the fitting for the boom mast gooseneck only involved a trip to a local marine hardware store where I purchased a double-locking nut and some spares. Then it was a simple task to reset the boom in place.

I was worried that the SatNav would be a bigger problem. Why had it given me such erroneous readings during the storm when I really needed it to work? Two antennae used the backstay as a ground, the SatNav and the SSB radio. It didn't take long to figure out the problem. The SSB radio was erasing the SatNav memory. Solution: shut off the SatNav when using the SSB. Funny how sometimes the biggest problems turn out to have the simplest solutions. My big jobs done, I turned my attention to helping Sherry.

We inventoried our medical kit. A doctor in California, who was also our friend, had provided everything we might possibly need from antibiotics to painkillers to packaged IV injections for unexpected crises like snakebite or allergic reaction. We had remedies for colds and flu and sunburn, bandages of all shapes and sizes, pressure pads to stop bleeding, ace bandages for sprains and strains, even a suture kit with instructions.

And for Sherry an adequate supply of seasick tablets called Stugeron. This is the remedy recommended by the British Navy. It has the advantage of combating nausea without putting the user to sleep. Without this medication the voyage would have been impossible for Sherry.

We chose November 20 as our departure date. November 19 was spent tying up the loose ends. I made sure that our paperwork was in order. We wanted no last minute delays while we waited for stamps or signatures. For sure, we didn't want another trip to the police station. I checked and rechecked all the standing rigging, then inventoried my supply of spare parts and filled the water and fuel tanks. Sherry made her last visit to the supermarket for some fresh meat and vegetables which would see us through the first couple of days. She also bought a souvenir of Casablanca. We have decided to buy some small thing from each port of call to remember our journey.

If Sherry was experiencing any pre cast-off jitters, she showed no signs. Maybe she had ordered the butterflies in her stomach to cool it. Just like me.

But overshadowing all the preparations was a feeling of exhilaration. I felt like a bird tottering on the edge of the nest. It was time to leave but was I ready? Yes, oh yes – I was more than ready. The dream I had carried with me since childhood was about to become reality.

Tomorrow the voyage of *Baraka A*, our circumnavigation would really begin.

Chapter Six

Fog shrouded the Casablanca harbour on the morning of November 20, the day of our departure, a drifting sifting mist that made us dive for our jackets. We had planned to be up 'before the sun' and underway by 8 a.m. As we untied the lines a few minutes before the appointed hour, I congratulated myself that everything was going according to plan. Everything except the sun. The seagulls sitting on the dock pilings ruffled their feathers against the weather and glared at us morosely as if to say, 'How can you be so happy on such a gloomy day?' I grinned as I turned on the engine. Nothing, no nothing, could spoil this moment for me. I was ready, *Baraka A* was ready, and even Sherry, who'd had so many reservations about our voyage, was ready too. We slipped from our mooring with no fanfare, so unlike our departure from Gosport when friends had lined the jetty and chase boats had followed us to capture the moment on video.

Only Mohammed, who was a marine employee and native Moroccan, appeared on the dock to wish us farewell and good luck.

"When you return, I'll be here to welcome you home," he said, smiling broadly.

We had become friendly with this young man during the previous week and, like Josh, the taxi driver from Gosport, he had been a true friend. Funny how it's often the 'little guy' who remains etched in your memory while the bigger fish swim away into oblivion. Mohammed had been like our personal Yellow Pages during our days in Casablanca. He knew the best and cheapest places to buy provisions and often he would help us haul them back to the boat. If we needed information about anything, he would appear, as if by some prearranged signal, and tell us not to worry. How we had come to appreciate his advice and suggestions and his just being there. So many times we had looked at each other, nodded in unison and said, "Let's ask Mohammed." Such offers of friendship are rare, like polished gems hidden in a rock crevice full of ordinary stones. Mohammed had concurred with me on the advisability of leaving port early to avoid rush hour. Casablanca is a busy harbour with fishing boats, freighters and cruising sloops fighting for space in the narrow channel.

I remembered entering Casablanca Harbour the previous week. I had been so overjoyed to finally be near land, to have 'made it' through a succession of storms. Now I wondered if I had not appreciated how tricky the channel could be. Not a chance. Sherry estimated the breakers, which were rolling in from the open sea and crashing on shore, to be well over eight feet high. If *Baraka A* strayed from the channel and went aground in these shallow treacherous waters... I brushed the thought away as I listened to the steady even thump of the engine and checked the compass heading. Soon this channel would be a memory. Soon we would be out in open waters heading for the Canaries.

The pitching and rolling of the boat sent Sherry running for the bucket.

"What a way to celebrate our departure," she said.

"When we reach deeper water the swells should even out and we'll have a smoother ride," I assured her.

"Well, to be on the safe side, I think I'll take some Stugeron. Hope they stay down," she replied ruefully. "Why didn't I think to take a couple before we left the harbour?"

"If you can manage it, find a spot on the horizon and glue your eye to it. Sometimes that helps."

Sherry looked over her shoulder at the disappearing shoreline.

"I think I can still see Mohammed," she said.

I passed her the binoculars.

"Yes, it's him," she said. He's standing on a spit of land by the harbour entrance waving like crazy. This will be the final nice thing he does for us. I'll keep my eye pinned on him, then maybe I won't get sick again."

Great idea, but it didn't work. Sherry continued to be seasick.

***Baraka A* Log – November 20**

After clearing the channel, I raised the main and then the genoa. The sea was still rough. Sherry took some more Stugeron and then lay down on her bunk and slept like a baby. After all the frantic days in Casablanca I knew that I should also be tired but I was too excited.

As we sailed into deeper water the pitching motion lessened and the sun came out. One minute we were in the mist and then it disappeared, just like someone had opened the curtains to let in the sunshine.

Today we began to sort ourselves out. At sea there must be an order to the day and everyone must know his or her tasks. We decided to take four hour shifts at the helm. After Sherry woke up from her nap, she came and took her turn. The sea continued to moderate and the temperature to climb. I noticed that Sherry was smiling.

Tonight Sherry passed a milestone, standing watch alone at night while I slept. To my great surprise, my sleep was real and deep, not a quasi-slumber with one ear cocked towards the helm.

Sherry's Journal, November 20

In spite of being sick on this, our first day out, I am enjoying the trip and am not feeling scared. Well, maybe a little scared when Jameel disappeared into the cabin tonight and told me that I was in charge. Actually the autopilot does the work. I kept scanning the horizon for freighters but saw none. This morning I sat in the cockpit and welcomed the dawn. I saw the sun coming up and it was a beautiful sight. Today we phoned our families and let them know that we were at sea and okay. My family was not as surprised as I expected them to be. But they are still very concerned about our safety.

On our second morning at sea, I noticed that the barometer had fallen a little. I hoped we would not experience a nose-dive but, to be cautious, I reefed both the main and genoa and set the sails wing to wing which increased the rolling motion but also increased the speed. I thought back to my sail to Vilamoura with Roy, like a wild ride at Disneyland. The combined forces of the time constraints we were under and Roy's love of going fast and pushing a boat to its max., meant that we never took a reef. No criticism intended There are many ways to sail a boat, an argument when taken to its logical conclusion, was as encompassing as life itself. It came down to a matter of preference, a personal choice. There are as many unique sailing styles as skippers at the helm or birds in the sky. Roy's love was ocean racing; mine was cruising along enjoying the view and making sure that Sherry wasn't scared out of her wits. I thought how differently I behaved on land behind the wheel of my car where I relished the challenge of manoeuvring the vehicle quickly through traffic. Roy told me that behind the wheel he was a dawdler. Most of the time he didn't even bother with a car, preferring a bicycle instead.

While Sherry was on watch, I decided to check out the *Walker Log* to see if it was functioning properly. While at sea there always seemed to be an endless list of things to check and while the weather was co-operative these tasks filled the empty moments.

It was imperative to have an accurate measure of the distance travelled. Luckily all that was needed was some lubrication so I doctored the apparatus with some '3 in 1' oil and then lowered it back into the water where it trailed in the boat's wake.

Sherry's Journal, November 21

The sea today is good and it is warm, with not so much wind as yesterday. Also my fear is less. I just have to keep my mind off the boat's motion so I will not get seasick again. This morning we had breakfast in the cockpit. This is real freedom. The seagulls which have been following us since we left Casablanca have disappeared so I know we are far from land. This afternoon we went forward to the bow and sunbathed while the autopilot did all the work and kept us on a steady course. We each had a nap during the day so we would be alert for our night watches. Nothing out here but us and a couple of fishing boats off in the distance.

Our captain/crew roles seemed to be failing into place. I explained to Sherry that, on a boat, there could only be one person in charge. If we had an emergency I would take the responsibility for making the decision on what to do or not to do. In emergencies there would be no time for debates. And Sherry must trust that I knew what I was doing. On big ships, they called this 'following orders'. On *Baraka A* I preferred to say 'following directions'.

Safety was a major concern to me. Remembering my experience when the boat and I had almost parted company off the African coast, I stressed the importance of not wandering around the deck without a safety harness. In fact, I asked Sherry not to wander from the cockpit, at least for the present. If she wanted to sunbathe on the foredeck, I would put the boat on autopilot and go forward with her.

I was really proud of Sherry and her enthusiasm to learn all she could about our boat. She seemed a natural on the tiller and almost immediately was able to sense changes in wind direction or speed.

Also she didn't grumble about standing watch at night - lonely hours, scary hours when the possibility of a freighter suddenly appearing out of the darkness was very real.

Sherry's Journal, November 22

The sea wasn't as calm today. By afternoon the waves were steep but not monstrous like Jameel has seen. The wind velocity also increased, which meant a rough ride but the good part was, that we made excellent time, sometimes surfing along at 6.5 knots. Today we had to fill the diesel tanks from the jerry cans. It was a messy job. There is nothing out here but blue water all around. We saw two ships today far, far away. If they had come close to us, I would have waved. How lonely it can be on the ocean. So much time and so little to do. Tonight the temperature was much cooler. Does this mean a weather change?

Baraka A Log – November 23

The SatNav is giving me problems again. I cannot believe the figures I am getting are correct because they are so far off a previous fix. Should I believe the equipment or my gut instinct, which tells something is wrong? I know the error is not caused by the SSB wiping out the SatNav memory because I turned off the SatNav when I used the radio. Could there be a difference between the deduced reckoning position and the fixed position? You bet! More than 30 n miles. I entered the DR position and the next SatNav fix came out okay. Bravo! Usually all that is needed to set things right is a little perseverance.

Today was our fourth day at sea. So far I would rate this trip as excellent. I could tell that Sherry was apprehensive about the erroneous reading from the SatNav and worried that I had solved the problem too easily. I tried to reassure her that everything was okay.

"Even if we don't use the SatNav, I know where we are," I assured her. "Besides, if we don't sight the Canaries on schedule, we will turn and sail east, back to Africa until we find land."

When we left the Canaries, we wouldn't have contingency plans like that, but I kept those thoughts to myself. In truth I had no worries. I believed my navigation was right on, a fact I hoped would be confirmed the next day, when we sighted land.

The barometer dropped this afternoon and we spent a miserable evening lashed by rain and wind. Luckily it didn't last too long, which put a smile back on Sherry's face.

Early on the morning of November 24 I saw lights on the horizon, two hours later than I'd predicted. Still Sherry was impressed.

"Navigation is not magic," I explained. "I have pilot charts, a compass and the means to fix our position. I always know where we are."

Sherry just nodded. I wondered if she thought that we just pushed off from the dock, bobbed around the ocean for a few days and by sheer luck made it to our destination. I decided to encourage her to take a more active role. Let her take the sextant shots and check the compass bearing. Just like me, she'd learn by doing.

Sherry's Journal, November 24

At 5.30 a.m. this morning I watched the horizon as the island of Tenerife slowly appeared out of the haze, almost like a mirage in the desert. I stood with Jameel in the cockpit welcoming the dawn and the new day and congratulating ourselves on the successful completion of the first leg of our journey. I felt proud of Jameel for his navigational skills, proud of Baraka A for being a sturdy, trustworthy vessel and proud of myself for signing on as first mate and even enjoying most of the moments. I wanted to jump up and down and shout, "We made it, we made it!" but instead I gave Jameel a congratulatory hug.

Jameel said that sighting land was always a thrill but reaching it would be an even bigger one. That wouldn't happen for another 5–6 hours. Our morale got an extra boost when a school of dolphins, numbering at least thirty, surrounded the boat and put on a spectacular show. Jumping and cavorting, they seemed to hang suspended in mid-air, nodding their heads and uttering friendly welcoming squeaks. Were they trying to communicate with us? I wished we could answer. Jameel captured the moment on both the video and still cameras.

Sherry had decided to use our voyage around the world as a geography and history lesson, hoping to learn all she could about the people and places we would visit. To this end we had gathered together a fairly substantial library. While we ate breakfast, Sherry filled me in on the Canary Islands.

"The Canaries belong to Spain and consist of seven islands, the largest of which is Tenerife," she read. "The capital of the country is Santa Cruz which has a good deepwater harbour." She paused and gazed at the islands in the distance. "Why aren't we going to Santa Cruz?" she asked.

"From what I've read, Santa Cruz is a big commercial harbour with lots of traffic. The harbour at Darsena Pesquera will have more room. And we'll still be close enough to Tenerife to pick up supplies."

Sherry's Journal, November 24

I was disappointed when we entered Darsena Pesquera harbour. It looked so primitive but I took comfort in the fact that it was crammed with sailing boats from everywhere, almost like a mini United Nations. As I looked around at all the flags from different countries snapping in the breeze, I noticed that there was just one Saudi flag and one Egyptian flag. And they were ours! Tears stung the corners of my eyes and I wiped them away impatiently. Why was I glassy-eyed on such a happy occasion? Jameel must have read my mind because he came up with the perfect answer.

"Look around the harbour, Sherry. We are the only Arabs here. It makes me so proud to represent our people this way."

Not trusting myself to speak, I squeezed his hand. I stood in the cockpit drinking in the sights and sounds while Jameel puttered around looking for an empty berth, which turned out to be a 'mission impossible'. In the end we rafted up next to a French couple.

As we were securing the lines and adjusting the fenders we saw an ageing hippie-type man in tattered blue jeans waving at us from the dock.

"Where did y'all get the Saudi flag?" he asked in the slow molasses drawl of the Southern United States.

"It's ours. My husband's family is from Saudi Arabia. And mine is from Egypt," I answered, then introduced him to Jameel.

"Well, I'll be!" the man retorted. "I lived in the Kingdom in the late Seventies, early Eighties, the oil boom days. Worked for Aramco. I knew quite a few Saudis and not one of them ever talked of going to sea. In fact you're the first Arabs I've ever seen on a sailboat. Some liked them fast speedboats, but never a sailboat."

"We hope we are the first of many to take this wonderful trip," said Jameel.

The man held his hand to his forehead like a visor and squinted into the blinding late afternoon sun.

"Used to know some Arabic," he said. "Baraka." He pursed his lips in concentration, then shook his head impatiently. "No, can't remember."

"It means Blessing," said Jameel.

The man nodded in agreement.

"Yes, that's it. But what's the 'A' for?"

And so Jameel again told the story of how our boat got its very unique name. We had been determined to paint 'Baraka' on the hull from the beginning but unfortunately that name had already been taken by someone else. So we simply added the A. If we ever had another boat we would probably name her Baraka B.

We talked with the man for a few more minutes and then he waved goodbye and walked away, still muttering and shaking his head.

"I guess we really are different," I told Jameel.

After tidying up the boat, we set out to explore the town. It seemed a pleasant enough place but a bit 'touristy' which is natural, I guess, because tourism is one of the prime industries here. What we were looking for we found very quickly – an open restaurant with an appealing menu. How lovely it was to sit outside on the terrace and admire the gulls swooping over the harbour while enjoying a delicious dinner of steak and shrimp with delicately seasoned rice. And after dinner, two cups of espresso coffee while we watched the sun dip beneath the horizon. This sailing life might not be too bad after all!

I found out why the harbour was so jammed with boats. The annual Atlantic Cruiser Race was due to start off Grand Canary in a few days' time. There was a carnival atmosphere around the marina as hordes of sailors made final preparations, loaded supplies and gave each other hot tips on rigging and sailing strategies. Even though we weren't racing, we felt as though we were truly part of the sailing fraternity. I thought back to the time I had towed that disabled sailboat into Casablanca harbour. I realised then that people who spend their time on sailboats are a special breed and enjoy a special bond with one another. Could the same be said of other sports, like racing car drivers or cross country skiers?

That night, before going to sleep, I filled in the log for this, the last day of our first leg.

Baraka A **Log – November 23**

Arrival: 25-11-86
Mileage: 537 N miles.
Heading: 237 degrees

The trip so far has been fantastic. The near perfect weather conditions have, I hope, given Sherry the confidence to sign on as first mate for the next leg, across the Atlantic.

After a few days in Darsena Pesquera, we decided to cast off the lines and head for the harbour of Los Cristianos near the southern tip of the island. The crowded holiday atmosphere of sailors tuning up for a race had not provided the restful atmosphere we needed to recharge our batteries before heading for Antigua. We had heard that Los Cristianos was quiet and had an abundant supply of water for cleaning the boat and ourselves.

We decided to inch our way along the coast keeping in sight of land. The forty-five mile trip took eight hours under motor as the winds were light to non-existent.

Sherry's Journal, November 29

A nice sail today which ended in disappointment. Los Cristianos is even more crowded than Darsena Pesquera. I read that this harbour used to be an old fishing port which has been renovated into a modern yacht harbour. I was happy to hear that the shopping facilities were excellent. But it is going to be very difficult to load the boat because we were forced to anchor out. This means a dinghy trip each time we have to go to shore.

We spent four days in Los Cristianos. The harbour was crammed with boats, mostly English and Scandinavian. Lots of blond heads. Again we were an oddity, the first Arab couple to ever drop a hook in these waters. Sherry kept herself busy making shopping lists, buying the provisions and storing them, which turned out to be as big a pain in the neck as we anticipated. Also the fresh water supply was meagre. In the end we had to rent a hotel room if we wanted to take a shower.

But nothing could dampen my good mood. Sherry had made her decision. She would cross the Atlantic with me.

"When I get scared," she said, "I think of you all alone in the middle of the ocean and I know I must be with you. And then I think of the trip here from Casablanca, which was okay most of the time and hope the next weeks at sea will be the same."

Well, so did I. But I knew the Atlantic could be a fearsome stretch of water. We would take each day as it came and we would be okay. Somehow, I just knew that to be the truth.

Sherry's Journal, December 1, The Canaries

I have been spending my days shopping and talking to the people in the harbour. One fellow told me that I was the only Egyptian he had ever met. This surprised me as Egyptians live in every country in the world. I told him if he wanted to meet some more of us he should take a trip to my country and visit the pyramids.

"On this journey," he said, "you will be so lonely. You will never meet any other people from your country."

'That is probably true,' I thought. 'But I will meet people from other countries. And I will always have Jameel.'

Jameel has been bombarded with the usual round of questions from people here in the harbour. I imagine that this is going to be the routine everywhere but he doesn't mind. In fact, Jameel loves talking to people.

So many boats here have cats on board. Why didn't we think to bring ours? They would have been very good company. I guess our boat is too small for people and cats and a litter tray. Also, there are quarantine restrictions in Australia and maybe other places too.

We have decided to begin our next leg on December 3, which should get us to Antigua by Christmas. The morning before our departure I dropped a case of ravioli, all twenty-four cans of it, into the murky polluted waters of the harbour. I put on my snorkel and mask and tried to retrieve it. Not a pleasant task and I gave up after rescuing a few visible cans from the gunky bottom. We inventoried the supplies and figured that we had enough food without the ravioli. And then we rented a hotel room for our last shower. This may have been a luxury for Sherry, but for me it was a necessity. The stench of the harbour water seemed to have invaded my pores. I hoped I hadn't picked up any nasty microbes, germs, diseases or whatever else happened to be lurking in that water. Tonight, our last in port, I could tell that Sherry's stomach was churning with butterflies. As she gazed at the boats in the harbour, I detected a haunted, tormented expression in her eyes. I knew that she was frightened. So was I. But that was normal. I reminded myself again that a little healthy fear was good because it kept me alert. There was no room for complacence aboard *Baraka A*.

I took her hand in mine.

"Look, Sherry," I said. "See all these sailboats here. They are leaving right after us for an ocean race. We won't be out there alone. There'll be boats in front of us, boats behind us, boats all around us." I hoped I was varnishing the truth a bit because the last thing I wanted was to be part of a flotilla.

"I know you have some reservations," I continued, "but, please believe me, everything will be okay. Remember how scared you were when we left Casablanca? This will be the same, only longer."

How I wished that I had been able to say, 'I promise.' But oceans, I knew, did not honour the promises made by men.

Sherry squeezed my hand and laid her head on my shoulder.

"I'm glad we're leaving tomorrow, before I have a chance to change my mind."

Yes, I was glad too. The sooner we weighed anchor, the better.

Chapter Seven

We hoisted the anchor and departed Los Cristianos just after lunch on December 3. As we threaded our way through the flotilla of boats which had gathered for the races, we realised how much we were going to miss the company of other sailors during the coming weeks. Most of the yachtsmen had heard about us and we were given a grand send-off complete with waves and shouts and cheers.

Once clear of the traffic, I raised the main and genoa. Grasping the tiller in my hand, I felt the boat respond to my touch. How exciting it was to watch the sails capturing the wind and to feel *Baraka A* heeling over gently as her bow sliced cleanly through the waves.

This was it: the real beginning of the voyage. I realised that I had uttered these same words at other jumping-off points. Sherry said that I sounded like a tape with only one soundtrack. The other beginnings had been like practice sprints before the final whistle, but, even so, when taken in context, they became the benchmark against which all future experiences would be measured.

To my mind our journey so far had been crammed with firsts. My *first* attempt at single-handling had ended with a quick return to port with a line around the prop. The next time out of Plymouth harbour with Roy Mullender on board counted as a first as well, my *first* successful attempt sailing offshore into the Atlantic, which was soon followed by my *first* successful single-handed voyage. Sailing *Baraka A* from Portugal to Casablanca through a succession of storms had bolstered my self-confidence and confirmed I was a survivor. Sherry's *first* ocean crossing – albeit a short, easy one – from Casablanca to the Canaries had taught her that sailing could sometimes be fun. And now here we were, the *first* Arabs to ever attempt an Atlantic crossing in a small vessel.

Destination: Antigua. Distance: 2582 nautical miles according to my calculations. I didn't expect to be far off.

The young call it being 'pumped'. At least, that's what our son Essam used to say when he was really excited about something. I was that and more – exhilarated, energetic, confident and brimming with enthusiasm. The pure simple joy of being master of this vessel brought a lump to my throat.

I stopped my musing for a moment and glanced at Sherry who was staring intently at the receding shoreline. Was she trying to quell a queasy stomach or was she awash in nostalgia for terra firma and the life she used to know? How would she cope in the confines of a 31 foot sailboat? Would she be homesick for the life she had left behind – especially our home in California with the beautiful gardens she'd so carefully cultivated? I shook my head. No use 'what iffing' and worrying. Sherry's ability to cope was quite unique. After all, she'd been coping with me for all the years of our marriage. She was amazingly adaptable: one moment resilient as steel, the next as pliable as a feather pillow.

Dared I hope that her enthusiasm would ever match mine? Unlikely, but then I remembered when her enthusiasm level had registered zero. We were definitely making progress!

The wind dropped to nothing by mid-afternoon. We had a choice – wallow and drift or rev the engines and continue on our course, hoping that wind lay ahead of us. Impatient to get some miles behind us, I turned on the engine. Fuel consumption had to be carefully rationed as there would be no friendly marinas along the way where we could duck in to replenish fuel and food or get out of the weather.

By evening the wind picked up again and I quickly shut down the engine and reverted to sail power.

Sherry's Journal, December 4th

We called our families this morning and told them that we were fine and headed for Antigua. I know that they are worried sick about us. We promised to call them every 10 days. Every penny we spent on the SSB radio has been worth it. When we call home we are hooked up by means of a maritime satellite relay station. The marvels of modern technology.

Today we had wind all day and made good time. We sighted another boat crossing in front of us, 24 metres, (almost 3 times bigger than Baraka A*) named* Mistere of London. *Jameel contacted the skipper on the VHF and learned that he, too, is heading for Antigua. I am learning that a bigger hull means a bigger hull speed and the boat soon disappeared over the horizon. Tonight the wind died down again and the sea was like glass the sky carpeted with stars.*

Our third morning out and we were without wind again. I thought it always blew like crazy on the ocean. At least that had been my experience! Again we had to make a choice - drift or motor - and again I turned on the engine. Then suddenly there was a school of dolphins frolicking beside the boat, which gave our morale a real boost. They stayed with us for about five minutes and then disappeared. Sherry wondered if they were off on their rounds to cheer up other becalmed sailors.

We were really becoming worried about the lack of wind. How long would it take to motor and drift across this vast ocean? How could we make the supplies last? As a first step we decided that the dishes could survive a saltwater wash.

***Baraka A* Log - December 5**

We finally got some wind but it is coming from the wrong direction and hitting us in the face. Where are the trade winds I've read so much about? Nothing to do but alter course and sail with the wind on our beam and hope that it swings around behind us again.

We rearranged our watch schedule from four hours off, four hours on to a three hour stint during the night and six hour watches during the day. I didn't like being out of the cockpit for long periods at night. I asked Sherry to call me if anything worried her, even if she thought it trivial, and to always alert me if she sighted another vessel. How quickly it could change from a dot on the horizon to a threatening looming presence on a collision course with *Baraka A*.

Tonight, as Sherry was getting ready to take over the helm for her 2 a.m. watch, the boat was suddenly hit broadside by one of those freak waves that come out of nowhere. Suddenly she found herself careening across the cockpit where her head collided with a handrail. I heard the thump and Sherry cry out in pain. In a just a few minutes I could tell that she was going to have a whopper of a black eye and a bruised cheek. I was very proud of my first mate when she insisted on standing her watch.

Sherry's Journal, December 6

I slept for 6 straight hours this morning. I am still not used to these night watches. We are both trusting ourselves and the boat more each day. But we have not found much time for eating. The wind comes and goes and changes direction so the windvane is not doing much work for us. We have to steer by hand. And there always seems to be deck work to interrupt mealtimes. There were all kinds of clouds in the sky today, different shapes and sizes and some of them quite black. The sun paid us a brief visit while Jameel slept. He looks very tired.

Baraka Log – December 7

Many problems today. First Sherry and I had a fight. Then we discovered that the toilet was plugged. Also I had a terrible earache. I'm betting that my dive for the ravioli in Los Cristianos harbour is the cause. Our wonderful complete medical kit had everything but ear drops. To make my day complete, what little wind there was shifted constantly. The windvane could not do its job so someone had to be on the tiller. And then, as a bonus, setting the whisker pole proved to be more of a challenge than I had anticipated.

Sherry's Journal, December 7

I know Jameel wrote about this bad day in the log. What can I add? This was the worst day we've had aboard the boat, perhaps the worst day ever. We were both in a very bad frame of mind. We went to opposite ends of the boat to get away from

> *each other, which is not easy on a 31 foot sailboat. I guess we both realised that we could not cross the ocean like this so we made peace.*

We were able to talk about our disagreement this evening and have decided that two people living so close together are destined to get on each other's nerves. Since we didn't have the option of walking around the block to blow off steam and jumping overboard seemed impractical, we agreed to give each other space. I would take the helmsman's seat in the stern and Sherry would hunker down on the starboard bunk where she couldn't see me and I couldn't see her. There we would stay until we both cooled off.

We had never expected living on a small boat to be a picnic but, then, we'd never really talked about our expectations or how we would deal with so much togetherness. For a start, we decided to begin each day in a positive frame of mind, leaving yesterday buried at the bottom of the sleeping bag. There were so many things to keep us occupied and happy. For instance, we could take the opportunity to talk about any subject that interested us, to remember past times and plan for future ones. We could take pleasure from the scenery. Like a black velvet sky washed with stars or pink edged clouds banked along the horizon at sunset. We promised ourselves that we would keep busy. Boredom is the foundation of many disagreements. We would learn to tie every knot in our book, *Knots and Splices*. Another book in our library, *Instant Weather Forecasting*, would help us fine-tune our knowledge of clouds and weather systems.

The next morning I decided to tackle another problem – the knot metre, which in fact is a through hull fitting in the form of a small paddle wheel. The water flows over the wheel, making it turn, and records the speed. I suspected that the erratic readings we'd been getting were caused by a build-up of seaweed or barnacles. There was a way to get to this from inside, which involved removing the fitting and jamming the space with a plug, a manoeuvre we should have practised on dry land a few times. What if the plug didn't fit and fell through to the ocean bottom? Then we'd face the possibility of sinking or non-stop bailing. In the end I made the decision to go overboard and tackle the problem from the outside. I tied a line around my waist and secured the other end to a stern cleat. Then, as

Sherry eased it out, I dropped into the water. The current immediately grabbed me, sucking me under the boat. I could feel the barnacles digging into my bare back, but of more immediate concern was the boat's hull which was directly above me, crashing through the waves with me trapped underneath. I swam free, came to the surface, took a gulp of air and foolishly decided to try once more. When I kicked myself free for the second time, I signalled Sherry to winch me in. Climbing back on board was no school holiday either. Finally I grabbed the back stay and hauled myself into the cockpit where I collapsed on the floor.

"That," I confided to Sherry, "was probably the most foolhardy thing I have ever done."

"Jameel, look at your back. It's bleeding."

She grabbed a towel and dabbed at the cuts. I sat numbed with exhaustion while Sherry dived for the medical kit. Soon she reappeared with cotton swabs and hydrogen peroxide, which stung like murder. I vowed never, except in case of dire emergency, to attempt an overboard repair again.

***Baraka A* Log - December 8**

Beautiful sailing today with the wind behind us. Occasionally we hit 7.2 knots. I hope it continues so we can make up for some lost time. This afternoon I again had trouble setting the whisker pole (the one Roy made), and in the end it broke. Luckily I had another one on board and soon we were sailing wing to wing. But we are rolling and Sherry and I got sick of the motion. So I tried rigging the spitfire to the jackstay and, boy, did it work, just like magic - wonderful.

The wind has been increasing steadily and I have been putting reef after reef in the main. By 13.30 I had put in the third reef. The genoa is still up but I winched it in to a sliver. The breeze is very strong and the wind and sea are high. The wind continued to increase during the evening so I put a fourth reef in the main. The spitfire was still in place and doing its job.

As I sat in the cockpit today, watching *Baraka A* being buffeted and slammed by the wind and the sea, I again took comfort that she was a well-built, sturdy boat. I also congratulated myself on having the foresight to insist on certain modifications. Like the spitfire, which kept us from rolling and broaching in the heavy seas. Most sloops only carry a head and main sail while cutters carry two sails in front of the mast. I guess you could call it an extra jib. We also had a tri-sail which worked as a storm main. I had asked that an extra slot be put in the mast so that I could exchange the mainsail as easily as reefing the jib with roller furling.

I also had Camper Nicholson raise the height of the stern seat so that I could see over the cabin top when I was sitting down. I had found this a real bonus during the days when the windvane wasn't functioning. Also, the single large window on each side of the cabin had been removed and replaced by three smaller windows. The plus was if a small window broke, less water would flood into the cabin. The minus was that three windows on each side increased the likelihood that one of them would leak. But the trade-off was clearly in favour of the smaller windows.

Sherry had suggested that the hatchboards be made of Plexiglas, reasoning that, during storms, she would be unable to sit closed up inside not knowing if I was okay out in the cockpit. If she could see me, her mind would not imagine all sorts of worst-case scenarios.

We had a good laugh today about my contortions last night while I was struggling to put a fourth reef in the main, a procedure I had never attempted before. At the time, however, neither of us was even smiling. While Sherry sat in the cabin behind the Plexiglas clenching and unclenching her fists, I stood in the pitch-black night with a flashlight in my mouth, trying to read Roy's instructions, *19 Steps To Easy Reefing,* which I'd put into a ziplock bag to protect it from the rain.

I always wondered why this operation was called 'jiffy reefing' because it was never done in the blink of an eye, as the term suggests. Reefing sails was an arduous task. Reefing sails was prompted by the weather, which was always worsening, always nasty. Standing on the hatch, clutching the boom and the mast in a pitching sea was difficult and often dangerous. Now, taking out the reef was a child's game.

Sherry's Journal, December 8-9

Our fresh produce is almost gone except for onions and potatoes. I tried to buy twice as much as I thought we would need. Next time I'll double that amount again. We keep coming back to the question of a refrigerator. I dream of a cold drink and some fresh bread and fresh food for more than just a couple of days. We are not eating very well. The canned food, especially the meat, is not very tasty and if Jameel doesn't like something, he dumps it overboard.

This morning we saw a sailboat quite far away. We tried to contact him on the VHF but got no response.

I am still hurting from my crash into the handrail and the bump on my face is now blue, as Jameel predicted. Tonight the sky was overcast. But other times, when the sky is clear and I am on watch, I just sit and observe the stars and the moon, which has reappeared. After a few nights I could pick out the constellations. Also I use the quiet nights to think about all sorts of things. Sometimes I am lucky and find Radio Cairo and listen to Arabic songs.

Today, the 9th, marks one week at sea for us. Still 20 more days to go, which seems like a long time. I know that below us the sea is full of life but up here on the surface there is nothing but blue water all around. It's a bit boring and killing time is a major problem. Today we played cards, cleaned the boat and did the laundry in saltwater. Unfortunately, while I was hanging the clothes out to dry, some of Jameel's underwear blew away. We also used saltwater for a shower today and it felt good.

The boat is rolling so much that it is impossible to sleep, stand up or prepare a meal. I had better get used to it for this is how we'll be sailing as long as the trade winds are at our back. Tonight we will try sleeping on the floor. We might as well start out there because that's where we end up when we are pitched out of our bunks.

As the days slipped by, we felt a growing confidence in *Baraka A* to manage whatever Mother Nature might dish up. And confidence in ourselves to chart a safe course through these ocean waters. I was peacock proud of Sherry and her growing nautical knowledge. She proved to be a natural with the sextant and soon was taking shots as good as mine. Also, her confidence to manage the boat on watch had leapfrogged to the point where she hardly consulted me at all. How different from the first days when she would call me for any triviality. I remembered how I had treated these cries for help with patience and diligence and now I could see how it had paid off.

To hope that Sherry's enjoyment equalled mine was the stuff of cobweb dreams. I contented myself with the fact that she was coping and even enjoying some of the moments. Boredom plagued her, even with books to read and sunsets to dream on. I managed to keep myself busy doing 'boat things', like checking the rigging, tightening screws and plotting our course. Antigua, where are you?

Sherry's Journal, December 10-11

We called our families today and what a boost it gave us to talk to the outside world. The weather is fair, our speed too. Jameel says that if everything goes well we should be in Antigua by Christmas Day. We are both counting the hours.

What keeps me going is the knowledge that I will be the first Arabic woman to cross the Atlantic Ocean in a small boat (or any sized boat at all). Also the possibility of flying to Cairo while Baraka A undergoes repairs keeps my spirits up. We have definitely decided to have a refrigerator installed.

For three days we have not seen one boat. Except for some small black birds that come from nowhere for a visit each day, there is nothing out here. The wind has been moderate and we are making about 6 knots.

During my night watch a soft gentle rain fell; so soothing, so fresh and so unlike the infrequent pounding storms we have in Jeddah. Later the moon and stars came out, bright and twinkling. From time to time there were strong gusts which caused the boat to roll. We are both sick of the constant motion even though the spitfire makes it almost bearable. Sleeping on the floor is not very comfortable and my back aches. In fact, my entire body aches.

It gets lonely, especially on watch. I sit in the cockpit thinking of my friends and my cats. I miss them so much.

Sherry grinned and gave me a hug when I told her today that for sure the boat had to go in for repairs and some modifications while in Antigua. And we would find it less expensive to fly home than stay in a hotel while the work was being done.

Another reason for going home was to show our families that we really were okay and to tell them that, yes, we were planning to continue on through the Panama Canal and across the Pacific. Also, we hoped to convey the message that a little financial support would be very much appreciated.

Top on my repair list was the windvane, which had been malfunctioning, closely followed by the leaks around the windows and in the compass housing. And then came the wish list: a refrigerator, a wind speed indicator so I would not have to guess or estimate even though I thought I'd done a pretty fair job of it; a speed log. I had not lost faith in the *Walker Log* but to my mind there could never be too much 'fact gathering' apparatus aboard *Baraka A*.

I was happy that the leak over the chart table had sorted itself out. How frustrating to find water all over the charts, to check the window seal and find not one drop. This was a problem destined to drive a sailor mad. At least this sailor. I checked and rechecked, even stood in the cockpit and threw buckets of saltwater at the window. Nothing. But still I continued to find annoying puddles. Then, one night, after a nasty squall, I discovered that the source of the leak was me. It was my routine, on entering the cabin, to grab the handrail over the chart table. This stormy night I watched as water from my oilskins collected in the cuff then dribbled on to the handrail. When enough accumulated it dropped on to the chart table. Could I blame Sherry for doubling over with laughter?

Sherry's Journal, December 12-15

Late at night on the 11th, a low pressure system moved in. Jameel knew what we were in for when the barometric pressure began dropping like a stone. I had only to look at the worsening weather – dark menacing clouds and the angry sea whipped into a froth by a rising wind. Just like the English Channel.

Unfortunately this was not an isolated storm but a series of fronts which battered us for four long miserable days – thunder, lightening, rain and the highest seas I'd ever seen. Nothing but crests all around us. We couldn't even see the horizon.

Again, we felt so alone out here on this surging grey sea. Even the little black birds deserted us. Standing watch alone at night was the loneliest time of all.

By the 15th, the fury of the storm had lessened. I was sitting in the cockpit on the 2 a.m. watch feeling bored and lonely and very tired when suddenly I saw a racing yacht passing by us at very close range. I counted 8 crew on deck as I waved and shouted to them in English and French and Arabic. They shouted back in some language I did not recognise and then gave me a cheer. Before I knew it, the yacht had disappeared into the black night. I wondered if it had all been a dream.

Baraka A passed this latest test of her durability like a pro: no gear or rigging failure, no broken windows, no shredded sails. Again I had occasion to remember Jeremy Lines's words: 'The secret to surviving storms at sea is the boat; a sturdy, reliable vessel will take you through it. Even the best sailor will face danger in a flimsy, poorly designed boat.'

As for our durability – mentally we'd endured the onslaught better than we expected. But physically we were worn out. No decent food or sleep for four days had taken its toll.

I didn't know how to say thank you to *Baraka A* for keeping us safe other than to give her a thorough scrubbing inside and out. As Sherry and I sat in the sunny cockpit that afternoon talking about nothing at all, the way married people often do, our conversation naturally drifted to the storm. Had we been scared? Yes, of course. Had we expected not to come through it? Never for a moment. Not with the trust we had in our boat and in God.

"I'm so grateful we called her Baraka," said Sherry. "She is a blessing. She keeps us safe."

I nodded in agreement. The perfect name for the perfect boat.

"If we had some milk and honey aboard, we could commission her again, just like the first time," I said.

"Wrong, Jameel," Sherry retorted. "If we had those items on board, we'd eat them for lunch."

I propped a cushion against the stern pulpit, lay back and let the sun lull me into a lazy dreamy doze. My thoughts drifted back to the day *Baraka A* had been officially commissioned. The folks at Camper Nicholson would probably never forget that day either. No doubt they had expected that this launching would proceed within the customary guidelines which meant cracking a bottle of champagne on the bow of the boat. But champagne was not part of our Islamic culture. Could we possibly substitute milk and honey? They admitted that they had never had such a request before, but yes, a milk and honey ceremony would be no problem. Later Jeremy Lines told me that finding the right sized receptacle to fit the standard champagne bottle holder had been a challenge but in the end they found a suitable narrow-necked ceramic container.

The other commissioning custom, having a lady do the honours, we followed to the letter. At the appointed time and place, Sherry stood in the sun-speckled boatyard and shattered the bottle of milk and honey against the bow on her first swing.

"May God bless this boat and all who sail on her," she said, then turned to Jeremy Lines and the other officials from the boatyard. "And blessings to all of you whose efforts made this day possible."

I remembered too, that after *Baraka A* slipped smoothly into the waters of Gosport harbour, she was just as smoothly hauled out again a few hours later to complete the finishing touches. But not before we admired her sitting so saucily in the water, like a beautiful, impudent scamp ready for adventure. Our friends came on board overflowing with compliments and best wishes. Later we raised our glasses in a toast to a successful voyage and gorged ourselves on the delicious buffet Camper Nicholson provided.

Visions of that sumptuous feast hauled me back to the present. I sat up and opened my eyes.

"Do we have anything to eat?" I asked.

"Nothing you like," Sherry answered. "Sure wish we had some more of that ravioli."

***Baraka A* Log – December 16**

We found 2 flying-fish in the cockpit this morning and ate them for breakfast. Sherry fried them, heads and all, in a skillet and they were delicious (my opinion only). After 4 days of bad weather, the weather is now perfect: warm and

sunny. We took the reefs out of the sails and cruised along enjoying the day. Treated ourselves to a saltwater bath and hair wash and I even shaved.

December 17

No wind at all so we have been motoring. The weather is great for going to the beach and lying around being lazy in the sun. The sea is calm, calm, calm. I hope that tonight or tomorrow the wind picks up. The autopilot broke today. Another item for my repair list.

As we motored across the flat sea I wondered again why the wind had to be so inconsistent. One moment a raging gale, the next a dead calm. How about a nice steady 20 knots?

Last night we again had visitors, this time during my evening watch. I usually divided my time between the helm and the chart table, unlike Sherry who preferred to hunker down in the cockpit and admire the stars. About midnight I came on deck for a quick look around and, to my surprise and horror, saw a substantial sailboat without any navigation lights about two hundred yards to our stern and closing fast on what looked like a collision course. Hadn't they seen us? Suddenly the screech of a siren shattered the silence. Before I could flash our lights or blow the air horn, they overtook and passed us with only feet to spare. I noticed the crew members laughing and pointing and shouting, apparently pleased with their prank. I filed the yacht's name in my memory bank then calmed Sherry, who had been rousted from her bunk by the commotion.

Courtesy is a way of life in the yachting world, a fact these fellows had apparently forgotten. If I met them again, they'd get a refresher course! Sailing on the ocean is so quiet. Only the slap of the waves against the hull and the whisper of the sails harnessing the wind break the silence, except of course during storms when there is too much noise. To sneak up on a small boat in the middle of the night with no intention other than harassment smacked of bullying, pure and simple.

Our food stores had dwindled to practically nothing. We still had spaghetti, macaroni, tuna and rice. Not many interesting meals on the table lately. Even foul medames, our favourite beans, were less than delicious. We spent most of our leisure time talking about what we were going to eat once we reached Antigua.

Sherry's Journal, December 17

No wind at all. Weather is so hot that it is hard to stay long in the cockpit but inside the cabin it is stifling. The sky is like washed blue denim, clear except for the trade wind clouds which look like puffs of smoke from an old steam engine. No flying-fish in the cockpit. I wonder if the sound of the engine keeps them away.

I've decided to call Jameel, 'The Man Who Never Says Ouch'. When he bangs into something and hurts himself, he says nothing. Not like me: I yell and screech. I noticed that he has a large bruise on his upper leg but he can't remember where or when he got it.

We have a new visitor, a seagull who has been with us since the storm. He comes every afternoon, flies around us, sits on the spreaders and then disappears until the next day.

Today when Jameel woke up from his nap, he asked, "Did anyone ask about me?" I looked around, then replied, "No phone calls for you today." And I didn't even crack a smile.

Only one thousand miles to go but it could have been a million. Where was the wind? I'd even have welcomed a nice friendly storm – anything to get us moving again. We had calculated that December 20 was the last day we could turn on the engine if we hoped to reserve enough fuel to charge the batteries and get us into English harbour. Entering an unfamiliar harbour under sail power alone ranked high on the list of sailing nightmares.

Tonight on watch, again becalmed, I remembered the lines of a poem by Samuel Coleridge that Essam had memorised and recited to us during his California school days.

> Down dropped the wind, the sails dropped down,
> 'Twas sad as sad could be,

And we did speak only to break
The silence of the sea.

All in a hot and copper sky,
The bloody sun at noon
Right above the mast did stand
No bigger than the moon.

Day after day, day after day,
We stuck, nor breath nor motion,
As idle as a painted ship
Upon a painted ocean.

And wasn't there supposed to be an albatross in the rigging mocking the becalmed sailor who was slowly and surely going mad? Well, we hadn't had one of those yet, unless our friendly seagull was acting as a stand-in.

Sherry's Journal, December 18

There is so little to record because nothing is happening. We are drifting and motoring. The thumping of the engine disturbs my peace of mind and reminds me that soon we will shut the engine off for good. To pass the time today we took pictures and shot miles of video including a spectacular sunset, all orange and red like a huge beach ball on the horizon. We are seeing lots of flying-fish but none on board. Too bad. I might be less fussy about how they taste now.

For many days we have not seen any ships. But we did see two huge kingfish come to the surface and follow the boat, paying no attention to Jameel's trolling lines. They were so big that at first I thought they were sharks. The sun beats down on us and it is hotter than the Arabian Desert. We take bucket showers to cool off.

Our snack bag for evening watches now holds two pieces of chocolate and one can of fruit salad. What happened to all the food we bought in Los Cristianos and ferried out to the boat in our dinghy? Next time I won't be caught short. There really is merit to that old cliché: live and learn.

Today was 'shut off the engine' day. We had reached the point of drifting and hoping. Our morale was in the basement. At the time we had thought the series of storms was our low point but we found that sitting motionless won those honours hands down. Sherry said we'd seen it all: good weather, bad weather and what she called 'the calms', which we agreed was the worst of all. I liked Sherry's new label – 'the calms'. Every other weather system had a name, so why not this one?

We resigned ourselves to the fact that we would not reach Antigua by the 25th. We would be out here eating fruit salad and spaghetti, not the holiday feast I had expected.

Every morning we woke up hoping for wind and finding not a breeze or a ripple. I explained the trade wind current to Sherry and told her that we were being slowly pulled along to our destination at 2-3 knots and that she shouldn't worry. We would arrive sooner or later. We wallowed and drifted, trying to keep the boat on course. I tried not to think about how much longer we'd be stuck here. Too depressing. Tonight we read the Koran and prayed that God would help us by sending some wind.

Sherry's Journal, December 22

God listened to our prayers. The wind is back and if it stays with us we will be in Antigua on the 27th. The wind is no longer at our back but has swung around so that we are sailing on a beam reach which helps the rolling. Are these still the trade winds? Jameel explained that the sailors on trading ships in ancient times gave these winds their name. He said that they usually blow from the north and east to the south-west and then pointed out that usually does not mean always.

Baraka A Log – December 22

Ran into two squalls which lasted less than an hour each. But the storms brought the wind we'd been hoping for. We raised the sails and flew through the water. I recorded a hull speed of 9.3 knots for a very brief interval.

The following day we were back to the status quo: no wind. I called the weather station in Antigua and asked them for a forecast. They predicted Force 4 tomorrow and Force 5 the next day with the wind swinging around to our stern, which would mean a greater speed. Both Sherry and I were itching to get off this boat. Today we passed some of the time discussing what we would do first when we disembarked. A delicious meal topped my list. Sherry was torn between that and a hot shower.

Sherry's Journal, December 24

Yesterday I called my family to wish them Merry Christmas. I sensed that they were proud of me and Jameel for successfully crossing the Atlantic. They always ask me the same question – 'Aren't you scared?' If they only knew. There are stories I will tell them some day. At the beginning of the last storm I was so scared that my bladder just let go all over my shoes!

Today was Christmas Eve. Usually I prepare a lovely dinner and we have friends in for a meal. Tonight I couldn't even offer a can of fruit cocktail. We ate the last one yesterday. So instead I took a couple of Stugeron and went to bed.

I should be happy that the wind is back but why must it be so strong? As I lay in my bunk, I could hear the rain pounding on the cabin top and the wind howling. Poor Jameel is out in the cockpit on watch. The wind is back at our stern and the waves are enormous. Jameel says it's a bad combination because the boat is rolling very badly again. But he says it's also a good combination because we're going 6 knots and even faster.

Merry Christmas! I asked for wind and got it. It rained today and the seas seemed even more menacing. White water all around us. Sherry spent most of the day huddled down in the cabin. I knew that she was badly frightened and probably thinking the worst and praying very hard. I couldn't say that I enjoyed the day but I was happy to see the knot metre reading 6.9-7.0 knots.

Sherry's Journal, December 26

I am exhausted and counting the minutes until we see land. What a last day. I surely hope it is the last one! Jameel seems as anxious to sight land as I am. I think we've both had enough of sailing for a while and are ready and eager for some comfort. The rain hasn't stopped all day, which prompted Jameel to shower, wash his hair and shave in lovely, clear, salt-free, rainwater.

We decided to both stay on watch tonight in case we are closer to land than we think. Just as a precaution. I believe Jameel is an excellent navigator and I told him so.

***Baraka A* Log - December 27**

At 06.30 this morning we sighted land. Saw groups of lights strung along the shore. Is this Antigua? We hoped so, though I did not recognise any landmarks. We switched on the engine and continued towards land and reached the entrance to English harbour. Mission partially accomplished. I thanked God for our health and safety.

As soon as we entered the harbour I look around for the customs shed. I asked directions from another yachtsman and he said not to worry. First, find a vacant buoy, tie up and when we were ready, go to shore. Customs was on the main dock. 'A considerably more relaxed attitude than Casablanca,' I thought as we searched for a comfortable anchorage in Freeman Bay. Sherry and I were beyond exhilaration to simple exhausted joy at having done it! We were the first Arabs to ever have attempted an Atlantic crossing.

"Attempted and *completed*," I told Sherry. "Don't forget the last part."

We had survived twenty-four days at sea, enduring the storms and the doldrums with what I hoped was stoic resolve. And we had enjoyed the good days in light-hearted camaraderie with gratitude and thanks to the sun and the sea for the respite.

Sherry and I could hardly wait to get off the boat. We quickly inflated the Avon, found the oars and rowed to shore. I wondered if I should mention my gun. Would honesty mean hours at the police station? I simply didn't know. When we finally found customs, the officials seemed so friendly that I decided to follow what is always the best course – tell the truth.

"A gun? No problem," they said. They advised me that if I was planning to leave the boat unattended it would be wise to turn the gun in for safekeeping.

"Bandits," one of the officers announced solemnly. "We have big problems here."

Which meant that I would be turning the gun over to them in a few days' time. My repair and wish list had grown longer as the voyage progressed. I estimated that the local boatyard would need at least three to four weeks to order and install the new equipment, especially the refrigerator.

Customs formalities completed, we returned to the boat, gathered together our laundry, saving the cleanest clothes for immediate use. Then we locked *Baraka A* and jumped back into the Avon. We hoped there was a decent inexpensive hotel with lots of hot water, and a laundry service. An ice cream kiosk nearby. Sherry had been dreaming about a cool, sweet, icy scoop of caramel with chocolate and nuts for weeks. But somehow I knew that she'd settle for just plain old vanilla.

Sherry's Log – Reflections on an Ocean Crossing

Eventually the boat becomes your cell. You cannot go anywhere. You don't see or talk to anybody. You are disciplined as to when to eat, what to eat, when to sleep and for how long. Also, when to shower, when to work and when to rest.

Except for boat handling and divine attention, there is little else you can do. It is definitely a learning experience and a disciplinary one for the soul and the body. It is an experience I will never forget. As long as I live I will remember those 24 days and the Atlantic Ocean.

Chapter Eight

We flew back to Antigua from London on January 31, arriving at 8 p.m. Even though it was late and we were jet-lagged, we headed straight for the boatyard, expecting to see *Baraka A* back in the water, all ready to sail to our next port of call. Our hearts plunged to our boots and beyond when we discovered the boat still on blocks with the promised work not completed and the boat in disarray. Nothing to do but walk back into town and find lodgings at the Deck Resort – which we would have to call home until the work was done. 'No,' I thought as we checked into a barely adequate room, 'not home.' It was just a place to stay. Home was *Baraka A*, the only place which could rightfully lay claim to that moniker. I glanced at Sherry and knew that she was feeling the same sense of disappointment. Like weary vacationers everywhere, we had been looking forward to this homecoming. The need to occupy space that was uniquely ours was almost tangible.

I looked back on the month long holiday and counted it a success. Cairo was our first stop. I listened in amazement and pride as Sherry recounted the Atlantic crossing. All the negatives seemed to evaporate in the warm Cairo sunshine. While I expected tales of seasickness, terror and boredom, Sherry revelled in recounting the positive: the breathtaking sunsets, her feelings of accomplishment at mastering various nautical tasks, like taking sun shots with the sextant and standing watch alone at night. But top on the list was the pride she felt in being the first woman from the Arab world to cross the Atlantic in a sailboat. Bravo Sherry, I wanted to shout. Sherry's aura of confidence and enthusiasm proved to be contagious. By the time we left Cairo her family were, if not enthusiastic, then at least stoically resigned to the fact that we were going to carry on. The Pacific Ocean was waiting for us.

Next stop Jeddah. My father's demeanour was predictable. Yes, he was proud of me and grateful that I had come back none the worse for wear. But surely I had proved my point. Would it not be foolhardy to continue? I brushed my father's concerns aside. He knew me well enough to realise that I never left a job half finished. If he had been unable to discourage me at the outset, what chance did he have after the successful completion of the first leg? I concluded that parents are born to fret and worry no matter what their offspring are doing. It is expected of them, part of the job.

Essam was in Jeddah visiting his grandparents for the school holidays. We tried to squeeze all the months we'd missed into a few short weeks. He wanted to know every single detail about our trip and, from the number of 'wows' that peppered his conversation, I guessed he was impressed. And envious. I thought how wonderful it would be to have Essam on board. But not, I reasoned, in the confined space of *Baraka A* where Sherry and I struggled for every square inch of privacy. But another voyage in another boat – yes!

Again the media were anxious for interviews. Predictably, topping the list of questions was why we had decided to sail around the world? A childhood dream fulfilled? A chance to counter the stereotype of Arabs as terrorists? An opportunity to prove that Arabs are courageous people who enjoy adventure and challenges? All of these reasons were valid in varying degrees but none could claim to be the *real reason*. What if I'd said, "Well, I'm sailing around the world for the pure joy of it. Forget the altruistic motives. I'm having fun?" Simplistic statements don't make good copy, even if they're true.

We stopped briefly in England on our return trip to Antigua. We were given a warm welcome at Camper Nicholson where we visited with Jeremy Lines and Roy Mullender and picked up some spare cleats and winches. These we crammed into our suitcases which were already past the bursting point with stuffed dates, halawa, kounafa, loukoum and kaak. They are all Arabic sweets which were, if not a necessity, then very welcome during the long night watches. Sherry had vowed never again to run short of these treats.

Our second day in Antigua, we began chasing down workmen and concluded that, if we wanted the work done quickly and properly, we'd have to be there to supervise it ourselves. Some completed jobs had been done incorrectly, like the new cabinets we'd ordered.

They'd been made to our specifications and installed but had not been treated with silicone to make them waterproof. I insisted on a redo. There would be no marinas or boatyards in the middle of the ocean.

Our days took on a numbing sameness. After breakfast we would plod down to the marina where Sherry would groan, sometimes quite loudly, at the mess the workmen had left and then put everything back in its proper place. The list of jobs seemed endless: repairing and installing a saltwater pump for the sink; repairing a sea cock under the sink in the head; rigging a top for the galley, one with braces so the pots could be secured; converting the icebox to a real refrigerator; and widening both berths, which we hoped would lessen or eliminate the time spent sleeping on the floor.

While I scraped the hull and checked the rigging, Sherry began making her shopping lists. Never again did we plan to be on the high seas with only one can of fruit and some dry spaghetti for company. Sherry felt that she had learned a lot from the Atlantic crossing. Although Roy Mullender had called her a 'first-class quartermaster' she felt that she'd fallen a little short of the mark!

"Look," I consoled her, "last time you stowed enough food on board, but not the kind of food we like. Like all that tinned meat. Might be all right for an Englishman but I can't stomach the stuff."

Sherry nodded.

"I noticed. I wonder if the fish gobbled up everything you threw overboard. This time I promise that the only food from tins will be fruits and vegetables and beans."

"And salami," I said. "Don't forget the dried salami. It keeps for ever and doesn't even need refrigeration. That's important now we have a refrigerator!"

Sherry's Journal, English Harbour, Antigua

During the day while we work on the boat it gets to be very hot, especially inside. Every morning I tidy up the mess left by the workmen. It's like a tornado has hit the inside of the boat. We work hard all day and when we go back to the motel at night our bodies ache all over.

The island scenery is beautiful, with wonderful deserted beaches along the coast. In Jeddah the beaches are walled off so that families can enjoy their privacy, which is an integral part of the Saudi way of life.

The island was occupied by the British for many years so the natives speak some kind of English which we find impossible to understand because they speak it so fast. The people are relaxed, a bit too relaxed perhaps. Things move at a slow pace so we must keep putting pressure on the workmen to hurry up. Even going out for dinner takes a lot of time, like an Arabic feast instead of a simple meal. We are learning to say, "I'm cool, man," like everybody else here.

We called our families to let them know about the delay. They told us that the second segment of our TV interview had appeared on Saudi TV and that we looked confident. They have recorded both portions and we will see it when we get back.

On February 7 we moved our belongings back on to the boat and the next day I began buying our food for the next leg. We're anxious to leave and excited to continue our little adventure.

We sailed out of English harbour bound for Sint Maarten, a distance of 104.3 nautical miles, early in the morning on February 10. Sherry leaned over the rail waving goodbye to the sea turtles, those beautiful creatures which had shared our anchorage those last days in Antigua and had provided so many hours of enjoyment. We were both looking forward to seeing the turtles on the Galapagos Islands.

I hoped the weather that day would be a harbinger for the rest of the trip. Even though we passed through a few brief showers, the sun always quickly reappeared like the star of a play who only occasionally leaves centre stage for the wings.

"It's nice to be at sea again," Sherry commented as she fixed lunch.

If she noticed the surprised but elated glance I threw her way, she took no notice. I let the words roll around in my head and kept coming back to 'again'. Was this the same wife who had jumped ship in Plymouth vowing, 'Never again?' Well, at least not today with the wind pushing us along at nearly 5 knots and the sun dancing on the wave crests. Not today, with our vessel scrubbed and polished and sporting all her new gear.

Baraka A **Log – February 10**

I decided to double reef the main and genoa to slow our boat speed so that we would not arrive in St Martin in the middle of the night.

Sherry's Journal, Bobby's Marina, Sint Maarten, February 11

This tiny island, only 34 square miles – no bigger than a grain of sand on the map – goes by two names depending which side you're on, the Dutch or the French. We arrived at the Dutch port of Sint Maarten at 7.30 a.m. and decided to anchor out rather than tie up to the dock, which was too crowded for us. Everyone seemed to be asleep except the men who were cleaning the beach. Later, after attending to our morning boat chores and pumping up the dinghy, we rowed to shore, checked in with the customs office and filled out the necessary papers. The town appeared to be filled with tourists and duty free shops.

At the top of our shopping list was an outboard motor for the dinghy. We had decided that the last thing we wanted to do when we arrived at a port was row to shore. So tiring and slow and, after days or weeks on board the boat, we wanted to get to land fast! Jameel said that safety was another factor. Sometimes the current and the tides can overwhelm an oarsmen, even someone as strong as Jameel. Sometimes it is more peaceful to row. We can turn off the engine and use the oars any time it suits us.

We were lucky to find a good outboard motor right at Bobby's Marina, a Mercury for $290. The next task was to figure out how to mount it on the transom of the dinghy. A local carpenter fashioned a motor mount in double-quick time. Both Sherry and I were impressed by the efficiency of the Dutch and the service at Bobby's Marina.

I decided that this was the place to resolve a problem that had been nagging at the corners of my mind ever since we left English harbour - the autohelm. I remembered how that piece of equipment had failed during the Atlantic crossing. It had been repaired and seemed to be functioning perfectly but I didn't quite trust it. What if it failed again in the middle of the Pacific? It just made sense to have a back-up. Bobby's Marina offered to order one for me and promised delivery in less than a week. Although we hadn't planned on such a long stop over in the Leewards we decided that safety must have precedence over time schedules. We spent the days hiking around town, purchasing extra lines which we would need for the Panama Canal passage and buying more groceries. Sherry was determined that the sail to Panama would be remembered for its gourmet meals! How much easier it was to motor back and forth to *Baraka A* with cartons of provisions than to row! When the new autohelm arrived, as promised, in less than a week, we installed it immediately and stowed the other one away.

***Baraka A* Log - At anchor, Sint Maarten**

A warship came into the anchorage today, small and grey in colour, but it looked awesome. Tomorrow we will set sail for Colón, Panama, a distance of 1112 nautical miles, about 9-10 days' sailing which is better than a hundred a day with no stops in between. I'm really looking forward to sailing the Caribbean Sea. From what I've read, the wind changes and varies often, so sailing will be very different from crossing the Atlantic. Maybe being near land is what makes the difference. Today is a lovely day. The sun is shining, with a few clouds, which give us a break from the heat while we finish up some little jobs - greasing the winches and scrubbing the hull.

Our departure from Sint Maarten was delayed for three days. First, Sherry didn't feel well and wanted a day to sort herself out. The next morning we woke to pounding rain and no wind, hardly an auspicious beginning for a ten day voyage, so we again stayed put. Then the 20th was my birthday, my thirty-eighth. Sherry wanted to celebrate the occasion with a dinner at one of the island's many restaurants. How could I refuse?

As I sat in the cockpit enjoying the afternoon sun, I marvelled at how quickly the years pass. I could look back and see myself as a teenager glued to the TV screen watching Adam Troy sailing his boat *Tiki* from one adventure in paradise to the next. As soon as we passed through the Panama Canal, we'd be heading for those same tropical islands that had so captured my imagination and my heart. All kids have dreams but, sadly, most are shoved aside or forgotten when the real world intrudes. It wasn't luck or good fortune which had made my dreams come true but stubborn determination. I had made myself a promise: I would never be an old man with rheumy eyes looking down the staircase of my life, mourning the steps I'd missed along the way.

That evening, after my birthday dinner, I deflated the dinghy and stowed it and the new motor away. Life on a mooring without transportation would certainly guarantee departure the next morning.

We left Sint Maarten harbour on February 21 under fair skies and gentle breezes. I spent most of the day doing a thorough 'Frank Mulville Inspection' and was pleased that all the rigging and equipment seemed to be in tip-top shape. Sherry lay in the cockpit with her face to the sun as *Baraka A* sliced cleanly through the water. Now if sailing could only be like this all the time...

***Baraka A* Log – February 21**

At 1600 the SatNav began to malfunction and I knew we had to change our plans and our course. Decided to head for St Croix in the American Virgin Islands. Arrived there at 07.00 and was advised to go to St Thomas in the British Virgin Islands, 60 miles north, for better service.

Sherry's Journal, St Thomas

It took us 7 hours to sail to St Thomas, beam reach all the way. It was a good ride with some bumpy waves. At first glance, St Thomas looked very nice, more like a city than an island. After clearing customs we walked around the harbour and even saw shopping malls! A bit too civilised for my taste. There were many beautiful boats at anchor all around us. Later today we watched as a British cruise ship, 'The Sea Princess', passed right by our anchorage. I wondered what the passengers thought as they looked down at our tiny boat bobbing in their wake like a toy. I wondered if any of them wanted to change places?

St Thomas had everything a sailor could want except someone to fix the SatNav. A fellow at the marina office said that St Croix was the place to go. Well, no way were we going to retrace our steps, going back and forth like a ping pong ball! Sherry and I looked at the charts and decided to continue north to Tortola and, if we got the same answer there, we would carry on to Puerto Rico. I hated to leave this very necessary repair job on the back burner until Panama. No repair facilities there really would mean some back-tracking.

We left St Thomas at 8 a.m. the following morning. The winds were light and in our face so we relied on an assist from the motor and arrived at 2 p.m. After clearing customs we headed into town and found Cay Electronics and a technician who promised that he could fix the SatNav. We arranged for him to come aboard the following morning.

Sherry's Journal, Tortola, February 2

The town is very quiet, as is the whole island. There are tiny roads leading into the hills, lined with boutiques and the usual souvenir shops. We spent the afternoon visiting the botanical gardens which made me homesick for my garden in Palo Alto, California.

The technician arrived, as promised, first thing in the morning and fixed the SatNav. I unearthed our spare autopilot from the V-berth storage area and asked the technician to take a look at it. The happy news was he declared it to be in top condition so we now have two fully functioning autopilots. Next we took care of some boat chores like cleaning the interior and hauling all our bedding to the laundromat, topping up the supplies of fresh fruit and bread and pipe tobacco for me. After filling the water and diesel tanks, we treated ourselves to a dinner out. Our last? How many times had we used that same excuse for a restaurant meal out and then discovered that we were heading to yet another port for repairs. Sherry reminded me that I had expressed a keen interest in sailing the Caribbean, that I had even written about it in the log. True, but I'd hoped to enjoy the scenery as it slipped by our hull rather than on land with my hand in my pocket searching for cash.

***Baraka A* Log – En route to Panama**

We left Tortola on February 28 under grey skies which cleared away. Two hours from port and the SatNav began malfunctioning again. After turning it off and then on again, it appeared to be working perfectly. I am keeping an accurate DR in case it fails again.

Sherry's Journal, En route to Panama

We did 130 miles the first day. I was worried, as it was the first day of a long trip. Last night we put out a fishing line and, when we hauled it in the next morning, something had eaten the hook and the line. An army ship passed really close to us and I think they slowed down to check us out.

Jameel has been fiddling with the SatNav for 3 days and now thinks the problems are identical to the ones he experienced near Gibraltar. The interference between the SSB radio and SatNav has not been resolved. What to do?

March 2

The sea is very bumpy. I have finished my Stugeron seasick tablets and the ones I'm taking now make me sleepy. It's hard to kill the time. I've been listening to some nice Spanish music from Puerto Rico and recording it. Listening to the weather forecast this evening, we heard about a power boat which sank in the Caribbean with 27 people on board. Makes you scared, doesn't it?

March 3

The sea is rough, the motion tough. I feel very sick every time I'm inside the boat. A very boring day. What we're doing is so hard and takes so much out of us. I wonder what the purpose is? Jameel says there are only 5 more days to go.

March 4-5

The days passed like all the other days – long and boring. We had the sea all to ourselves, no sound, nothing to see except blue water all around. It gives you the blues after a while. We can't see land but we know that we are passing between the Dominican Republic and Venezuela.

I miss my friends a lot, especially my sister. I also miss civilisation. It's very lonely out here, especially at night.

It was difficult to see Sherry so miserable with seasickness and homesickness, especially while I felt only exhilaration at being back at the helm again. The winds were stiff at times, 18 knots gusting to 22 with a 5-8 foot sea but *Baraka A* responded beautifully, bounding through the steely-blue ocean with grace and agility. A lovely sail. I was enjoying every minute.

Sherry's Journal, March 6

At dawn the sky was very cloudy and I wondered if it would rain. My morale is very down and I am homesick. I wish I could open my eyes and be in the Red Sea. I know that won't happen for many months. We still have the whole Pacific and Indian Oceans to cross. God only knows what is ahead. It's

> *hard to be at sea because I'm never standing up straight and I feel sick when I'm bent over.*
>
> *In harbours, among other boats, I always feel good and ready for what lies ahead. But once we are at sea, alone, with no land in sight, all my good thoughts fade away and I feel very lonely. Many times I look at my country's flag and wonder if anyone knows what I'm doing or even cares.*

On March 7 we had another close call with a freighter. I had just slipped into a delicious slumber when suddenly I was yanked awake by Sherry's screams.

"Jameel! Jameel! Wake up!"

I leapt into the cockpit and, to my horror, saw a freighter heading straight for us and closing fast. Should I set off some flares? Did I have time to unearth them and figure out how they worked? Not a chance. I jumped back into the cabin and called the ship on the VHF radio, channel 16, which is the channel that all ships are supposed to monitor.

"Big ship, big ship, do you see us?"

No answer.

"Big ship, big ship, we are on a collision course. What are your intentions?"

Again, no answer.

By this time the freighter was, by my estimate, less than a quarter of a mile away – too close!

Sherry's face was ashen as she clutched my arm. Suddenly the freighter began to turn and, when it passed by us, there couldn't have been more than 150 metres separating us. As we wallowed in her wash, we saw the Russian lettering on the smokestack. A huge Russian freighter with the radio operator asleep at his post had almost run over us. I was fuming mad when I called the ship again on the VHF.

"Big Russian ship. You almost ran us down."

"No see you – sorry," came the reply in guttural English.

"It's a good thing we're alert on watch or we'd be dead by now."

A moment of silence followed by a grunt ended the conversation as the Russian radio operator signed off.

The next morning I made contact with the Panama traffic control station. After giving us a number, we motored past the breakwater with a tanker at our heels, into the quarantine area where we dropped anchor and joined the flotilla of other sailboats preparing to traverse the canal. First stop - customs where we presented our visas for Panama. We would never forget the weeks of anxiety and frustration while we waited in England for this very necessary paperwork to come through. We met some other sailors in the customs shed who advised us that Cristobal was a dirty and dangerous city and that we should exercise caution if venturing from the mooring. One tale making the circuit was about a sailor who had been mugged and robbed and when he finally returned to his boat he was stark naked. He was not as lucky as some others who had managed to hold on to their underwear.

Sherry's Journal, March 9-10

Jameel went into town on foot - no taxis available - to buy bread and fruit and returned empty-handed. All the shops were closed because it was Sunday. Jameel arrived back intact and fully clothed but he told me that he could sense the young thugs were watching him. Maybe they knew that Jameel was not afraid of them. With his training in boxing and karate, Jameel isn't afraid of many things. The following day I accompanied Jameel to town where he visited the immigration office. We found out that sailboats can cross the canal only on Tuesdays and Thursdays. We would like to get out of here as soon as possible.

Unfortunately we did not make the Tuesday crossing - more forms to fill out and then the wait for canal staff to measure our boat and assign us a number. We learned that you can either go through the canal alone - expensive - or rafted to other sailboats which means that you share the line handlers and therefore save money. We naturally chose the latter course. We hope to go on Thursday. Wednesday, we found a reliable taxi driver to take us to town and the supermarket which really was *super*! Everything we could possibly need was there on the shelves except replacement fishing tackle, lines and hooks, which we found in a fish and bait shop. Wednesday night, we flushed the water tanks and refilled them.

Sherry's Journal, March 11, Cristobal, Panama

I am anxious to leave this place. I know that many countries have problems with poverty and Egypt is no exception. But, after this, I think Egypt is doing a better job than Panama. With all the problems we face at home, it's nothing compared to what I've seen here. I wish we had videotaped this city so everyone could see what it's like. Not a good idea. One sailor at the anchorage had his camera stolen while on a trip to town.

Our line handlers, Mr Wolf, a Panamanian named Alphonse and a Canadian named Ray, appeared, as promised, early in the morning on March 12 in their pilot boat and led us towards the locks. Before entering the Gatun locks, we lashed three boats together, with *Baraka A* ending up on the port side.

Sherry sat on the foredeck immersed in an article she'd clipped about the Panama Canal, occasionally throwing me titbits of information over her shoulder.

"The Gatun locks look like giant steps and consist of three pairs of concrete chambers to accommodate boats going both ways." She paused. "That's right, Jameel, they do look like steps. It says here that we will rise a total of 85 feet before we enter Gatun Lake."

I managed a 'hmm' as Sherry again focused on her article. Along with the two other skippers, I was intent on adjusting the fenders so the boats wouldn't crash into one another as the water rushed into the first lock.

"It cost $380,000,000 and took ten years to build this," Sherry continued. She looked at me quizzically. "That doesn't seem like very much money at least today but I guess in 1914 it was a huge sum."

I took reels of video footage as we passed through the locks and afterwards when we undid the lines lashing the three boats together and then raced each other across Gatun Lake. Overhead, the sun rode high in the sky against a backdrop of cotton candy clouds. The scenery was something from an artist's sketchbook – lots of tiny islands and pine trees punctuating the shimmering blue water of the lake. And, to make the day perfect, we found some new friends to share our anchorage for the evening. We anchored out to get away from the mosquitoes but our linehandlers chose to nose their vessel into the shore. Mr Wolf told Sherry that he thought we were the first Arab sailors to pass through the Panama Canal! And for sure *Baraka A* was the first sailboat flying the Saudi and Egyptian flags to make this trip.

As we rocked at anchor that evening, we reflected that up to this point we had not really had time to relax and enjoy the social part of sailing. Usually we had been so busy chasing down equipment or readying the boat for the next leg that we had put social interaction on the back burner except for the occasional hand wave or casual greeting.

The next morning our linehandlers were raring to go by 7 a.m. We followed them like ducks in a row for about eight miles through the Gaillard Cut until we reached the Pedro Miguel locks where we again lashed ourselves together. Our first descent took us down 31 feet to Miraflores Lake. We then crossed the lake to the Miraflores Locks where we entered the first of two chambers which would lower us to the level of the Pacific Ocean. Sherry commented that going through the locks was like climbing up a mountain and then coming down the other side.

Our plan was to sail to the island of Taboga which lies in the Gulf of Panama about ten miles from Panama City, with the yacht *Lady Helen*, one of the members of our flotilla. Our pilot, Mr Wolf, kindly offered to take our broken whisker pole, which had snapped in two in the Caribbean, to a welding shop in Panama City and then bring it back to us via ferry, a gesture of friendship that brought a lump to my throat.

Our anchorage in Taboga offered little protection, which made for a bumpy, rolly night. I slept fitfully, fearing that the rising wind would cause our anchor to drag.

The next morning *Lady Helen* weighed anchor and headed for an island called Las Perlas, six hours away, which would be the first stop on the voyage back to San Francisco. We would miss these new-found friends. Saying hello and then goodbye too quickly was, I concluded, part of what life at sea was all about. We would find other friends at other anchorages. But it was neither practical nor possible to sail in tandem with another vessel. Every sailboat had a different hull speed based on design, rigging and the know-how of the helmsman. Part of the joy of sailing was, for me, the freedom to set my own pace, to revel in the luxury of being master of my time and space.

While we watched *Lady Helen* disappear over the horizon, Sherry perused her shopping lists. We planned to take the ferry to Panama City and restock the boat for the next leg. The Galapagos were eight hundred miles away. I kept telling Sherry that this would be a shorter sail than the one from Tortola to Panama, possibly eight days if the winds are steady.

***Baraka A* Log – at anchor, Taboga Island, Panama City**

During our stay here we took the ferry to Panama City to buy provisions and to look for some Stugeron for Sherry. She was overjoyed when she found some in a pharmacy and bought most of their stock. On the way back I observed two dolphins. They looked different from the ones we'd seen in the Atlantic, bigger but just as playful.

The mountain facing the anchorage was on fire for two days and the wind-blown debris, burned trees and ashes fell on the boat. We were very annoyed at having to clean up the mess. We hope to leave here tomorrow.

Sherry's Journal, March 14 – Taboga Island

I threw my other seasick pills, the ones that made me sleepy, overboard. We went ashore this afternoon. Luckily it was just a sightseeing trip, not a shopping expedition because there was not much to buy in the stores. As soon as Mr Wolf arrives with the whisker pole we will leave. Jameel is anxious to be underway.

We had planned to bid farewell to Taboga as soon as the whisker pole was back on board, which was accomplished the evening of

March 16 when Mr Wolf delivered it in person – another example of the extraordinary generosity of members of the sailing community. There was nothing standing in the way; we planned a March 17th departure wearing whatever green garments we owned in honour of St Patrick's Day. But, as has become our custom, we put off our departure for one more day so that Sherry could ready herself and the boat for yet another ocean passage. I appreciated how weary she was of being a dot on the ocean in a 31 foot sailboat. She would count the moments while *Baraka A* ploughed through eight hundred miles of wind and waves until the outline of the Galapagos Islands appeared on the horizon. Memorable days, when the sea and wind were in perfect tune, were a bonus that Sherry never counted on. Did she know how I appreciated her participation in this crazy venture of mine or how much I admired her pluck? It's one thing for a sailing enthusiast to jump on board a sailboat and winch in the sheets and say, 'Let's go!' but quite another for a person like Sherry, for whom sailing the world's oceans was an endurance test.

I had heard on the sailor's grapevine that the authorities in the Marquesas, which is part of French Polynesia, required proof of means, i.e. that you have the wherewithal to get yourself home if something happens to you or your boat while visiting our shores. They had neither the desire nor the resources to take care of stranded sailors.

I called home and talked to my cousin. We agreed that I would phone him when we arrived at Hiva Oa. If we needed proof of solvency, he would send us a couple of airline tickets. I also asked him to send some money from my Jeddah account to the British Consulate in Tahiti. By the time we arrived there we'd be flat stony broke.

Then I phoned Essam at school in England. How refreshing it was to hear the enthusiasm in his voice. How he wished he could be with us instead of imprisoned at a school desk, watching dust motes drift in the stale air.

"Don't forget," he said. "Next time you do it, I'm coming too."

We left Taboga, Panama at midmorning on March 18. Destination: Academy Bay in the Galapagos. We motored from our mooring under a relentless sun with not a whisper of wind. How I'd hoped for a snappy breeze to fill the sails on this *first* day of our journey across the Pacific. Yes, another first. Ahead lay the adventures in paradise I'd dreamed about since I was a kid. I could hardly wait for the fun to start.

Chapter Nine

Sherry's Journal, March 18, en route to the Galapagos

Today I am 28 years old and I hope I have become a lot wiser. This year I have travelled a lot; Casablanca to the Canaries and then to the Caribbean and on to Panama. I've seen lots of different cultures and different ways of living, some good and some really primitive, some nice places and some ugly ones too. We've still got a long way to go. I hope we will always be careful and safe in our travels. I am looking forward to seeing some beautiful landfalls in the Pacific soon.

Jameel apologised for not celebrating my birthday with a meal out and a birthday cake and candles. I told him, 'Never mind. All I want for my birthday is smooth sailing back to Casablanca.'

We spent the first few days at sea battling what Sherry called 'the calms'. And the unrelenting heat. Without the cooling effects of a breeze, we felt like toast on the griddle. Nothing to do but motor and try to capture what little wind there was and hope that friendlier weather conditions lay ahead. According to some sailors we had talked to in Tabago, this stretch of ocean was notorious for its flat seas. Some sailors had taken as long as twenty days to make the passage.

The days passed slowly as we chugged and wallowed across the ocean under a blazing and occasionally hazy sun. We passed the long daylight hours fishing, with no luck, admiring the dolphins that visited us periodically. At night we lay in the cockpit studying the constellations of stars scattered like diamonds on a velvet sky. But all the while we kept a wary eye out for tankers and freighters heading for the Panama Canal.

We decided to stick with the same watch schedule which had worked well for us during the Atlantic crossing. In the daylight hours we each stood a six hour watch and during the evening hours we broke that up into shorter periods of three hours. I was uncomfortable being away from the tiller at night. When Sherry was on watch I found that I was unable to sleep and instead thrashed around in my bunk with one ear tuned to the cockpit. I put it down to 'just back at sea jitters' and figured that, once we'd been at sea a few weeks and far away from the shipping lanes, I'd learn to relax. Sherry also loved this timetable. Being alone at night in the cockpit when, according to Sherry, people are supposed to be in bed, was never easy for her.

***Baraka A* Log – March 20-21**

There is a serious leak in the boat. Today we found the floorboards floating and I immediately pumped the water out. In the bilge I found a piece of fibreglass packing material which makes me think that the water is coming in through the shaft. I hope the leak doesn't become worse. The good news is that we have been gaining 20 miles a day from the current. With this leak we need to get to the Galapagos as fast as we can. I am averaging about 60 pumps every two hours which makes for a lot of water over a 24 hour period. Why didn't I buy an electric pump?

I tried to reassure Sherry that the leak was nothing to worry about but I could hardly fool her when she saw me pumping the bilges almost constantly. We had plenty of fuel so, if necessary, we could motor all the way to the Galapagos. Fortunately the wind picked up the fifth day out and we were able to sail all day, making about 4-5 knots. Sherry called it a perfect day: calm seas and wind, a rare combination. But tonight a strange thing happened. Sitting in the cockpit we were suddenly overwhelmed by the stench of rotting fish. Sherry wanted to know what it was. I had no explanation.

Sherry's Journal, en route to the Galapagos

I think, from my own experience, that the Pacific is richer in sea life than the Atlantic. We have seen more fish and dolphins and today a sea turtle lying on its back clapping his hands. I guess they're called flippers. I even saw a shark – my first – but just his back fin and tail as he cruised by checking out the boat.

One night a bird paid us a visit, and sat on our whisker pole, keeping us company all night. Jameel took a picture of him. In the morning he flew away. I was sad to see him go.

Since the wind returned we have had perfect sailing. In the afternoons I take a shower or listen to music on the tape recorder and just enjoy the absolute privacy. We have the whole horizon to ourselves. What a life – lying in the sun eating the watermelons we bought in Panama.

All good things must end. The wind shifted around, hitting us head on, which made for lumpy seas and a bumpy ride. We winched in the genoa and reefed the main and, with a motor assist, continued to make good time. The leak had not worsened but the effort of pumping hundreds of gallon of water out of the boat every day was taking its toll. Galapagos, where are you?

We watched thunderheads massing on the horizon like an invading army readying itself for attack. We were not disappointed. Thunder boomed across the sky ahead of the rain, which pelted the boat with machine-gun ferocity. I didn't miss the opportunity to take a warm freshwater shower, so unlike the cold water variety in the North Atlantic!

We had to fill the diesel tanks, a messy chore in the choppy seas but necessary with two hundred and twenty miles to go.

Sherry's Journal, nearing the Galapagos

Jameel said that we should arrive at the Galapagos today. This morning was like a picture postcard, the sun and the sea in concert again to create a perfect day. And an added bonus – entertainment! A school of dolphins and some sea lions frolicked around the boat for over an hour and Jameel was able to capture the action on video. I wondered if this is a usual thing. Do these two animals usually play together like chums on a cricket field? Fantastic end to this leg of the journey.

We arrived at Santa Cruz Island in the Galapagos chain at 13.30 hours. Mission accomplished. We anchored in Academy Bay, one of the two permitted anchorages in the entire archipelago, which, according to Sherry's research, covers an area of 3029 square miles and is made up of five main islands and several smaller ones.

But history and geography had to take a back seat to my main concern – the leak. In the calm water of the anchorage, I went over the side and soon located the problem. As I had suspected, the water was leaking in through the propeller shaft housing. It was a simple matter to reset the packing and tighten the screws, then pump the boat dry. I chuckled to myself, remembering another day which now seemed so long ago – that day in Plymouth harbour when *Baraka A* had been hauled for propeller/shaft repairs. The word 'packing' had not been part of my vocabulary then though I had pretended to know exactly what the mechanic was talking about. Now, here I was resetting the stuff myself. Nothing like 'on the job' training, I concluded.

Meanwhile, Sherry had discovered that John on *Mr John IV* was anchored just a few metres away from us. We first met this charming, single-handed sailor from England in Cristobal. He had heard about our adventures and took the opportunity to wish us good luck on our round-the-world voyage. "We'll be seeing each other along the way," he promised. We hoped that might happen some time, some place, but not in the Galapagos, our first landfall. We arranged to meet for dinner on shore.

Next we unpacked and inflated the dinghy and secured the outboard to its transom. I gave the cord a mighty pull. Not a sputter, not a cough, not a wheeze. I then went through all the futile exercises outboard owners try when the motor refuses to start like checking the gas tank, opening the air vent and wiggling the spark plug wires. Still nothing. And so we rowed to shore, completed the customs formalities and walked to the village to shop for supplies. We found out that supplies came by ferry from Ecuador every two weeks. The empty state of the shelves told us that the supply ship was long overdue. We bought what we could – onions, eggs and butter.

We spent the next three days trying to provision *Baraka A* for the trip to the Marquesas. Water was available only by the jug – we bought six of them which we rowed back to *Baraka A*. By chance I met an Ecuadorean fellow who said that he could provide me with one barrel of diesel fuel. Since selling diesel to sailboats was illegal we made arrangements for him to ferry it out to us after dark. Except I hadn't counted on the night being as black as the inside of an inkwell. I felt like a drug smuggler as I lifted the cans on board and then paid 'my source' $60 for third grade diesel. The fuel was so dirty we had to run it through a filter on its way to our tank. Sherry and I agreed that fooling around with diesel fuel was our least favourite pastime. But all the hard work was worth it. We ended up with full diesel tanks and four extra gallons which we stored on deck.

No sooner had we said goodbye to the diesel man, than, out of nowhere, a ferocious searing pain hit my stomach like a bolt of lightning. I sank to the cabin floor writhing and groaning. With Sherry's help I crawled to the head where my body tried to rid itself of whatever nasty thing I'd eaten. Sherry sponged my forehead and murmured comforting words and wondered if she should go to shore and try to find a doctor.

"I'll be fine," I said as another spasm hit. Just before dawn I felt well enough to crawl into my bunk where I spent most of the day.

That evening I decided to treat myself to a haircut. My hair was growing shaggy and I feared I'd resemble an ageing hippie by the time we reached the Marquesas in about a month's time. Leaving Sherry aboard the boat reading a book, I rowed the dinghy to shore and asked one of the residents where I could find the barbershop. She just laughed.

"None here," she replied. "You want your hair cut? I can do it."

She led me along the path to a restaurant which her mother owned. I followed her into the kitchen where she pointed to a wooden Pepsi crate. "Sit there," she said, then rummaged through a drawer full of cutlery till she found some scissors. When she finished she gave me a sliver of mirror. Not bad, I concluded. I thanked her, offered her payment which she refused. Too bad I also had to refuse her invitation to have dinner at the restaurant. My stomach was still growling at me.

Every day we went shopping in hope of finding some food, any kind, canned or fresh. The difficulties in purchasing a good supply of food, water and fuel frustrated and astounded us. From this port of call there would be no opportunity to provision the boat for the next three thousand miles. Sherry had done a mammoth shopping at the supermarket in Panama City and we had enough of the staples to see us through to Hiva Oa. But we were dismally short of what Sherry called 'goodies', the sweets we loved for night watches. We thought we'd found gold when we discovered four cases of Pepsi and Seven Up in one shop. We bought it all.

We learned that the Galapagos was one of Ecuador's National Parks and the lack of facilities was deliberate. Their first concern was to protect the fragile ecosystem. Catering to visitors was a distant second.

Sherry's Journal, Galapagos Islands

I read in one of my books that these islands used to be called the Enchanted Isles. Pirates buried their treasure here. The islands are volcanic, mostly black rocks covered with low bushes and cactus. There are swampy areas which breed mosquitoes and little black flies that bite. We did not find any beaches, just rocky shorelines with lots of iguanas.

There are many beautiful birds, butterflies and sea creatures here, even pelicans which I thought only lived in Antarctica. One morning we went to the Darwin Institute and saw the famous Galapagos turtles and more iguanas.

About 6000 people live here. They seem to be very poor and have a low standard of living. Maybe you don't need much money to be happy here. The people are contented and friendly.

The anchorage here is calm and pleasant, the water a light blue. We have seals, puffer fish, and a big pelican for company. Still, we are anxious to leave for Hiva Oa in the Marquesas. Hopefully tomorrow.

Chapter Ten

We left the Galapagos on the last day of March, destination Hiva Oa, the most northerly inhabited landfall in the Marquesas. Sherry commented that French Polynesia looked like sprinkles of salt on a vast blue tablecloth. I wondered how sailors in days gone by had found these tiny specks with only the stars to guide them. We had those same stars but fortunately we also had a SatNav, which appeared to be operating without any kinks. I crossed my fingers that this vital piece of equipment would continue to behave.

We sailed out of the anchorage with our good friend John, on *Mr John IV*, under a bright, hot sky and continued in tandem until the wind dropped to nothing. On with the motor, which pushed us along and charged our batteries. This leg would be our longest to date, 3000 miles as compared to the Atlantic crossing which clocked in at 2582 miles. The need to monitor fuel consumption was again a top priority.

During the late afternoon we lost sight of Mr John as he disappeared over the horizon. We knew that we would be seeing him again in the Marquesas. Although his boat was bigger and therefore his hull speed faster, he would only beat us by hours, or at the most, a day.

Our first night out, Sherry created a wonderful dinner for us using the perishable produce - some tomatoes, green onions and cabbage - which we had purchased in the Galapagos. The carrots and yellow onions and potatoes would keep for a while. Although we had a refrigerator, it didn't measure up to a domestic kitchen model with an uninterrupted power source. Running the refrigerator drained our batteries which then had to be recharged by turning on the engine. A never-ending circle which always came back to fuel consumption. So we tried to content ourselves with a 'just barely cool' setting but there were so many times when we yearned for a really cold drink.

After dinner we sat in the cockpit sipping coffee and enjoying our cigarettes. How happy I was to be back at sea. In the harbour I always felt penned in, like a horse in the corral, kicking at the rail fence in search of freedom and open spaces. I knew that Sherry preferred those days when we were tied to a buoy or a dock. Harbours were safe places, unlike the sea which could delight, surprise or terrify us. As far as Sherry was concerned the terrifying moments outnumbered all the others and stuck in her memory like Velcro to a shag rug while the placid times quickly faded into the tapestry of life at sea.

But, this first night out Sherry was in a positive frame of mind. I watched her adjust the pillow behind her head, then sigh and wriggle her toes.

"It is beautiful out here tonight, isn't it, Jameel? I wish it would stay like this all the way to the Marquesas."

But that was not to be!

Baraka Log – March 31

A good sail today but which ended at 23.00 when we encountered a heavy squall with winds gusting to 20 knots. I took down the genoa and put 3 reefs in the main.

Tonight there were no moon or stars, just fog and mist and rain and wind. Suddenly in front of me I saw a mountain rising out of the sea. No time to turn away. I thought well – this is it. The boat would crash on to the shore and Sherry and I would be killed or hurt and the boat would become a heap of splinters. I held fast to the tiller and waited for the worst. But nothing happened. Even the knot metre was still registering 6 knots and the mountain was still right there off my bow. I called to Sherry to come topside. How could we continue to slice through the water towards a huge land mass and not at least hear a crunch? Sherry suggested that perhaps the combination of the masthead light, the dark night and the swirling mist had created an optical illusion.

Sherry's Journal, March 31

Tonight it rained viciously. I have never seen such rain anywhere. It was pounding down so hard that I could not even open my eyes. In the desert climate of Saudi Arabia and Egypt it sometimes rains hard too. But mostly we have sandstorms, when the wind whirls across the flat open spaces like a tornado, blasting sand and grit in every direction. If you're caught out in a sandstorm, it's a good idea to keep your eyes closed, also to cover your mouth and nose. Sandstorms leave heaps of sand in all the wrong places. Rainstorms like this one, gave us the opportunity to fill our tanks with water, which sweetened the bottled stuff we had bought in the Galapagos.

During the storm, a wounded bird fell into our cockpit. I think it was a petrel - black, small and scruffy. I wondered how he had found the safety of our boat in this enormous ocean. I tried to feed him some scraps of food but he didn't want to eat anything. He crawled into my bunk and fell asleep. My cat often used to curl up at the bottom of my bed but this was the first time a bird had ever shared my sleeping space. The next morning I couldn't find him anywhere and assumed that he had flown away but, while I was searching for some clean clothes in the V-berth, I found him asleep on a cushion. Jameel carried him out to the cockpit but he didn't seem interested in leaving. He spent the day hopping around the cabin and the night flying around, perhaps practising take-offs? In the morning Jameel again took him outside. He hopped around the cockpit a bit, then found a perch on the stern pulpit. And then suddenly he was gone, flying back to the Galapagos or whatever land lies behind us. I crossed my fingers, hoping he would make it. He seemed so small, so tired for such a long journey. After the bird left, I felt very lonely for his company. He kept us entertained for 2 days and was not afraid of us.

For three days and nights we passed through squalls and rain with intermittent periods of calm when we had to turn the engines on and motor. Sometimes the wind shifted around and hit us in the face, forcing us to beat into the wind in order to hold our south-westerly course. Sherry found the motion bumpy and complained that inside the cabin everything was moving. During our brief calm and sunny periods, Sherry hung all our damp bedding and clothing out to dry on the lifelines.

***Baraka A* Log – En route to the Marquesas, April 4-15**

> **Every day I turn the engine on for 2-3 hours to charge our batteries. The rest of the time we sail. The wind has been fair to squally, sometimes gusting to 25 knots. The boat is performing like a pro, slicing cleanly through the water under reefed main. Though Sherry complains of the lurching and rolling, all I can say is 'nice'. A continuing mystery at sea! What is that foul fishy odour and where is it coming from? Sometimes it is just a whiff, sometimes it's overpowering. Sherry wants to know what and why. I told her maybe schools of dead or dying fish. But that doesn't make sense.**

As we continued our westward course towards the Marquesas, our days fell into a routine. Every morning and evening I conducted a thorough 'Frank Mulville Inspection' of *Baraka A*. I concluded that my attention to detail must be paying off because we had suffered no traumatic gear failure. I thought back to the first days of the circumnavigation when exactly the reverse had been true. I found that I could keep myself busy doing 'boat things': checking our position, adjusting the sails, altering our course and recording our progress in the log; but time hung more heavily on Sherry's hands. The domestic chores, which she claimed as her own, were hardly time-consuming. If the day was sunny, she would wash our clothes and hang them out to dry in the rigging. Tidying the cabin took only a fraction of an hour. 31 feet was not a huge space to keep organised, not like our houses in Palo Alto or Jeddah.

Preparing three tasty appealing meals each day was the greatest challenge Sherry faced. Breakfast was perhaps the easiest and the most enjoyable. There was something magical about the morning sky as the sun broke over the horizon, staining the lingering clouds with traces of pink. Then we would sit in the cockpit eating cereal and milk out of long-life paper cartons or toast and jam, although keeping fresh bread aboard for more than a few days out of port was a problem we never solved. Unless you count melba toast a solution! When morning greeted us with rain and gloomy clouds clustered overhead, we ate inside, usually sitting on our bunks since the cabin table had been removed after Sherry bashed her legs to bits on it during our voyage to Plymouth.

Foul medames, which is a well-known bean in the Arab world, was a favourite meal which we ate over and over again, sometimes even for breakfast. A good source of protein, it was a meal in itself but Sherry experimented and presented this standby in many different guises: cooked with oil and a squeeze of lemon or fried with onions and canned tomatoes and a pinch of cumin or coriander or as an accompaniment to rice or pasta. We had been lucky to find foul medames in the supermarket in Panama City. They are not universally available. While we were loading the beans on board *Baraka A*, Sherry had not been able to resist the temptation to toss a few well earned barbs in my direction: "Don't drop these overboard, Jameel. Remember the ravioli in Tenerife."

During the daylight hours the windvane and autopilot did most of the work, leaving us free to nap or read or daydream. Daytime was my sleeping time. During the night I still found myself unable to relax. I kept seeing freighters looming on the horizon. Every creak of the rigging made my imagination work overtime and I would bound from my bed into the cockpit. And so we continued with the schedule we had begun while crossing the Atlantic - six hour watches during the day, switching to three hours during the night. The words from Frank Mulville's book had become imprinted on my brain - 'the night time hours are the most dangerous hours at sea'. Sherry preferred this schedule too. Being alone in the cockpit at night for three hours was all she could manage, even though I was just a whisper away.

Sherry spent most of her spare time reading. Not only the sailing books I preferred but every sort of fiction and non-fiction in Arabic and English and French. One favourite way to pass the hours was to open the atlas and travel books and read up on our next landfall. We counted it a lucky day when we picked up a radio programme on the short wave, especially one in Arabic. Then we dropped whatever we were doing and just listened.

To my mind, Sherry seemed more relaxed aboard *Baraka A* than during the Atlantic crossing. Although she never experienced or understood the exhilaration I felt at matching my wits against the elements and coming out the winner, her terror of high winds and rough seas seemed to have abated. I keep coming back to what Roy Mullender told me on our way to Portugal – 'You have a fine little vessel here; she will take you anywhere.' The longer I sailed *Baraka A*, the more I believed that the secret of a successful voyage lay not in the experience or expertise of the skipper but in the boat. Even the finest skipper in the world would not fare well in an inadequate vessel. But an inexperienced sailor like myself could do just fine in a sturdy, trustworthy boat like the 'Nick 31'. Wasn't I, as the English are fond of saying, the proof of the pudding?

Sherry had also come to believe in the integrity of *Baraka A*. The boat had brought us safely through waves as high as mountains, gale force winds screeching through the rigging and white water boiling over the decks. And after each encounter with bad weather we'd said, 'See, the boat can take it. She was built to handle the worst Mother Nature sends our way.'

I always imagined that Sherry added a silent addendum: 'Please send us more of the nice stuff. Storms aren't any fun.'

Sherry's Journal, en route to the Marquesas. Day 2-15

It is hard to believe that we have not caught one single fish. We have fishing lines, fishing hooks and the hope that when we throw the line into the water something will happen. It would be a treat to have some fresh fish for dinner instead of the usual pasta and rice and foul medames. We hear of other sailors catching fish all the time but we have not caught even one since the beginning of this voyage. Are we doing something wrong? We have seen schools of flying-fish jumping out of the sea and diving back in. Sometimes they land on the deck but before we can catch them, they wriggle off. Why don't they fall into the cockpit? One morning we managed to capture two but they were so small that we threw them back. Jameel finds it funny that I now want to eat some of these flying-fish. He teases me about the ones he cooked up for me on our way across the Atlantic, the ones I refused to eat! Our diet is very boring. All the fresh produce we bought in the Galapagos rotted so we are now eating everything from tins. I have been reading about the Marquesas. We will find every kind of fresh fruit there. I can hardly wait.

The weather has been fair to bad with some nice days now and again. The wind will go from 10 knots to 25 in a split second, usually accompanied by heavy showers. When the wind blows hard, the sea builds up. Then the bow disappears under the water and the waves crash against the side of the boat. Inside, everything flies around. One morning the foul medames I was preparing for breakfast ended up on the floor. We had canned fruit instead. I hate the days when the sun never comes out and all I can see are black clouds.

So far my impression is that the Pacific Ocean is not that calm at all. If pacific means peace, I wonder how this ocean got its name. I have taken a seasick pill every day. One morning the sky was red. Jameel recited an old sailor's rhyme, 'Red sky in the morning, sailors take warning. Red sky at night, sailors delight', which I now know is true. That was a terrible day, howling wind up to 28 knots, accompanied by nasty squalls with pounding unfriendly rain. The sea became very agitated with froth-covered whitecaps churning around the boat. Jameel reefed both the main and the genoa. The next morning the sky was red again and predictably we had another horrible day with even higher winds. Jameel furled in the genoa and put up the spitfire. I wonder how the other boats we met in the Galapagos are doing. Especially our friend John. He's out here alone battling this weather.

We had been at sea seventeen days before the winds stopped shifting around us and settled into a steady following breeze. Sherry found sailing a beam reach more comfortable than running wing to wing before the wind. But, comfortable or not, we made better time with the wind behind us and the current giving us a nice boost. And that was the bottom line – how far did we go today? How many more miles to Hiva Oa?

Sherry decided to mend our Egyptian and Saudi flags, which had become shredded along the edges. From our own experience as spectators on a buoy or a dock, we knew that, when a vessel enters a harbour, all eyes immediately zoom in on the flags. Since ours were unique, we wanted them to look as perfect as possible - no limp bedraggled scraps of fabric would fly from our lanyards!

Both Sherry and I kept a written record of our voyage. Mine took the form of cryptic log notes, dealing with wind velocity, compass settings, hull speed and the choice of sails or reefing points to suit the weather. As Essam would have said, 'Same old, same old,' which I guessed was a current popular phrase. In direct contrast, Sherry hardly ever wrote about the mechanics of sailing a boat. But the weather yes, especially if it was nasty. Then she would write in large block letters at the bottom of the page BAD WEATHER or HORRIBLE DAY. But she also recorded the good moments - spectacular sunset, beautiful sunrise, so peaceful out here, but usually in her ordinary handwriting, as if ordinary days deserved no special attention. But mostly Sherry wrote about her feelings and emotions, something women do well and men hardly bother with. So I considered we had a good balance and at journey's end our records would complement one another.

Sherry's Journal, April 15

What a surprise! Just before dawn we found 27 flying-fish on the deck and in the cockpit. Jameel was overjoyed. He waited for the sun to break over the horizon and give us some light before he attempted to clean and cook them. Why so many flying-fish when there were none before? Could it be the full moon? After Jameel cleaned the fish there was a stinky mess of fish remains to clean up. But it was worth it. What a treat to have some fresh food to eat.

Another bonus - today was sunny and the wind moderate. But after two weeks out here on this boat I decided that I had had it with the view outside so I spent my time on watch inside, reading and writing in my journal and just stepped out into the cockpit for a check every 15 to 30 minutes. We still have 1700 miles to go, which means at least another 2 weeks at sea. It's hard to imagine staying at sea for so long, so we just do our best and try to take it one day at a time and try to keep occupied so boredom doesn't suffocate us. Can't wait to get to land and have a really cold drink and some fresh fruit. We miss this food item the most. Right next in line is fresh meat. How we would love a good steak or lamb kebabs or chicken 'broast', which is popular in Jeddah. I guess it's a combination of roasting and broiling which is unique and delicious.

We took advantage of the fair weather and had a shower. First we washed with saltwater and then rinsed off with fresh water to take away the stickiness.

I have been watching the sky and reading my book on cloud formations and learning what they tell us about the weather. I know about the red sky in the morning but I have also learned that the clouds which look like mare's tails, especially in a mackerel-coloured sky, mean there's a storm brewing somewhere. It always seems to blow harder at night which really scares me. Somehow Jameel never seems scared.

After seeing nothing but flying-fish and the petrel for two weeks, we were amazed to sight three big ships, two freighters and what we thought was a cruising ship because of all the lights on her decks. Sherry's imagination went into overdrive.

"I wonder what the passengers are doing. Probably having a delicious meal or dancing or watching a movie. Maybe even playing cards in the casino. Some big ships have casinos now."

"Maybe someday we will go on a ship like that. But right now I have to make sure that this one doesn't run us over," I said. "We're back in the shipping lanes, that's for certain."

Which meant, I knew, that we had to be vigilant twenty-four hours a day.

Every week we called our families in Cairo and Jeddah to let them know that we were safe. On April 20 I reported that we had reached the half-way point in our circumnavigation.

"But isn't that enough?" my mother answered. "Surely you have proven that you can do it. Maybe you should consider turning back and coming home."

"But it's just as far to turn around as to keep going. Besides, all the good stuff lies ahead of us, all the islands I've been dreaming of visiting since I was a small boy."

Sherry's family worried about our health and the weather.

"We're taking a multi-vitamin each day," she assured them. But when it came to the weather, Sherry still found it easier to fib.

"It's lovely out here, so beautiful," she'd say even though the reality was wind-flogged sails and scudding spray and the wind piping up to 25 knots.

Sherry's Journal, April 18

The boat is sailing well and we are trying to keep busy to make the days disappear. When it is clear, the sea is especially beautiful at night with the stars and the moon and the planets. Everything we see makes us think of freedom and greatness and unqualified nobility.

We have 1015 miles to go. I miss land. I admit that so far this trip has gone very well for us. I hope it stays this way till the end.

***Baraka A* – Log April 19**

Around midnight I saw what looked like a flare in the sky to the north of us. I called Sherry to come and take a look. The light was bright orange and yellow and it kept moving up behind the clouds with a tremendous speed before veering south in lines of shimmering brightness, more spectacular than fireworks. We agreed that it was not a falling star and could find no ready explanation. Was this a show just for us? We are the only ones out here.

Sherry's Journal, April 21

We covered 120 miles today, the best mileage so far. Our morale is up as we think about the Marquesas. In preparation for our arrival, I scrubbed the cabin and took a shower. We now know that we have enough water to finish the trip even without any more rain. Will the butane hold out?

April 25

Unfortunately the wind died and our speed dropped to 1 knot. We were so close to land yet so far away. We saw a sailboat in the distance and tried to call them on the radio but got no response. Later we learned that it was some people we'd met in the Galapagos, the Watchorn family sailing Canada Goose.

Our patience is running out as we advance towards land. Same weather pattern – fluttering wind or none at all and flat seas. We motor for a couple of hours and then drift. We must save enough fuel to get us into the harbour at Hiva Oa. We saw some big fish jumping out of the water. Does this mean land is near? We hope so.

***Baraka A* Log – April 26, En route to the Marquesas**

We had a break from our usual boring day today with a fire in the cabin. Sherry lit a cigarette and then threw the match into the trash before checking that it was out. Then she went out on deck to read. Unfortunately the bin caught fire and luckily I smelled something burning and went into the cabin to find the whole galley on fire. I used the fire extinguisher to put the fire out. Must remember to get it recharged in the Marquesas.

April 28

I have recalibrated the speed and log indicator after taking several fixes. The build-up of barnacles on the hull

has impeded the propeller from recording the distance travelled accurately.

Sherry's Journal, March 29

At dawn the sky was blanketed with thick dark ugly clouds, relieved only by an orange glow along the horizon. A red sky in the morning? Suddenly it began to rain and the wind picked up to 16 knots. I thought we were in for a horrible day but in less than an hour blue began poking through the overcast and the wind dropped to a comfortable 12 knots. If this was to be our last day at sea, I would leave this leg with good memories. Jameel said that we would slow the boat down if necessary so that we do not arrive at Hiva Oa in the dark. Again I followed the same routine as last week in preparation for our arrival - a shower for myself and a scrubbing for the cabin.

Our last night out, *Baraka A* collided with an unknown object. We heard a bang and felt a tremendous thump. Sherry was very frightened. I checked the boat thoroughly and could find no leaks or other damage. What was it? A shark or a whale or perhaps a piece of driftwood. I presumed that it was not a reef or atoll because I had our position pinpointed exactly on the chart and I assumed we were sailing in safe waters. Tiny but deadly land masses lurking just below the surface of the waves are a sailor's nightmare. Hit one and your hull can be ripped to shreds.

We first sighted Hiva Oa on March 29 at 5 a.m., at first just the outline of a mountain rising in the mist ahead of us. Nothing to do but change course and kill time until the sun came up and burned off some of the cloud cover. At 5.30 a.m. the weather took a turn for the worse with low, menacing clouds gathering overhead and the all too familiar red morning sky barely visible on the horizon. The wind picked up to 28 knots and then the island disappeared from view behind the clouds. To be so near to land and not be able to see it was a very frightening experience. I tacked out to sea and sailed in circles waiting for the weather to clear. I had read that the entrance to the harbour at Hiva Oa could be tricky, even elusive in bad weather.

I have tried to remember how I felt on reaching our first landfall in the Pacific. Proud that I had embraced the challenge of sailing 3000 miles in a 31 foot boat and succeeded? Grateful that we had arrived safely and in good health without even one bruise to show off? Overjoyed that the boat had performed so well? We'd had no gear failure, damaged sails, or leaks. There would be no need to haul the boat for extensive repairs. We would spend our time in this beautiful place exploring and relaxing.

I guess what I felt was a sense of contentment, a feeling that this was how it was supposed to be. You leave one port, casting off the lines as you edge away from the dock, sail across the open sea and arrive unscathed at the next port.

There was no mystery as to how Sherry felt as we anchored in Traitor Bay, Atuona in Hiva Oa. No philosophical ponderings for my wife. She was, as the English say, over the moon.

"Land, land! I see land," she shouted. "I want to go for a walk, eat a banana, drink a coke, a nice cold coke. Please, Jameel, get out the dinghy and the motor. I want to go to shore more than I have ever wanted anything."

I nodded and ducked into the cabin. The dinghy part would be easy but the outboard motor - well, that was an entirely different matter!

Chapter Eleven

Sherry's Journal, April 29

Today we arrived safely in Hiva Oa in the Marquesas. I felt like jumping overboard and swimming to shore but I restrained myself and waited while Jameel pumped up the dinghy and tried to get the motor working. No go! So we rowed. After checking in with customs, we walked to town, which took us half an hour. Although there were buses and taxis here, we wanted to stretch our muscles, which haven't had much exercise in the last thirty days. My first impression of this place was the beauty all around us: lush green trees sagging with fruit; high mountain peaks; valleys and clear streams; palm trees growing from the beaches right up to the base of the mountains, in straight rows like soldiers on parade. The sand on the beaches was black but fine like our sand beaches back home. Another first for us – black sand!

After 30 days with no scenery except the blue sea and mottled sky in all its various moods, the vistas here were magnificent, almost overwhelming. Even the town was lush, green and pretty with quaint cottages lining the streets. Our first stop was the post office where we found a telephone and called our families. They were overjoyed that we had arrived safely.

To our surprise, our friend John, from Mr John IV, *was not waiting for us when we arrived. He sailed into the bay that afternoon and that evening we joined him for a beautiful dinner of fresh fish! I have never tasted anything so delicious. All the people here in the anchorage seemed very friendly and helpful telling us where to buy diesel and food and offering to exchange books. That was important for me because I was nearly out of reading material.*

To me, being at sea always meant freedom. And conversely being at anchor meant that the practical world intruded, forcing me to deal with problems which always seemed more complicated than simply getting *Baraka A* to the next port of call. Hiva Oa was no exception.

At the top of my worry list was the matter of a visitor's visa for French Polynesia. I had heard through the grapevine that it was necessary to post a bond or show proof that we were financially solvent and able to leave the country should the need arise. Usually an airline ticket home sufficed, which was something I didn't have although I had explored the option of my cousin sending them to us if the need arose.

I decided to go in to see the customs officials in a positive frame of mind. In the past I had found that the rumours passed from boat to boat at anchor tended to be of the worst-case scenario variety. So I simply told the two officers in the customs shed the truth - we were just passing through on our way around the world. It helped that I was able to back up my rhetoric with newspaper articles and photos. No, I didn't have much cash with me but I had made arrangements with my family in Jeddah to send me money via the British Consulate in Tahiti. If I needed to show proof of solvency I could do so after I reached Papeete.

The senior customs man frowned then stared at me as he shrugged his shoulders. Did he not understand? I began to tell my story again but had barely finished the first sentence when his junior assistant stopped me with a wave of his hand.

"But sir, there is no British Consulate in Tahiti."

Sherry's face turned the colour of chalk. I swallowed hard before answering.

"Impossible. An Englishman in Antigua told me about the Consulate and I told my cousin." An icy fear gripped my chest. "What has happened to my money?"

Another shrug.

"Impossible to say, sir, but it is certainly not waiting for you at a Consulate that does not exist."

"I assure you that I will straighten this matter out once we reach Tahiti," I said with a confidence I did not feel.

"Not to worry, sir. Your money has probably found its way to the bank. We will issue you visas here. You may pick them up before you leave for Tahiti."

I smiled and thanked the two gentlemen for their kindness and consideration. And I'd been worried about something as simple as visas! Now money – that was a real problem. As I walked down the street with Sherry, my mind was churning. We were too close to being flat stony broke for comfort. Our financial woes had begun in Antigua when the boat repairs had chewed a deeper hole into our financial reserves than we had counted on. But after talking to that English fellow, a misinformed English fellow as it turned out, I had felt an enormous weight lift from my shoulders. It had been so easy! I had contacted my cousin who replied that he would take care of the money transfer.

Now what were we to do? The first thing was to promise myself to never again take at face value casual words exchanged in a boat harbour. The second was to find us a few dollars so we could resupply the boat. I decided to sell our marine radio, which I had purchased for $200, for a mere $60, but that was the only offer going and we needed the cash. After budgeting this tiny nest egg down to the last penny, we decided to forget about money and enjoy our stay on this beautiful island. We had enough to see us through until we picked up the money in Tahiti. We didn't allow ourselves to say 'if'. Things would work out. They always had in the past.

Sherry's Journal, Hiva Oa

Have been spending our days discovering more of the enchantment of this island and not worrying about our nearly empty wallets. This morning we walked to town again, picking and eating mangoes along the way. Tomorrow we will come and pick some green ones for the boat. Unlike the Galapagos, the land here is very fertile and everything grows. The wildflowers are magnificent. In the afternoon we sat on the beach and watched some horses galloping across the sand, nostrils flared, manes streaming behind them in the wind. Breathtaking! Who would ever want to leave this place – it's Paradise.

Hiva Oa was like the Galapagos in that there were no marine facilities, which meant that we would again haul the diesel from shore and row it out to *Baraka A*. But first we had to await its arrival on the supply boat which was always due 'any day now'. And although there was no limit to the fresh produce we could pick off the trees, the supplies in the stores were limited. It rained almost every afternoon so we were able to fill our water tanks the easy way, just like we'd done at sea. Just collect it in buckets and pour it in the water tanks. And while doing this chore, enjoy a warm shower.

What impressed me most about Hiva Oa was the friendliness of the people, both the natives and the French. Thanks to Sherry's fluency in that language, we were able to establish real contact with the French inhabitants of the island. One, a shopkeeper, offered to let us use his TV and VCR so we could review the rolls of film we'd shot since the beginning of the voyage. Unfortunately the tape wasn't that clear, which was disappointing and we hoped that the VCR, not our tape, was the cause. The best shots were of the Botanical Garden in Tortolla and the various dolphins we had encountered in our travels.

One afternoon, while I was bartering for a basket of fruit with a young Marquesan, I found out that he was an amateur boxer. Nothing to do but follow him to his cottage where we spent several hours talking about boxing and actually sparring a little. In the end he wouldn't let me pay for the fruit.

Again we found that we were unique, the first Arab sailors to have stopped at these islands. And again people seemed surprised that we were just ordinary folk. No, we were not fabulously wealthy. Oh, if they only knew! No, we did not live next door to an oil well. Yes, these were our everyday clothes: jeans, T-shirts and bathing suits. Yes, many Arabs wore robes and head-dresses but many didn't and we fell into that latter category, especially on the boat.

Sherry and I were conscious of the fact that the impression we made on people would be a lasting one and we tried very hard to make it positive. Which wasn't that difficult. To my mind the secret lay in just being ourselves.

I felt relieved that our longest ocean passage lay behind us. From Hiva Oa to Australia we would be 'island hopping', never too far from repair facilities or the corner store. Still, I spent considerable time while we were at anchor giving the boat a thorough check-over.

I examined the shrouds and stays to make sure that they were not frayed, the same for the sheets and halyards. I greased the winches and checked the blocks and shackles. Everything appeared to be in fine working order except the outboard motor. I was beginning to regret ever buying the thing. In the end I stowed it away, thinking that in Tahiti I was more likely to find an expert in outboard motor repairs. I obviously did not qualify!

Sherry's Journal, Hiva Oa

Most days it is very hot but it cools off during the afternoon after the rain. If I forget to bring the laundry in, it gets wet. Finally I have had some luck fishing! I caught a baby shark, an ugly looking creature. Still I didn't want to kill a baby, no matter what the species. A journalist from the island visited us and said he was going to write a story about us, the first Arabs to ever visit this island.

Every day new people arrived on sailboats form every corner of the world. We enjoyed meeting and talking to them and answering their questions. Top on the list was why we chose to attempt this voyage in a 31 foot boat followed by what life was like in Saudi Arabia.

Another popular topic was prayers – do Muslims really pray five times a day? How to Answer? In some Muslim countries attention to prayers is somewhat relaxed, unlike Saudi Arabia where adherence to the prayer schedule defines the day. The first prayer, Fajr, begins about an hour before sunrise. Around noon the muezzin calls the faithful to the Dhuhr Prayer. All the shops close and do not open until after the Asr prayer in late afternoon. Then the shopping frenzy begins. The Maghrib Prayer follows about two hours later and the Isha Prayer, which is the final prayer of the day, ninety minutes after that. Each day the prayer schedule is posted in the newspaper, as the times change according to the rising and setting of the sun. But not too dramatically as Saudi Arabia lies close to the equator where the length of the days and nights do not change that much with the seasons. I could never imagine sailing across the world's oceans without a deep faith in God. Our prayers kept us strong and protected us at sea. Many times during storms we prayed non-stop that God would take care of us.

We enjoyed our time in Hiva Oa so much that it was difficult to think of leaving it. It came as no surprise that the island was beautiful. All the words I had read about the South Pacific filled my mind with pictures more breathtaking than a painted canvas. We had not expected anything but friendly, hospitable people. But so approachable, so outgoing, so genuinely interested in interacting with us – that came as a delightful and welcome bonus. The same affability permeated the population of 'boat people' at anchor with us and, even though sailors arrived and left in succession, there was a continuity to the congenial tempo in the harbour. Sherry did not even want to discuss leaving.

"It's so peaceful here, Jameel. Why can't we just stay for ever?" she asked more than once.

"Because there are many more islands waiting for us, maybe even more beautiful than this one," I said.

"Impossible," she replied with a frown.

"Well there's another reason. We have to keep pushing westward so that we don't find ourselves caught in the Indian Ocean during the monsoon season."

I remembered our days in the English Channel during 'gale season' and remembered too the lesson I had learned. There really is an order to the weather seasons that sweep the globe, be they typhoons, monsoons, gales or hurricanes. The prudent sailor pays attention and sets his timetable accordingly.

During the next few days I knew by the way Sherry was cleaning the boat, sorting out the interior and loading supplies that she had accepted the inevitable. Yes, our time on Hiva Oa must end.

On the morning of May 5 the supply boat finally arrived with its cargo of diesel fuel and other essentials. We filled our diesel cans and rowed them out to *Baraka A* where we spent several messy hours filling our tanks. If all went well, I planned to leave the following morning for Manihi Island, another speck in the ocean.

Sherry's Journal, Hiva Oa, May 5

Tonight we had a barbecue on shore. Almost everyone came, bringing an assortment of food. We sat around the campfire, stimulated and entertained by the conversation with the other sailors. So unlike our usual routine of early to bed. A young Marquesan chap kept us entertained by telling us stories about the cannibalism which was still a common practice on the island during his grandfather's lifetime. The brain, which was the choicest bit, always went to the chief. Fortunately we had finished dinner before he began telling his stories.

Tomorrow we leave this gorgeous place. I will always remember Hiva Oa for its lush, green beauty and its warm-hearted, generous and kind people.

***Baraka A* Log – En route to the Tuamotu Archipelago – Distance 511 miles**

We left Hiva Oa at 15.00 with 1 reef in the main. Just outside the anchorage we encountered 26 knot winds for a brief period. Later, wind steadied and we had a smooth sail. At 2100 the SatNav began to malfunction. Discovered a loose connection which I fixed. When we reach Tahiti I will have it repaired professionally.

In the atlas the Tuamotu Archipelago appears as a crescent-shaped string of approximately seventy-six coral islands stretching over one thousand miles in length, lying between Hiva Oa and the Society Islands. Our destination was the island of Manihi. The sailing conditions were ideal: the winds between 10-14 knots, sunny and hot during the day and cool at night. The boat was handling beautifully and we made good time. The only clinker was the SatNav which seemed to have a life of its own. It died, was revived, then died again. All attempts at resuscitation failed so we reverted to DR.

After five days we arrived at the island of Manihi. In nautical literature, this archipelago went by another name, 'The Dangerous

Archipelago' because of the numerous coral reefs lurking just below the surface of the water. I had also read stories of ships going aground in these waters, so I approached the island cautiously. After proceeding through a very poorly marked channel, we entered the harbour to find that we were the only sailboat there. A more thorough perusal of the charts showed the presence of a large number of coral reefs. That, combined with the strong current running through the anchorage, convinced us to head for Rangiroa, the main island in the archipelago which lay ninety miles further down the chain. I had visions of *Baraka A* dragging her anchor and the current carrying us on to a reef where we would become matchsticks. Even so the beautiful sand beaches looked inviting as we turned and sailed away.

We wondered if we had made the right decision when we encountered strong squalls and rain almost as soon as we were clear of Manihi. But the weather cleared almost immediately and we had a pleasant sail until the wind dropped to nothing and we were forced to resort to engine power for the rest of the day and through the night.

***Baraka A* Log - Rangiroa Island, May 11**

Sighted land at 07.30 and did not drop anchor inside the lagoon until 12.30. I sailed back and forth along the reef for 4 hours looking for the entrance to the harbour. I finally found it 2 miles north of the position indicated in the Admiralty Pilot Book. Must be a misprint as these pilot books are always right on. A school of dolphins came out to greet us, our welcoming committee. They played around the boat then disappeared, only to reappear again. We again took lots of video footage.

Sherry's Journal, Rangiroa Island

Jameel was right. There are islands as beautiful as Hiva Oa and this is one of them. This island is flatter but very green with lots of birds. Inside the lagoon the water is so clear that we can see the fish swimming on the bottom. I spied a sandshark with its baby floating lazily, just inches above the sand under our keel. Mama was immense but the man in the next boat put my mind at ease when he explained that they were harmless because they cannot bite. That was reassuring, especially because we want to spend lots of time in the water. Again the people are very friendly, especially the kids who say bonjour and smile at us.

Ignoring the sandshark, we jumped into the water and cleaned the hull. It was hard work but easy in a way because the water was so clear that we could see every barnacle and patch of growth, which was green and slimy. It is hard to find words to describe the water – translucent, crystalline, aquamarine in colour and as warm as a bath. Even our hard work turned out to be fun. To make the day perfect, the wife of the local police chief gave us four fish which I cooked for dinner.

We were invited to go snorkelling. The beauty took my breath away. I have never seen so many colourful exotic fish. The Red Sea coral reefs are reputed to be some of the best in the world. Jameel, who spends many free moments diving in the Red Sea, could not believe how clear the water was on Rangiroa. An unforgettable day.

Sherry learned from her reading that the economy of the island depends on the coconut palm. Coconut meat and milk are the mainstay of the diet here, along with fish, but only a fraction of the harvest is consumed this way. The rest of the coconut meat is left to dry in the sun and then made into coconut oil. The thick outer shell is not discarded but stripped and made into rope.

Like Sherry, I was overwhelmed by this place. This was my dream come true, my fantasies of sailing to remote beautiful unspoiled islands realised. Sherry told me that she now understood what forces had driven me to undertake this voyage. And also how much she was enjoying herself even though the long sea passages would always be an endurance test.

Sherry's Journal, Rangiroa

I hope the day never comes when big hotels line this beach. We met an American couple named Kay and Rick and spent the afternoon talking on our boat. Then we moved our boat to an anchorage near them, which was right in front of a hotel. But this hotel was charming: small, with a thatched roof and open-air porches on three sides. We had dinner together. I prepared fish again, and she made tabbouleh, which surprised me because it is a dish from Lebanon which is very popular in Saudi Arabia. Tabbouleh is made from chopped parsley and bulgar wheat.

We hated to leave Rangiroa but Tahiti lay a mere 180 miles away. But Tahiti offered more than beauty. Like a bank, hopefully, with a nice bank draft made out in our names, just waiting for us. We needed money for the usual replenishing of the boat stores. And also to have our autohelms repaired (again), an expense which seemed never-ending. We heard from other sailors that autohelm failure was a fact of life at sea. After digesting this bit of nautical lore, I began to view the autohelm in a more friendly fashion. I asked myself what other piece of equipment was on the job round the clock for weeks on end. Maybe repairs were just a natural part of the life cycle of an autohelm. So I stopped hitting myself over the head for gear failure which was, if not inevitable, at least likely. At the same time I gave myself a congratulatory pat on the back for fixing the SatNav (again). I determined that this piece of equipment and I were destined to have a love/hate relationship for the duration of the voyage. Sailing with the help of the SatNav, made navigation almost effortless and I would never think of undertaking any sort of voyage without one. But, on the flip side of the coin, I took comfort from the fact that I had proven myself to be a competent navigator doing it the 'old way'. Sherry and I had never missed a landfall or a harbour due to a malfunctioning SatNav. So I promised myself to remain calm if the SatNav malfunctioned, to fix it if I could and, if I could not, then to proceed to the next port of call and hand it over to an expert. Looking back, I concluded that I had had just as much success repairing this capricious piece of equipment as the professionals.

We left Rangiroa after lunch on May 15. Sherry stowed the shells that she had gathered on the beach that morning in the V-berth, which had become a catch-all for everything including coconuts and every kind of fresh fruit imaginable, especially bananas. The tide and current were with us as we departed. We could see a group of native children standing on the beach waving to us and grinning broadly. So happy, so peaceful, so unencumbered by material possessions. Maybe the world would be a better place if we all lived this way.

Baraka A Log – May 15

> **Radar went crazy tonight. It indicated that land lay ahead of us less than two miles which really frightened me. How could my navigation be that far off? After some close observations and calculations I concluded that the radar was giving me the opposite picture. Example: if land was behind, it would indicate that land was ahead. Also right and left were switched. Another item to be fixed in Tahiti. I spent many miserable moments wondering where we were. Later the moon came out and we were able to confirm that we were on the right course heading for Tahiti.**

Sherry happened to read this log entry the following morning and had a good chuckle.

"I think there are a few missing parts to this story," she said. "Like how I tried to tell you something was wrong but you wouldn't believe me. How could your wife know more than the radar?"

I grinned sheepishly.

"Honestly, Sherry, I will never say that you are crazy again."

It had all happened so quickly. One moment we were sailing along on what I thought was the right heading when I heard Sherry screaming in the cockpit.

"Jameel, Jameel, we are close to land. Come out here."

"Impossible," I had replied. "We are miles from land. I see nothing on the radar."

"I don't care about the radar. I can hear waves crashing on the shore."

"Can you see the shore?"

"Of course not, it's dark as ink out here, but I can hear breakers. We're going to hit land," Sherry screeched. "Jameel, get out here!"

"Oh, all right," I replied nonchalantly. "But who do you expect me to believe, you or the radar?"

"Well, you'd better believe me. Now I see a light flashing just ahead of us."

This statement had propelled me from the cabin like an Olympic sprinter and to my horror I saw that Sherry had been making all the right calls. We were almost on top of some small atoll. No doubt the light was a hand held flashlight which someone was waving frantically in the hope that we would see it in time and turn back. I grabbed the tiller and threw it over hard. *Baraka A* spun like a top on a marble floor, coming about smoothly and quickly and soon we were heading out to the open sea and safety. How could I explain to Sherry that recording the screw-ups was never easy for a skipper, especially this skipper!

Chapter Twelve

We sighted the island of Tahiti basking in the rays of the rising sun at 07.30 on Sunday, May 17. The wind was blowing furiously as we approached Papeete harbour, gusting to 24 knots which predictably churned the waves into a vicious chop. As we entered the channel we found that the current was running strongly against us. But beyond the breakwater, the calm waters of the harbour beckoned us so we continued cautiously, albeit slowly, but with no mishaps. After dropping anchor, we went through our usual routine of launching the dinghy and rowing to shore, only to find that all the shops were closed because it was a holiday. Even so, we got the impression that Papeete was a lively spot, with lots of shops and cafes and tourist attractions.

We were up with the sun on Monday morning, hoping to be on the steps of the bank when it opened. Our financial situation had escalated from precarious to downright scary. I considered us close to destitute, with only $1.50 in the pocket of my jeans. But no use getting into a stew before we knew what was up, I reasoned, as we walked down the street towards the bank. Perhaps the money was already there, as the customs official in Hiva Oa had suggested.

But those dreams disappeared like morning fog on the horizon when we talked to the vice president of the bank. No, there had been no money transfer. No, he did not know what might have happened to funds sent to a non existent address. Yes, money transfers from the Middle East, though not common in this part of the world, should only take two or three days.

I patted my jeans pocket to make sure our money stash was still there and then thanked the bank VP and headed to the post office to place a call to Jeddah – a collect call. When I got my mother on the line I asked her to contact my cousin and have him send us a bank draft immediately.

"But didn't he send you some money already?" she asked.

Squashing my mounting irritation, I fought the phone static to tell my mother about the non-existent embassy and the money mix-up.

"Please speak to the bank today," I said. "Sherry and I are really in a bad state here."

After ringing off, we plodded along the sidewalk dodging the morning shoppers. How I wished I had been able to speak to my father directly. After lecturing me a bit about spending too much money he would have gone directly to the bank and arranged for an immediate transfer. Instead we had to rely on the circuitous route through my mother to my cousin. I hoped she had understood the urgency of the situation.

I pulled our cash supply from my pocket and asked Sherry how we should spend our last few cents.

"I need some cigarettes," she replied.

"Cigarettes?" While we're starving here, you want cigarettes? I have plenty of pipe tobacco; you can smoke my pipe."

Sherry wrinkled her nose.

"That smelly thing? We're hardly starving, Jameel. We've still got lots of beans and rice and pasta."

"But no fresh meat. You don't know how hungry I am for a steak."

"We don't have enough money for a steak."

Across the street I spied a kiosk from which the smells of roasting chicken drifted on the still morning air.

"There," I said, pointing to the cheery tables under a red and white striped canopy. "Let's see if we can get a couple of chicken sandwiches."

As it turned out, we only had enough money for one but we savoured every bite. As it also turned out, Sherry, over the next few days, became quite attached to my smelly old pipe!

After eating every last crumb of our sandwich, we continued on through town until we located the office of *La Dépêche Journal*, the main newspaper on the island. The editor greeted us warmly. Yes, he had read the numerous Reuters articles about our journey and was interested in doing a feature on us. Could a photographer and reporter come to the boat to interview us?

We, of course, agreed. We just hoped that our visitors would not expect too much in the way of refreshments.

After leaving the newspaper office, we located a shop and arranged for the repair of the recalcitrant outboard and the broken autohelms. Thank God they didn't ask for money up front.

Today, as I look back on our first few days in Tahiti, the memories that assail me are not of palm trees bending in the wind or gentle blue water lapping against the white sand beaches or exotic dancers in grass skirts with flowers in their hair undulating gracefully to the beat of the drums. No, what springs to mind is Sherry and I sitting in the cockpit of *Baraka A* eating rice decorated with canned tomatoes while the aroma of steaks sizzling on the grill and chickens turning on the barbecue spit wafted across the water from the cafes which lined the waterfront. I also recollect rowing the dinghy to shore first thing every morning so that we could be at the bank when it opened.

"Money here yet," I would ask, my brown eyes bright with anticipation like a child in front of the candy counter.

"Sorry, Mr Adnan. Nothing yet. Perhaps this afternoon or tomorrow morning."

Why didn't we explain the situation to the bank manager and ask for a small loan to tide us over? If there is one trait that distinguishes the Arab race from all others, it is our pride. Self-reliance is woven into the fabric of our makeup. Even the thought of asking for a hand-out was abhorrent. Hand in hand with our pride is a belief that 'whatever will be will be'. 'Inshallah' (God willing), the money would arrive quickly and, if it did not, we would continue to eat boiled pasta and rice supplemented by our supply of canned fruits and vegetables. They say that pride goeth before a fall. Luckily our money arrived before we fell flat on our faces!

Sherry's Journal, Tahiti, May 18-21

We have been walking everywhere (no spare cash for taxis), making lists of all the things we will need for the next leg. I heard someone say, 'When you buy a boat you buy a problem'. Sailing is fun but also a lot of hard work, with not too many luxuries like hot showers. For those, you must go to a hotel. But tonight, as we sat in the cockpit of Baraka A *and gazed at the mountains on the island of Mooréa in the distance, an island we hoped to visit soon, we agreed that we had never seen a more beautiful sight. Would the view have been as spectacular from a hotel balcony? No* Baraka A *was the place to be!*

John, from Mr John IV, *and the Watchorn family on* Canada Goose *arrived from Manihi and we spent a few happy hours comparing notes on our respective journeys. Met another couple, Canadians, aboard* Home Brew, *who invited us to have dinner with them, an invitation we accepted without one second of hesitation. I became intrigued when I discovered that the chicken that we so enjoyed had been cooked and canned months earlier and stored for future use. Since we already had a pressure cooker, an item which was essential for safe canning, I decided to become a home canner too. Jameel, who refused to eat commercially canned meat products, endorsed the idea and the next day I became an avid pupil and learned the technique. I figured that on long ocean passages, home canned meat would give us a change from dried salami. I wish I had learned how to do this before setting off across the Atlantic. I also wished that I had a ready supply of home canned meals in our galley!*

Sherry and I agreed that Tahiti was a beautiful place but after the tranquillity of our last two anchorages, perhaps a bit too busy? We were anchored a few feet off a beach behind which ran the island's main highway. It got noisy early and stayed noisy until late at night. The price you pay for civilisation. On the plus side, we found Papeete to be a vigorous commercial centre, very modern, but very expensive which proved a bit of an obstacle until my money came through. While we waited for the autopilots and the outboard to be repaired, we went sightseeing with John (*Mr John IV*) and the Watchorns (*Canada Goose*) and prowled through the wonderful markets where every fresh fruit imaginable was on sale. Strangely enough, we found hardly any vegetables and what few there were, carried an unreasonably high price tag, like $5 for a head of lettuce. Being a curious fellow, I asked questions until I found the answer. Polynesians don't eat vegetables; in fact they hardly know what a vegetable is. For years vegetables were not even cultivated on the islands. When foreigners arrived demanding vegetables and seemed willing to pay outrageous prices, some farmers planted vegetable crops. When I thought about this, it all made perfect sense. Fruit grows on trees and needs no looking after. You just watch it ripen, then you pick it. Vegetables grow in soil and need constant attention – weeding, watering, hoeing, fertilising: a labour-intensive enterprise. No wonder the Tahitians stuck to fruit. Another labour-intensive project, this time for us, was taking our water jugs to the beach and filling them at the communal tap, then rowing back to the boat and filling the water tanks. No afternoon rain to give us a break. Sherry used some of the fresh water to give our clothes a much needed wash but the deck and windows had to make do with water from the sea.

Sherry's Journal, at anchor, Papeete Harbour

It took us a few days to get used to 'city life' but now I am really enjoying myself, especially since our funds arrived and we have money to eat out in the numerous cafes which we have been eyeing hungrily. We went on a shopping spree and splurged on souvenirs for our friends and family. I've also had a chance to catch up on my letter writing. I don't often get this close to a post office and stamps. The article in La Dépêche Journal *was published as promised, a full page story with pictures. We were delighted.*

We haven't missed one celebration or festival. We couldn't stay away from the Mr and Miss Tahiti competition, the local version of a beauty pageant with men as co-contestants. The participants looked marvellous in their native costumes. So did the Tahitian dancers, who put on a performance that same evening. Such grace and beauty. The dancers were exquisite in their grass skirts with flowers in their hair. Again we took lots of video footage. The miracle of video is that our families will have the chance to enjoy these moments too.

The best thing about Tahiti is the weather. As we proceed south, it is becoming cooler. The days are lovely and sunny but the nights almost approach being chilly which makes for great sleeping.

We had to wait in Papeete for the autohelms and the outboard to be fixed, which stretched into twelve days, longer than we had anticipated. The radar, it appeared, could not be repaired. I could send but not receive so I decided to leave it on at night so that ships in the area would be aware of my existence. I would have to rely on my eyes and ears and that special 'gut feeling' to be aware of theirs.

Sherry was so excited to have a functioning outboard motor on the dinghy. At last power! She jumped on board, pulled the cord and took off for a spin around the anchorage, a journey which came to an abrupt end when the dinghy flipped over and the motor got a dousing. Lots of outboard motors survive a dunking and start up again with no problem but not this one. I didn't know whether to laugh or cry or yell in frustration. Sherry felt so guilty about the incident that I couldn't stay angry for more than a moment. I knew that we could not wait around Papeete for another twelve days getting the motor repaired again. The boat was scrubbed inside and out, the provisions were stored and we were ready to go.

Just as we were ready to leave, the weather changed for the worse. Departure day greeted us with high winds and pounding rain. *Mr John IV*, whose next port of call was also Mooréa, decided to brave the weather but he soon scooted back into the anchorage when he found that he could make no headway against the fierce winds.

There is a saying that 'ports rot ships and men' and oh, how that applied to me. Too long in a harbour and I began to feel antsy. Sherry, on the other hand, loved life in port and was always reluctant to leave.

We were behind schedule. I made the decision that, on May 29, we would leave Tahiti no matter what the weather, a decision that won no hearty round of applause from my wife!

***Baraka A* Log – May 29, Destination Mooréa, 25 miles**

Weighed anchor at 13.00 with 3 reefs in the main. Encountered very bad weather with winds gusting up to 39 knots with zero visibility. Mooréa island was shrouded in fog. Waited for the weather to clear before attempting to

enter the harbour. Once inside, the water was flat but the wind was still howling.

Sherry's Journal, Cook's Bay, Mooréa Island

I know I sound like a broken record but this place is the most beautiful so far. The harbour is shaped like a horseshoe with mountains on all sides, so close I feel as though I can touch them. All around us it is so lush, so green, so unlike the desert landscape we are used to.

Although we were in protected waters, the wind was blowing furiously. Jameel set the anchor quite a few times before he was satisfied that we would hold fast and not be blown on to the rocky shore. What a night, with the wind screeching around the mountains then slamming into Baraka A *broadside, causing her to heel like we were on a hard beat. Before dawn all the skippers were on deck with flashlights checking anchor lines. Unfortunately 3 boats tore loose and were blown on to the shore. We thanked God that we had held fast.*

We endured two days of stormy weather, thankful that we were in a protected harbour and not out on the open sea. Finally, on May 31, the storm blew itself out like an exhausted child after a prolonged temper tantrum and we were able to really appreciate the beauty of this anchorage. I pumped up the dinghy so we could get to shore which prompted Sherry to bemoan the fact that our motor was again not functioning.

Without consulting my first mate, I yanked the motor out of its storage spot under the V-berth.

"This motor's been nothing but a burr in my socks since we bought it," I announced, as I lugged it out on deck. "It's time for a burial at sea."

I lifted it over the lifelines and dropped it into the water. "May you rest in peace," I said as it gurgled and sank.

"No," replied Sherry, "now you will rest in peace."

I glanced over my shoulder at Sherry who was sitting in the cockpit. Was that a frown creasing her brow or a smile tickling the corners of her mouth? As usual her good mood surfaced and we had a good laugh.

Our good mood continued to escalate when old friends from *Mr John IV* and *Canada Goose* arrived at Cook's Bay. To our delight we also met some new sailors who soon became good friends, Claude and Emilia Allouch on *Pasha* and Roger and Jojo Lextrait on *Couscous*. Boat names fascinated me. *Couscous* is a Moroccan speciality, the base of which is a grain smaller and softer than rice. Sherry found couscous delicious. For me, they were merely okay. What would prompt a boat owner to give his vessel this name? We soon found out that Roger Lextrait was a master chef who, like Sherry, adored couscous. His wife, Jojo, was a Hawaiian beauty of Chinese descent.

I immediately recognised the name, *Pasha* which was the name of a Turkish lord who lived during the days when the Ottoman Empire controlled Turkey. At last, someone from our part of the world.

Claude and Emilia Allouch admitted to recognising the name Baraka and also our Egyptian and Saudi flags. Reluctantly they admitted that they were not Turkish, but Israelis and their national flag was hidden away in a sail bag. I don't think Sherry and I had ever met anyone from Israel before but after just a few moments we knew that these people were the same as everyone else we'd met in anchorages along the way; just ordinary folks with no axe to grind. We agreed that Israelis, like Arabs, were unique. Not many from either country cruised the South Seas. Would we be welcomed or shunned? Emilia and Claude had decided to play it safe. Sherry and I had taken the opposite tack, a difference which made for many lively discussions over the next few days.

A group of us, (like a mini United Nations) rented a car and drove around the island, almost mesmerised by the vistas of mountains and sea. Later we had dinner together at the Bali Hai Hotel.

I decided that, weather permitting, we would leave for the island of Aitutaki which lay south-west of us, a distance of 575 nautical miles, on June 3.

Sherry's Journal, Cook's Harbour, June 2

Tonight we were the guests of honour at a dinner aboard Pasha. *We had a good time but it was very sad too when it came time to say* goodbye *knowing that we might not ever see each other again. I think that all the sailors we have met are special people. If the whole world treated themselves so nicely, we would not have any wars or problems. We help each other, we get to know one another fast and then we leave each other with beautiful memories and best wishes.*

June 3, Cook's Bay

I wondered why Jameel was having such a struggle to raise the anchor. He heaved and pulled and finally wrapped the anchor line around the winch. The cause of all the problems was the outboard motor, which had become entangled in the anchor chain. Nothing to do but haul the motor aboard after which Jameel gave it another burial at sea. I laughed till my sides ached, unlike Jameel who could only manage a chilly smile. But too quickly the laughter faded and I found myself fighting back the tears as we sailed out of the harbour leaving a lot of friends behind. It's hardly likely that we will meet up again. We're pushing ahead and all the others are cruising from island to island with no timetable. Good luck to all of them and all our love.

Sherry didn't notice that my eyes were also on the damp side as we sailed out of Cook's Bay. These few days spent with bright, energetic, gracious people would remain a highlight of our trip. Sherry said it all – if the people of the world conducted themselves like sailors in an anchorage we would live in a better world. Problems between countries are caused by politicians, not ordinary people.

***Baraka A* Log – June 5**

Second day out and there are all the indications of a coming storm – high clouds interspersed with low clouds, wind dropping and rising and changing direction from W to N. The barometric pressure remains steady in spite of

ominous black clouds blanketing the horizon. Sailing under main (3 reefs) and genoa. Tonight, that fish stink again.

It was only 575 miles to Aitutaki but the wind, which should have been behind us came either straight at us, or across our beam, which made for a slogging, wallowing sail. Heavy rain squalls and flukey winds battered *Baraka A* as she made her way slowly across a pitching sea. Sherry swallowed her Stugeron and took to her bunk and tried to ignore the creaking and groaning of the boat as waves pummelled the hull with a boxer's precision.

On Sunday, June 7, we had a respite from the nasty weather when the wind died to nothing and the sun came out. Out too came all our soggy clothing which Sherry hung on the lifelines to dry. In the afternoon we treated ourselves to a shower, our first in many days. I wondered if it was ever possible to have 'just a nice breeze' while at sea. Must it either be dead calm or raging? Today we motored. With 240 miles to go we hoped for some increase in the wind velocity!

The next day, when the wind returned, it had shifted around so that we were again beating into it. Even with a motor assist we did the nautical equivalent of plodding, a slow, clumsy forward motion.

Sherry's Journal, June 9

We are 95 miles from Aitutaki and the weather is still not good. The sky is hiding behind a barricade of angry dark clouds. It rains and the wind blows hard. I hope that by the time we reach our destination, the weather has settled. Jameel read that the passage leading to the lagoon is narrow and shallow and full of coral heads.

We sighted the island of Aitutaki early in the morning. Unlike Tahiti and Mooréa, this island was a low flat atoll with no distinguishing landmarks. Unfortunately, the weather had not improved and we were still plagued by angry overcast skies, sullen seas, pounding rain and squalling winds. The weather forecast on the radio informed us that we were in for more of the same, the result of a series of depressions which seemed reluctant to disperse or move on.

Finding the harbour channel proved to be a more difficult task than I had ever imagined. We tacked back and forth hoping to locate the one elusive entrance. No go. Although I was always reluctant to ask for assistance – the macho syndrome which is also part of my Arab make-up. When I finally made radio contact I was advised *not* to attempt entering the harbour on my own but to wait for a tug assist.

Even with a tug pulling us, entering the harbour at Aitutaki was a scary experience. The current was running so strongly that the water bubbled up around us like a witch's cauldron. Then the boat began to yaw and swing on the end of the tow rope like a clock's pendulum. From the cockpit of *Baraka A* we could see a profusion of rocks and reefs on both sides of the boat. We breathed a sigh of relief when we reached the safety of the harbour and dropped anchor. Trying to enter this harbour against the current without an assist was, we learned from the one other boat there, an impossible task. We would time our departure to coincide with the outgoing current.

Sherry's Journal, Aitutaki, June 10-11

In the afternoon we took a long walk in the village and stopped at the post office where I called my family. As always, their first question was about the weather. And as always I gave them my standard response. "Lovely," I replied. "We've had a wonderful sail." What good could come of telling them stories of storms and rain and being seasick? Why should I cause them worry? I love them and miss them so much.

We discovered that the only petrol depot on the island was located several miles from the harbour. Sherry decided to stay behind to clean the boat and tackle our bug problem. Since the Galapagos we had been plagued by small flying insects, like tiny mosquitoes and the moment we thought that we had eradicated them for good, they reappeared. I didn't blame Sherry for finding something else to do. I knew I was in for a long, tiring, wet day.

First I loaded the jerry cans into the dinghy, rowed to shore against a vicious current then managed to hitch a ride with a passing motorist. At the gas station I filled the jerry cans, hitched another ride back to town, fought the current getting back to the boat and then unloaded the jerry cans and filled the diesel tanks. The weather complemented the task at hand - drumming rain whipped by the wind into a stinging spray. I lost count of the number of trips to and fro but finally the tanks were full and so were the jerry cans. Sherry announced that *Baraka A* was again 'bug free'. I was too tired to care.

Sherry's Journal, at anchor Aitutaki, June 12

Jameel says that we will leave on Monday, June 15, which is three days away. I hope the weather changes before we have to leave. It rains constantly and the wind blows so strongly that we fear the anchor will drag and we will end up on the coral reefs. I am lonely and bored. I miss our friends from the last anchorage and wonder where they are. I hope everyone is safe. There is only one other boat here, with a family from Denmark on board. When I told them that I had been unable to buy any books or mags here they very kindly gave me three books, one of which was 'Out of Africa'. Nice and thick! It will take a long time to read. The Danish family seems very pleasant but I can't summon up the energy to forge a real friendship like we enjoyed with our friends in Cook's Bay.

After a couple of days at anchor, we decided to forget the weather and go have some fun. As usual Sherry knew all the facts about the island of Aitutaki from her reading. It was, she informed me, one of the three principal islands that make up the southern tier of the Cook Islands. These were the islands that Captain Cook bumped into on his way to Australia and should not be confused with Cook's Bay on Mooréa. The island was small, only twenty square miles in area. Sherry and I rented motorbikes and went exploring. We stopped at beautiful secluded beaches and collected shells, walked barefoot on the hard-packed sand, then later stopped for a delicious lunch at the Aitutaki Resort. In the afternoon we did the laundry then treated ourselves to a dinner out at the Rapea Hotel in the village. Delicious seafood.

We wondered why the weather hadn't co-operated to make our stay on this lovely island idyllic instead of merely nice. No break in the rain or overcast to give us even a peep of sun. No respite from the wind which went from a howl to a shriek to 'blowing with rage', which is how Sherry described it in her journal. In truth it almost seemed as if the wind was out to get us, to tear us loose from our anchorage and fling us on to the rocks. Before retiring for the night, I always checked that the anchors were secure. That night the weather deteriorated to a new low. The wind whipped the waters of the harbour into a frenzy, which caused *Baraka A* to pitch and toss which meant that neither of us got much sleep.

***Baraka A* Log – June 13**

Anchorage here not good, mostly coral reefs right up to the shore. No firm sand to set the hook except where the Danish boat is anchored. Tonight the anchor dragged. God must have been watching over us because *Baraka A* miraculously ended up on the one patch of sandy beach in the whole lagoon. Before we realised what was happening, the boat was 'beached' on her side. All night we listened to the hull pounding and scraping against the sand and prayed that she would not be damaged. Decided that pulling the boat off the beach back into the water would be a tricky undertaking so will wait for daylight and the high tide and try to do it right.

Sherry's Journal, June 14

This morning our worst fears were realised. Jameel threw the anchor out more than a few times and slowly he was able to winch the boat back into deep water. We called our Danish neighbour for assistance and together he and Jameel were able to move Baraka A to safety. Jameel set another anchor – that made three, a record for us.

Tonight we accepted an invitation to go crabbing with some of the locals. The goal was to capture as many of the crabs as possible as they scurried from the sea to the protection of the bushes which line the road. We were amazed to see how easily the natives were able to spot the crabs in the dark. Again it was pouring with rain but we still had fun. Jameel and I were overwhelmed by the friendliness of the people. This was no put on smile to attract tourist dollars but a genuine desire to interact with us as fellow inhabitants of the same planet.

Jameel has delayed our departure until the 16th in hopes that the weather will clear. For once I am ready to depart. Maybe better weather lies ahead.

Chapter Thirteen

We set sail from the island of Aitutaki on June 16 in tandem with the Danish boat. I glanced at Sherry, who was sitting stone-faced in the cockpit gripping the lifelines as she stared at the coral heads and reefs slipping by our hull.

"It's okay, Sherry," I said. "Look, the water's flat, not even a ripple. This time we're going in the same direction as the current. We'll be fine."

Sherry did not loosen her grip or turn her head to acknowledge my cheery words. Not until we were safely out in the open sea did she come out of her trance like state and wave goodbye to our Danish friends, who were heading in the opposite direction.

"Sorry, Jameel," she said. "When I'm frightened there's nothing you can do or say to change it. Being scared is something I have to do alone." She paused. "Maybe even need to do alone."

She propped her chin in her hand and gazed at the island of Aitutaki which was fast becoming a smudge on the horizon.

I wondered if I would ever have any real appreciation of the terror Sherry felt at being at sea aboard a piece of floating fibreglass, her imagination working overtime about all the things that could go wrong. Nasty weather and gear failure? Those we had experienced and survived. We'd also hit or been hit by some object, perhaps a whale. A collision with a whale had sent many a boat to the bottom. Encounters with coral reefs and submerged atolls could tear *Baraka A* to shreds and perhaps her occupants as well.

I knew that Sherry would have preferred to remain in California or return to Cairo or Jeddah and live a conventional life. Yet here she was, aboard *Baraka A*, being first mate to a crazy guy who was trying to sail a 31 foot sailboat around the world. I'd always thought of Sherry as a special person: bright, talented, fun and very brave. Most of the other wives we'd met along the way had been almost as gung-ho as their husbands about sailing. Sherry found the cruising life a real struggle but she stuck with it and with me. Somehow that day, as we headed off towards American Samoa, the enormity of that commitment hit me square in the face.

Also hitting me square in the face were the headwinds as we put *Baraka A* on the right heading for American Samoa. Not an uphill battle again! Where were the gentle trade winds we'd heard so much about?

Our destination was Pago Pago (pronounced Pango Pango. Don't ask me why. Some Arabic words don't make sense either) which lay to the south-west, 682 miles away. It amazed me that we were beginning to view these voyages of several hundred miles as short hops compared to the Galapagos to Hiva Oa leg which clocked in at three thousand plus. Looking back, I remembered our short little sail to the Canary Islands. How adventurous we'd felt at being out on the open ocean. With every passing day, my confidence and ability to handle any kind of weather, was growing.

Except that I hadn't counted on a storm which came blasting out of nowhere when we were six days out. That time I was every bit as scared as Sherry.

***Baraka A* Log - June 22**

Storm began on Sherry's watch. Suddenly the wind went from 3 knots to 18 knots in a matter of seconds which made Sherry scream for me to come on deck. The wind kept escalating over the next few hours until we were battling 35 knots. Experienced a knock-down while in the cockpit. My face was just inches from the water. Held tight to the tiller and gradually the boat righted herself. Put a fourth reef in the main and furled in the genoa. Lashed the tiller to a stanchion on the lee side and hove to. Went below and closed the hatch. Nothing to do but wait it out till the weather improves.

Sherry's Journal, June 22

All night the wind screamed around us. The rain battered the hull and decks with a ferocious drumming sound. How could something as soft as water drops make so much noise? Locked inside the cabin with Jameel, I was more frightened than I can ever remember. The boat rolled and pitched, causing us to heel over until the spreaders were in the water. I thought – here we go, upside down with the mast pointing to the ocean bottom – but then, ever so slowly, the boat righted herself. The water crashing everywhere sounded like a bomb blast. Jameel and I said a lot of prayers that long terrible night. This was the worst storm so far, much worse, Jameel said, than the ones he encountered on the way to Casablanca.

The next morning the wind dropped back to a reasonable 8 knots but the sky was still lead pencil grey and the rain continued to pelt us. I spent the morning cleaning the cabin and putting everything back in its proper place. Even my basket of produce had become airborne during the storm. Fruits and vegetables were scattered all over the floor and even behind the cushions.

I spent the morning doing an extra-thorough 'Frank Mulville Inspection' of the rigging. By some miracle nothing was broken. In the afternoon the wind died to almost nothing except for intermittent squalls when it would pipe up to 15-20, but only for brief periods. We were behind schedule and hoped for a nice following breeze to push us the remaining 155 miles to American Samoa. For once I was as anxious as Sherry to see land.

Sherry's Journal, approaching American Samoa.

I have been sitting inside, out of the weather writing in my journal. A very important matter came to my mind: the Red Sea. Both Jameel and I have been astounded by the misinformation about this body of water – that it is dangerous, and that there are pirates. Never! There are pirates in parts of the Caribbean but not in the beautiful Red Sea. After sailing more than half-way around the world, I think that there are no prettier beaches anywhere. Almost all the sailors we've met say that the preferred route is via South Africa and the Cape of Good Hope. That is one of the stormiest and most dangerous patches of water in the world, unlike the Red Sea which is almost calm in comparison. All we can hope is that our voyage will help convince others that the Red Sea is not a dangerous place to be.

I have been reading a book, 'The Women's Room'. Every man who thought he understood women must read it. Also, every woman who thought she knew herself! I was feeling so homesick today that I decided to write a poem.

The land around is beautiful,
Where all the trees are fruitful,
The sea flows with grace
As if in a big race

But I miss home
Where my love had grown.
And I miss my sister
With whom my heart felt richer.
The land in which I lived
And where my parents sleep
Is in my heart as deep
As the colour of the sea.

Nasty weather continued to batter us as we proceeded toward America Samoa - squalls, rain, drizzle, and a constantly shifting wind which meant we could not just set the windvane and autohelm and disappear into the cabin out of the weather. In spite of my efforts to time our approach to a landfall during the daylight hours, we always seemed to miss, either arriving at night or very early morning. America Samoa was no exception. We sighted lights at 4 a.m. and then had to motor around in circles till dawn broke. The island, with its steep mountain peaks piercing the clouds was beautiful, a word we had used and again. But was there another that could do the job so well? The wind started to pick up as we entered the harbour but once inside the breakwater we found flat water and were able to anchor quickly and smoothly. Sherry got out the binoculars and scanned the anchorage for our friends. No one, at least not yet. Maybe before we *had* to leave. We were badly behind schedule and pressing on had become a priority. I decided not to share this thought with Sherry, who cherished her time in port and always wished that she could make every anchorage her permanent home.

After completing the customs formalities we went out for lunch and then to the outboard motor shop where we purchased a brand new 2.2 hp Yamaha.

"What happens if the motor gets wet?" Sherry asked the salesman.

"Nothing," he replied. "Always, it works fine."

That night we fell into our bunks early and slept like hibernating bears. A week with little sleep had taken its toll.

The next morning over breakfast Sherry read me excerpts from her travel book:

"Pago Pago is one of the finest harbours in the South Pacific with all the facilities visiting sailors might need close at hand."

"Look, Jameel," she continued. "Here's a picture of a cable car we can take to the top of the mountain. Let's do it."

"Look, Sherry," I said, pointing to a boat just entering the harbour. "Isn't that *Couscous*?"

In a flash we were in the dinghy and *motoring* across the anchorage to welcome our friends Roger and Jojo Lextrait. Sherry and Jojo fell on each other like long lost sisters which made me realise that there really did exist a bond stronger than superglue among the women who chose (maybe endured?) a life at sea. Over the next few days more friends appeared: *Mr John IV* and *Moline*, whom we'd last seen in Cook's Bay. A reunion so soon with people we thought we'd left behind, people we thought we'd never see again, made Sherry's eyes dance with happiness and anticipation. Soon a Canadian couple aboard *Justice II* joined the gang.

We bought ourselves a tiny black and white TV to take advantage of the American television programmes available here. Both Sherry and I loved watching TV. We weren't the 'glued to the screen' types, but there were several programmes we enjoyed. Some of the people in the harbour wouldn't have tolerated a TV near their boats as if TV and boating were arch enemies. Then I reminded myself that it was a TV programme that really fired my imagination about sailing the world's oceans. Maybe if I hadn't been consumed by *Adventures in*

Paradise when I was a kid, I wouldn't be out here as an adult enjoying the South Sea islands.

Sherry's Journal, American Samoa

Went shopping just with the girls, something I haven't done in many months. Then we went out to lunch. I think this island is the cheapest so far, especially for clothes. I bought shirts and shorts, pants and T-shirts for both me and Jameel. All our clothes are worn out from washing them in saltwater. While I was buying clothes, Jameel was prowling around the nautical shops buying boring things like oil filters and charts.

Parts of this island are magnificent. We went sightseeing with our friends. The mountains are breathtaking in their greenery, with every tree imaginable growing – mango, papaya, banana and breadfruit. I don't like breadfruit much. It tastes like a sweet potato.

The town itself has its pretty parts and its dingy parts which I know is typical of cities in every part of the world. I guess I've forgotten what cities are like. I haven't been in one since Panama.

In spite of our busy social life, we spent many hours stowing enough fuel and food on board to take us to Australia. I did my first canning – chicken and beef – which will give our meals at sea some variety.

The port captain here told us that he had never met anyone from the Arab world before. He thought that we had a lot in common because he was Mormon and allowed to have more than one wife. Well, not really. Having lived in America for many years, I knew there were laws against polygamy whereas in my country multiple marriages are sanctioned by law.

The idea of having more than one wife seemed to intrigue and fascinate the people we met during our circumnavigation, a conclusion we reached after fielding questions on the subject again and again and again. Yes, a man may take up to four wives but he must treat them in the same manner, which costs a lot of riyals. No, not everyone has four wives, in fact today very few do. Most men are like me and count themselves lucky to have just one wife!

I watched a man standing on shore throwing a net into the water, probably fishing for the 'catch of the day' for one of the restaurants in town. The people here survived on a diet rich in fish. Again I wondered why my luck at fishing had been so dismal. Perhaps the missing ingredient was patience.

Sherry's Journal, American Samoa, July 4

Today was the Fourth of July, American Independence Day. All the 'boat people' gathered for a barbecue ashore. What a great party! All our friends were with us and we had a wonderful time. But it was sad too. My friend Jojo from Couscous *is flying home tomorrow morning and we had to say* goodbye. *I gave her our black and white TV. We both cried. I know I'll miss her a lot and I hope so much that I will see her again. I expected lots of things while I was sailing around the world: storms, boredom, seasickness and fear. I never expected to find a really good friend.*

I had planned our departure from American Samoa for July 6. But then the Watchorns arrived on *Canada Goose* so we decided to stay on and visit with them for a couple of days. A lucky delay as it turned out, for the weather turned rotten once again, trapping us in the harbour for days. Winds gusting to 34 knots kept everyone aboard their boats on alert. One morning we woke up to find the dinghy line trailing forlornly in the water behind the boat. The motor was safe on its motor mount but what good was a motor without a dinghy? Were we destined to have only one of these items at any given time? Sherry spied the dinghy on shore, thankfully not flung on to the rocks but just bobbing gently by the water's edge. With the help of a neighbouring skipper, I retrieved it and tied it up with a bowline, not the granny knots Sherry liked to use.

The weather defied description. Wind driven rain made staying outside impossible, so we hunkered down inside and went over our checklists again. It might be a long time before we found a provisioning spot as complete as this one.

Sherry's Journal, American Samoa, July 7

Jameel hates being trapped in the harbour. This morning he said that the wind was good. Good for him but too hard for me. Jameel would like to sail from here straight to the Santa Cruz Islands, which are 1300 miles away and that means spending two weeks at sea. Not a happy thought.

This afternoon we went to town and ordered some business cards with our names and addresses (Cairo and Jeddah) and on the top:

BARAKA A
FIRST ARAB CIRCUMNAVIGATION ATTEMPT

Jameel agreed to wait two more days for the weather to clear. On Thursday we decided to give it yet one more day but to leave for certain on July 10. The last day in harbour is always very hard for me, knowing that we will be leaving land and civilisation behind. That night we went out for dinner with Canada Goose *and* Justice II. *We're all heading in different directions and we'll probably not see each other again. Jameel reminded me that I have said this many times in the past but this time I think it's true. We've been such good friends. We said goodbye remembering so many beautiful moments. Precious memories.*

The next morning, as we sailed out of the harbour, Sherry turned and waved goodbye to American Samoa.

"This is the hardest place to leave so far," she said. "We made so many good friends and now we have to leave them and go out to sea all by ourselves."

I knew I had a quick rejoinder if I wanted to use it – "You always say the same thing but we always meet up with old friends and make new ones in every harbour we visit." But I kept my mouth firmly shut. I remembered Sherry telling me that there was nothing I could do to stop her being scared and I figured the same argument applied to 'sad and lonely'. I knew that many enchanting islands lay ahead of us. I also knew that Sherry would again be in the middle of the social scene wherever we went. Making friends came so easily to her. Her congenial outgoing personality made everyone who met her feel comfortable and welcome. I wondered what my social life would have been like without Sherry around to get things moving. Probably okay but certainly not fantastic!

***Baraka A* Log – July 13**

The weather settled into a steady following breeze so we set the sails wing to wing which made for a very rolly ride. But the compensation was the miles quickly disappearing under our hull. Today I caught a fish, a big dorado, but it got away before I could get it aboard. Then I caught a second one, not quite as big, which I managed to land! When they are caught they change colour from silver to green, yellow and blue. Sherry took a video so we can prove to our families and friends back home that we really did catch fish.

Sherry's Journal, July 13

Jameel cleaned the fish in the cockpit which made a horrible mess. But that evening, when we ate a dinner of freshly cooked fish, we decided that cleaning up the mess was a small price to pay.

A perfect day except for the barometer which seemed to be falling. "Please," I prayed, "no more storms."

The falling barometer did not bring a storm but 'the calms'. The sky looked nasty, with thunderheads stretching from one horizon to the other like ugly balls of grey cotton candy. We put on the motor thinking that maybe nicer weather lay ahead. Although it finally rained, the wind never picked up. At night we again stuffed ourselves with dorado and threw what remained overboard.

Sherry's Journal, July 16

We are sitting here, still in the calms. I want some wind but not too much. Trouble is you can't specially order the wind velocity and, usually, you get more than you want.

During my watch last night I was sitting inside reading a book. Then I heard a noise from the cockpit so I went to investigate with a flashlight. Found a big flying-fish with its wings still open. I put it back into the sea. We've eaten enough fish for a while.

Still 270 miles to go but thankfully the wind picked up and we made good time. We hoped to make Rotuma in the next two days.

Flushed by the success of my first catch, I decided to pass the time trying my luck again, hoping that a smaller fish would take the bait. Not a nibble until we were in sight of Rotuma when I landed a huge tuna which filled the entire cockpit. Cleaning it created an even bigger mess than the dorado and by the time we were finished we were both covered in blood. Luckily it took three and a half hours to reach the island which gave us time to sluice down the boat and also ourselves.

On arrival we discovered that there really was no harbour on Rotuma, just a small bay open to the weather. We didn't see any hint of boats or people and decided that we would sail on after a short rest and a swim.

Sherry's Journal, Rotuma, July 20

After dropping the anchor we surveyed the small bay and suddenly realised how gorgeous everything was. Prettier than a postcard. On one side of the lagoon clear turquoise water lapped at a patch of white sand beach fringed with palm trees. On the other side, black rocks with tiny caves formed a backdrop for more palm trees which seemed to be growing right out of the rocks. And birds - they were everywhere, swooping and chirping. When I told Jameel that the beauty of this place took my breath away, he teased me, "You always use those same words, Sherry." Maybe so, but this time I really meant it.

Today, when I take a walk down memory lane recalling the various islands we visited during our circumnavigation, I always take an extra moment to remember Rotuma. Was it by chance that we decided to stop there just for a moment to have a rest and a swim? Or was our discovery of this island paradise a reward for all the miles we'd sailed or perhaps an incentive to continue on and find other places like it?

I remember Sherry drinking in the scenery like a thirsty camel who's gone too long without water. Then we noticed a group of natives gathered on the shore smiling broadly and waving at us.

Sherry pointed to the tuna.

"Let's take it to them. It will feed the whole village. We'll just end up throwing most of it away."

Agreed. We jumped into the dinghy and motored to shore. The head man, whose name was Victor, seemed overwhelmed by our gift. He offered to take us to the police station in the village to register our arrival and then drive us around the tiny island. The village boasted a hospital, a primary school to grade six, government offices and a bank.

Victor told us that Rotuma, which is the smallest and the most northerly of the Fiji Islands, did not have the facilities to attract tourists – no marina, not even a protected harbour and hardly any shops. He spoke of his island with pride referring to its occupants as 'Rotumans'.

"We're so far away we don't feel part of Fiji," he explained.

Without the influx of tourist dollars, the people lived a simple, almost primitive life, subsisting on a diet of fish and fruit. We would be allowed, Victor informed us, to pick all the fruit we wanted but first we had to ask permission. And we must be specific as to which fruits we wanted to pick. If we changed our minds or wanted to add to the list, we must ask permission again. Not that our requests would ever be refused, Victor assured us. I thought that maybe the 'civilised' people of the world could learn a thing or two about courtesy from these folks.

After being reassured that the small bay was safe for anchoring, we decided to stay for a couple of days and bask in the tranquillity of this place. So often our harbour time could be described as 'frantic time' as we chased here and there buying supplies or searching for repair facilities. Here we could relax and recharge our batteries. Sherry commented that this was a first for us, a holiday from reality.

The next morning, while we were eating breakfast, a contingent of visitors arrived: the police chief and his sergeant, the agricultural officer, postmaster and security officer. No, there was no problem. They just wanted to see the boat and talk to us. What did we think of their island?

"Beautiful," Sherry replied. "More beautiful than I can say."

Next to arrive was Victor, with some freshly baked bread and an invitation to take us fruit picking, to be followed by lunch at his home. I could see that Sherry's eyes were glassy with tears.

We spent the next few hours bouncing along a rutted road with Victor and some companions, thinking that we had never seen such a profusion of fruit trees. Lunch at Victor's home gave us the rare opportunity to see a typical native Fijian home. I had expected a dwelling with a thatched roof and bamboo stakes or coconut mats for walls. But Victor's home was made of cement blocks with a galvanised tin roof. There was only one opening, the entryway. Once inside I noticed that there were no windows and that all the rooms opened directly off the main room. Again no doors.

"You like my house?" Victor asked.

I nodded, then leaned over and whispered in his ear.

"There are no doors. How do you find some privacy when you want to make love?"

Victor rocked on his heals and laughed loudly.

"For that we go outside to the bushes."

Victor chattered on about his family and his island. One cultural taboo I found particularly interesting; when a man marries a woman he must never again see her mother.

"But if you don't have a mother-in-law, how can you tell mother-in-law jokes?" I asked Victor.

He didn't answer, only looked at me as if he couldn't decide whether to be perplexed or amused. But then his booming laugh told me that 'amused' had won the draw.

We met his father, who delighted in telling us tales of the old days. The most precious gift in the Fijian culture is the white mat made out of palm fronds, a gift usually reserved for a tribal chief or newlyweds. So different from our culture where the most precious gift is probably a Rolex watch or a diamond ring.

Driving back to the boat after lunch, we decided to stop and pick papayas. Under the papaya trees I noticed wooden stakes angled into the ground around the trunks. Victor explained that they were put there to dissuade animals from stealing the fruit. We picked a sackful and then I spied a particularly luscious papaya near the top of one of the trees. 'No problem,' I thought. 'I'll just climb up and get it.' A plan I immediately put into execution. Just as I was reaching for the elusive papaya, I heard an ominous splintering sound. As the branch broke, I came flying out of the tree and landed on my head, gouging my leg from ankle to groin on the bamboo stakes. Victor and his companions found my escapade a huge joke and couldn't stop laughing. As we drove back to town they stopped several times to talk with friends, conversations punctuated by loud guffaws and Victor pointing to me in the back seat where I was dabbing at my scratches and bruises which seemed to have multiplied. My underarm and chest had begun to ooze and throb and there was a huge scratch behind my ear and along my neck. I began to feel a bit miffed. Falling out of a tree was perhaps mildly amusing, but hilarious? Well, not to my mind since my head had taken quite a thump and I was a mass of abrasions. My irritation must have shown because Victor tried to keep a straight face.

"Everyone knows that you must never try to climb a papaya tree," he explained. "Even little children know this thing. The branches are hollow and brittle and," he paused to hide his smile behind his hand, "people who do it, fall, yes, they always fall." I made obligatory chuckling sounds and assured him that I wasn't really hurt.

I was silent as we bumped along the road back to town. Although the day was warm, I shivered as though someone had just 'walked over my grave', a phrase I'd picked up during my years in America.

My mind hurtled back in time to another day and another papaya tree. Sherry and I had been picking papayas up in the mountains on Hiva Oa. Suddenly I spied a tree on the cliff side of the road with a particularly delectable-looking papaya hanging in the high branches. As I began to step over the low fence which separated the tarmac from the sheer cliff face, Sherry grabbed my arm.

"Please, Jameel, we don't need any more papayas. That tree is not safe. Look how it is leaning way out over nothing. If you fall..." Her voice trailed off.

"Please, Jameel," Sherry pleaded again.

But as usual, I turned a deaf ear. Just as I placed my foot on the trunk and was reaching for an overhanging branch to hoist myself up, I glanced again at the papaya. Suddenly it didn't look so delicious. It appeared that a bird had beaten me to it and pecked a hole in the skin. Not to worry. I didn't really need that papaya especially since we had a bag full of perfect ones. I stepped back over the fence, picked up the sack of fruit and headed down the road to town.

Now, many weeks later on the island of Rotuma, I realised that I probably owed my life to a hungry bird.

Sherry's Journal, Rotuma

I have never met such kind, generous, honest people anywhere. They have nothing yet they are willing to share everything with us. Never have I seen so many fruits growing – pineapple, guava, mandarin, banana. Before we left, Victor and his friends came to the boat with baskets heaped with fruit, so much that I had to find new places to store it.

Jameel and I loved our time on Rotuma. This was the 'time out' we needed to be just Sherry and Jameel for a couple of days, not Arab circumnavigators. And to be alone. I know we are alone while we are sailing but that is not a relaxing time. When we are in port we relax but we are never alone. Rotuma gave us the best of both worlds. We will never forget our time there.

Chapter Fourteen

The first evening out of Rotuma the wind picked up and we found ourselves surfing along the crests of the waves at 6 knots. I hoped that these favourable winds would continue so we could cross these last few miles of the Pacific quickly.

Baraka A Log – July 24

Heard via the marine radio that there is a tropical storm with 120 knot winds to the north of us. The nice black bird which landed on our boat a few thousand miles ago is back with us! Now he is sleeping inside the boat. I am happy to give birds a spot to rest, especially after realising it was a bird that probably saved me from a horrible fall or worse! Sherry tells me that, of course, this is not the same bird. Maybe his cousin?

July 26

Lovely sailing tonight. The bird has gone after staying with us for 2 days. We tried to feed him but he refused all food and only took the water Sherry offered. Last night he flew around the cabin and kept us awake. Today I took him outside on my shoulder. He surveyed the situation for a few moments, then just flew away.

I called my cousin in Jeddah on the SSB radio to give him an address in Australia where he could contact us. I also asked him to withdraw money from my bank account and send a bank draft ASAP. I knew that we would be dropping more than a few dollars in Cairns, first to provision the boat and second to spruce up *Baraka A* before she tackled her third ocean. Top on the list was a scraping and repainting of the bottom. The weeks in the harbour in American Samoa had caused the gunge on the hull to thrive and grow like a scourge of weeds. I also wanted to have the dodger stanchion repaired, the same one I'd broken on the way to Casablanca when I flew from the chart table to the floor of the cockpit like some ungainly bird. Although the diesel engine had been a star performer for thousands of miles, the time for an overhaul was long overdue.

We also decided to have a canopy installed to give us some respite from the sun. And then there was a long list of 'little things', like more anchor chain, a couple more butane bottles, nautical charts and a dozen other items that we had found we couldn't do without. Whoever said that a boat was a hole in the water into which you poured money, certainly spoke the truth.

Sherry's Journal, July 27

During the early hours of the afternoon something happened which, at the outset, seemed a little scary until we got used to it. Out of nowhere appeared thousands of dolphins and pilot whales. They swam around the boat, alongside the boat and even under the boat, bumping the hull. We figured they must be migrating somewhere. After a while we began to see that there were two kinds of dolphins, one with a pointed nose and a whitish tip. The other type was distinguishable by its round mouth. They stayed with us for 5 hours, cavorting around the boat. Jameel shot miles of video tape.

July 28

We tried to enter the harbour at Vinikolo Island but we could not find the entrance. We remembered the island of Aitutaki where we'd also run into difficulty finding the way in and remembered too the nasty weather we had endured while we were at anchor there. Perhaps that was why Jameel decided to forget this island and push on westward to Cairns, Australia which is 1300 miles away. To my surprise, I accepted this change of plan calmly, as if 1300 miles were just a trip around the block. This is a distance that must be covered and whether we do it now or in a few days hardly makes any difference. Right now we are experiencing very steady following winds, strong at times, but not too strong. With a 2 knot boost from the current, we are making excellent time. Still, I am not excited about two more weeks at sea!

Sighting a ship was always a major event. After days all alone on this vast ocean any diversion was welcome. So when Sherry spied what looked like a container cargo ship on the horizon, I immediately got on the VHF radio and called them. No response. This didn't surprise me. All the skippers I'd met in the various ports along the way told the same story – big ships often don't respond to small sailing vessels. Of course, the radio operator could be asleep at his post. But the more likely reason was that the freighter remained silent in fear of being asked for a favour which might cause some delay. And, in the shipping business, delays cost money. Even though this argument had some merit, it worried me that the big boys were not following the rules of etiquette at sea. You should always answer your radio. In this case there was no harm done – we only wanted to say hello. But what if we had really needed help? I prayed that day would never come.

Sherry's Journal, en route to Cairns

The days flow together. Every day I write in my journal about the wind and weather conditions, about the fish we almost caught or the birds we saw or the freighter that didn't bother to say hello. But, mostly, all the days we spend at sea are alike and all are boring. The sea and sky are our only companions. I miss so many things that I cannot begin to mention them. To kill the time I have been reading a lot, sometimes a book a day. After so many days at sea, this boat is like a prison. Even Jameel, who enjoys the challenge of sailing more than I ever could imagine, said that he is anxious for this leg to be over. Australia, are you still 800 miles away? I pray these steady trade winds keep pushing us closer and closer. Every few days we experience that overwhelming fishy odour. We continue to wonder what it can be.

By my calculations, the moon should be full when we hit the Grafton Passage. I heard from other sailors that negotiating this 47 mile passage through the Great Barrier Reef could be tricky. Unfortunately, I couldn't predict the weather. A full moon would be of little help if it was hiding under a blanket of clouds.

We were hungry for some fresh fish to spice up our diet. But I hadn't had as much as a nibble unless you counted the time a huge fish had bitten the line in two and disappeared. I created a new lure which Sherry said looked like a scarecrow and predicted that only a stupid fish would take the bait. Well, a few days later, I landed one of these stupid fish, a huge dorado. Sherry cooked it for dinner and we stuffed ourselves to bursting.

The miles continued to disappear as we flew across the waves at 6-7 knots, making me wonder what our speed would have been with a clean bottom. The wind was steady and moderate, escalating to strong at times. This was our first storm-free leg which unfortunately did not mean rain free. We endured many dismal, drizzly, grey days which did little to lift Sherry's flagging spirits. I found that trying to cheer her up only made her more unhappy. I had come to accept the fact that Sherry did not like these long hauls and nothing I could say or do would change it.

As we got closer to Australia we began to pick up radio stations, which gave both of us a boost. Listening to radio talk shows made us feel that we were once again part of the universe. One night we sat in the cockpit tapping our feet in time to the lively music reverberating off the bulkheads while *Baraka A* ploughed on through the waves. Our first concert at sea in many months.

***Baraka A* Log - August 6**

Spotted another sailboat which we contacted on the VHF. Unlike the freighter, they answered immediately. They were Australians from Townsville bound for the Louisiade Archepelago in Papua New Guinea which is dead east of Cape York at the northernmost tip of Queensland.

According to my charts, their bearing had them headed for a reef which did not show up on their charts at all. They thanked us and adjusted their course. Again, one skipper helping another. I'm proud to be part of it.

Two days later, around 9 a.m. we sighted Bougainville Reef Lighthouse which meant that the Grafton Passage was only a few miles away. The weather turned nasty as we entered the passage – strong winds, pitching seas and a succession of rain squalls which soaked us to the marrow and reduced our visibility to near zero. Not good, since there were coral reefs on either side of us. Sherry positioned herself on the bow as a lookout and we continued cautiously through the passage. In English you say, 'with your heart in your mouth'. In Arabic you say, 'with a hand on your heart'. But, whatever the language, the meaning is the same.

As we approached land, the weather eased and the dolphin welcoming committee appeared, squealing and leaping around the boat. With each passing mile, Sherry's excitement grew. As usual she went on a cleaning frenzy so that we would arrive in port tidy and composed. I always appreciated Sherry's interest in keeping *Baraka A* shipshape.

I called the Cairns harbour-master and told him that we would arrive before nightfall. Sherry and I stood in the cockpit and gave each other a congratulatory hug. We had done it – crossed the Pacific Ocean, a huge and awesome expanse of water, in a 31 foot sailboat.

***Baraka A* Log – August 8**

While sailing up Grafton Passage, discovered that one of the lower front starboard shrouds had snapped. Another item to be replaced. Glad this happened here and not in mid-ocean. Was I capable of replacing a shroud on a pitching rolling deck? Yes. Did I want to? Definitely not. Arrived at Cairns harbour at 19.00 and immediately checked in with customs. As always, I declared the pistol. This time they took it and asked me to fill out a form. They said I could collect the pistol before leaving Australia. I will believe that when it happens!

I asked the customs officer where I could change some of my American dollars into Australian ones.

"Sorry, mate. Nothing's open till Monday, I'm afraid." He reached into his pocket and pulled out a wad of bills. "Maybe I can help you out," he said, peeling off some twenty dollar notes and pressing them into my hand.

"But you don't even know me," I said.

He waved aside my protests.

"No worries. You look like an honest bloke and I'm a pretty good judge of character. Have to be in my job."

"First thing Monday I'll go to the bank and pay you back."

"I know you will," the customs official replied and with a jaunty wave he turned and sauntered down the dock.

I turned to Sherry.

"I guess everything I've heard about Aussie generosity is true."

Sherry's Journal, Cairns, Queensland, Australia, August 8

We made it! I keep pinching myself to make sure it's not a dream. After clearing customs and pitching all our food, (even the canned stuff and the cartons of long-life milk) in accordance with the strict Australian import laws, I took my first hot shower in 7 months. I didn't care that the shower was in the gas station in a stall in the parking lot, or that it cost $5. Jameel said it felt weird to be pelted with hot fresh water. Weird for him, maybe, but wonderful for me. Standing under the stinging spray, I thought how simple things like a shower become a luxury when you have to go without.

Tonight we went out to dinner and later had coffee aboard the boat which is docked next to us. The city of Cairns seems to be very modern with lovely shops and supermarkets. And friendly people, so generous, just like the ones we met on the South Sea islands. Maybe Cairns is a unique blend of civilisation and wilderness, the best of both worlds in one tranquil place.

Early Monday morning we were awakened by a knocking on the hatch boards. To our surprise it was our friend, John from *Mr John*

IV, whom we'd last seen in American Samoa. Instead of his usual frayed cut-offs, T-shirt and sneakers, he was dressed in a shirt, tie and sports jacket like a business executive on the way to the office.

"Sorry to barge in on you like this," he said. "I just flew in from New Zealand and I thought I'd check the harbour to see if any of my friends were in town."

"No apologies necessary," said Sherry. "Come in. I'll make some coffee and then you can tell us all your news. Sorry it's only coffee but we just arrived yesterday and I haven't been to the supermarket yet."

While Sherry made coffee, John brought us up to date. While at anchor in American Samoa, he'd been offered a job as First Officer aboard a cruising yacht, *Sea Cloud*. He set sail immediately for New Zealand and, after arranging to moor his boat there, had jumped aboard a plane for Cairns. He would begin his new job on Tuesday morning.

"You must stay with us," said Sherry as she poured the coffee.

There followed a few rounds of good-natured bantering between Sherry and John.

"I don't want to put you out," from John followed by a "Don't be silly," from Sherry which ended with John shrugging his shoulders and saying, "Okay."

We spent the day together walking the streets of Cairns, shopping, gossiping and just enjoying each other's company. That night we celebrated his new job with a dinner out.

The next morning, John, decked out in his whites, waved a final goodbye from the bridge of *Sea Cloud*. We wondered if we would ever see him again.

I spent the next few days arranging for the boat to be hauled and waiting for the bank draft from Jeddah to arrive. Fortunately the repair work could begin without a deposit up front, another bit of Aussie generosity that I appreciated more than anyone knew.

Sherry was very impressed with the supermarkets and declared them better than anything she remembered in the States. She made extensive lists of what we needed so that when our money arrived she could head straight for the store. We changed our cash on hand to Aussie currency, paid back Andrew, the customs official, and still had enough to survive.

I called Camper Nicholson and told them that *Baraka A* and her crew of two had arrived safely in Australia.

"Such a strong sturdy boat," I said. "She could take whatever weather came our way and keep going."

Sherry's Journal, Cairns

It's so nice to be on land again after 18 days at sea. Just being around people feels good. We've decided to sleep on board the boat while the repair work is being done, mostly to save money. Jameel has determined that we must be frugal and make our money (when it arrives) last a long time. There are showers and laundry facilities at the repair yard so staying aboard will be no problem.

Finally on Monday, August 17, the bank draft arrived. Sherry almost sprinted to the supermarket and filled her shopping cart to overflowing. We would make many similar trips over the next couple of weeks. Provisioning the boat for three months, hopefully until we reached Jeddah, was a huge task. We had the engine serviced and the broken shroud replaced and bought some spare engine parts. I checked the batteries and repaired our whisker pole (again) which always seemed to take a thrashing on the downwind legs. Our 'must do' list was lengthy but every day we managed to chip away at it.

We took our films to be developed and were ecstatic at how well the pictures came out. I sent a package off to my family in Jeddah, hoping it would help them understand what 'this crazy circumnavigation' was all about.

Sherry's Journal, Cairns

Cairns is the kind of place anyone would like to live. It is clean and the sea and sand beaches are spectacular against a backdrop of mountains and forests. But what impresses me most is the people. Aussies are so honest, so straightforward, so 'dinkie die' which is an Australian expression with no counterpart in any language I know. I think it means nice. This would be the perfect place to stay forever if only it weren't so far from home and my family.

I discovered a book shop and broke the budget on reading material. But, as I told Jameel, reading is my only pleasure while we're at sea.

Baraka A was hauled out of the water on August 18. The workmen at the Cruising Yacht Squadron, which I thought was a curious name for a boatyard, were impressed with our collection of barnacles, embedded shells and slime. We began the attack with a power hose, finishing four days later with a power sander. After applying two coats of bottom paint we concluded that it was time to let the professionals take over the rest of the work.

Our days fell into a routine. After breakfast we cleared out and left *Baraka A* to the workmen, took a taxi into Cairns where we spent the day attending to errands. At night we would return to the boat after the workmen had left and Sherry would groan at the mess.

Sherry's Journal, Cruising Yacht Squadron Boatyard, Cairns

In the beginning I told Jameel that living on the boat while it was out of the water was almost like an adventure. The only inconvenience was not being able to use the toilet. Almost immediately the adventure turned into a nightmare. Every night when we returned to the boat there was black dust everywhere, dust which I had to clean up before we could go to bed. One high spot was the new friends we made, Lee and Leslie, whose boat was also up on blocks being repaired.

While the work on the boat continued, we went sightseeing with some other friends we'd made in Cairns, John and Cheryl Cornelius. John held the position of Port Captain for an ocean cruising yacht club, whose headquarters are in England. One day our destination was the village of Kurando in the rainforests. I had always imagined Australia being bone dry like Saudi Arabia. Parts of the interior would fit that description but Cairns is far enough north to be considered tropical.

I wondered if I could capture the enchantment of the rain forest on video: tiny lakes nestled among the trees which were home to exotic birds I'd previously only seen in aviaries, rivers gurgling over pebbly bottoms, parrots screeching in the still air. It came to us with the force of a boxer's punch – this world is a beautiful place and we must all work together to make sure it stays that way.

We discovered that the Australians worked very productively during the week but, come the weekend, everything shut down: banks, shops, even some restaurants, and of course, the boatyard. Weekend hours were designated for pleasure whether it was swimming, diving, strolling sand beaches, picnicking with the family, playing football or just hanging around 'throwing shrimps on the barbie'. I thought back to life in Jeddah. On Friday, which is equivalent to Sunday in many parts of the world, all the shops are closed in the morning and remain closed until after the Asr prayer in the late afternoon. But, after that, Jeddah once again becomes a thriving bustling metropolis with people rushing to the souks.

Though I applauded the Australian way of life, which guaranteed everyone 'time off for play', at the same time I had to admit to a bit of resentment that no one appeared willing to work overtime to get my boat ready. Yes, I was getting antsy again. We had many miles to sail before we could count the circumnavigation finished and say proudly, "Yes, we did it. We sailed around the world."

Sherry's Journal, Cruising Yacht Squadron, Cairns

I have been spending a lot of time shopping for souvenirs and writing postcards to family, friends and the newspapers which have asked us to keep in touch. Words cannot describe this place, yes again – the most beautiful we have seen so far. A turquoise sea, a sky so blue it must be painted, clear air, sunshine and friendly, outgoing people. But the time to leave creeps closer every day. I am really worried about the Indian Ocean. Every passage will be long – 18 days or more. And the weather. Everyone says the Indian Ocean can be really fierce. Jameel calls it challenging. Staying on land makes you lose your sea legs. I will have to get used to everything again: the motion, the solitude, the noise that the wind and sea make.

On Friday August 28, *Baraka A* slipped back into the water with a heartfelt, 'Thank God' from her skipper and first mate that the work was finally finished. Sherry's knees still ached from the two days she had spent fastening the safety net to the lifelines. We decided to send the sunshade back for a redo, insisting on stronger fabric and smaller, more discreet letters for our boat name.

Our last three days in port were, as usual, hectic. We made our final trip to the 'Woolies' grocery store and emerged with three trolleys piled to the brim, which we pushed right to the marina. I must confess that I left Sherry to deal with the mess, to sort and label all the canned goods and stow the fresh produce, while I went off with John Cornelius to purchase an Australian bush hat. On the way back to the boat we passed a marine supply store so naturally I had to stop and take a look. Sherry never could understand what had compelled me to buy that kayak.

"I'll use it," I explained as I stood on the dock, my new toy at my feet.

Sherry sighed. "Where?"

"I don't know. Maybe I'll kayak down the Nile one day. But for now I can use it to paddle around the anchorage."

"But it's so big, Jameel. Where are we going to store it?"

"On the bow some place. I'll lash it down."

"But there's no room, Jameel, not with all the jerry cans."

"I'll make room," I replied heaving the kayak over the lifelines.

Sherry sighed again then threw up her hands in defeat. After stowing the kayak, I scrambled back to the cockpit.

"How do you like my hat?" I asked, hoping to shift the focus away from the kayak. "I had a choice of grey rabbit fur or brown kangaroo hide for the trim."

"I'm glad you chose the rabbit fur. I can't think of killing a kangaroo to make a hat."

"Both John and the shopkeeper pronounced it 'beaut'!" I replied as I tried it on.

"You could pass for Crocodile Dundee," said Sherry, then paused, her chin cupped in her hand as she looked me up and down. "Well, maybe, if you dyed your hair blond. But Crocodile Dundee in a kayak – now that would really be something to see."

The last day in port I filled our diesel tanks and jerry cans, estimating that we had about 600 miles worth of reserve fuel. That night we invited Cheryl and John Cornelius and Andrew, our friendly customs agent, for a goodbye dinner. Though Sherry claimed the chicken tasted like rubber, no one noticed the food. This last night together we were focused on having a good time and leaving each other with pleasant memories. As always, we exchanged addresses and promised to keep in touch.

For Sherry, saying goodbye to new-found friends was a painful experience only outranked by the terror she felt on leaving the safety of the anchorage. I promised her that our first days would be short hops from one anchorage to another as we wended our way up the coast inside the Great Barrier Reef on our way to the Arafura Sea.

"No big deal," I promised. "We'll take it slow and easy."

Sherry managed a slow smile.

"That's what you always say, Jameel."

Chapter Fifteen

A hazy sun poked through the clouds as we motored out of Cairns Harbour on September 1. Destination – Low Isles, a mere 35 miles away. The choppy sea looked like a marine freeway. Even the colour complemented the analogy – dull grey, like cement, as did the traffic, with every sort of vessel imaginable – sailboats, fishing boats, tugboats and pleasure yachts – in a gridlock fighting for space and creating wakes which hit us from all sides.

While I concentrated on taking the worst of the wash head on, Sherry kept her eyes focused on the disappearing shoreline.

"I hate to leave Australia," she confessed. "It's such a beautiful country with beautiful friendly people. Maybe one day we will come back here, Inshallah."

"We aren't really leaving Australia until we enter Torres Strait. You'll love this part of the trip," I promised. "Every day we will sail for a few miles to the next anchorage, drop the hook and relax. It's a boater's paradise."

Sherry ducked into the cabin and reappeared with her world atlas.

"Show me, where we're going, Jameel. Maps, I can understand. You, sometimes no."

She flipped through the book until she found the map of Australia. I leaned over her shoulder, tracing our route with my finger. "Here we are, leaving Cairns and there is Cape York, right at the northern tip of Queensland. We will follow the coast here with the Barrier Reef to starboard and the York Peninsula to port. We can stop at any one of these islands until we turn to westward into the Torres Strait. That takes us to the Arafura Sea and then the Timor Sea where we will find Christmas Island."

"But exactly where is Christmas Island? That's what I want to know," said Sherry, flipping to the glossary at the back of the atlas. "Page 110, P8," she muttered as she thumbed through the pages.

"There," she announced, pointing to a small black speck in the middle of a vast blue area. She raised her eyes from the atlas and gazed at me over steepled fingers.

"Guess what, Jameel. When we get to Christmas Island we'll be back in Australia - at least that what the map shows. I wonder if they'll be as nice as the folks we met in Cairns."

"Everyone in this part of the world is nice so why should the folks on Christmas Island be any different? It's a long hard sail to get there. That's why we should look at these next few days as a holiday. There'll be lots of people to meet and things to do."

"And *not* do, like night watches," Sherry replied. "For me, that's a real plus."

For me night watches were neither a plus nor a minus. Sometimes I enjoyed the tranquillity that accompanied the night. There really was nothing to do but keep *Baraka A* on course and watch out for freighters. Freed from the necessity or compulsion to keep myself occupied with boat chores like deck scrubbing, I would stretch out in the cockpit and revel in the silence broken only by the slapping of the waves on the hull or the crack of the sail as it captured the wind.

If there was a plus to anchoring for the night, it was Sherry's enthusiasm to cook us a really good dinner which she often found impossible while we were underway. We had a good supply of fresh fruits and vegetables and fresh meat which would see us through the first few days.

***Baraka A* Log**

Back at sea! Sailing with main and Genoa, wing to wing. Average speed is close to 6.5 knots - thanks to a clean bottom.

Sherry's Journal, Island hopping along the great Barrier Reef

September 2, Low Isles to Cape Bedford, 70 miles

We woke up early and left our first overnight anchorage. We met a lot of fishing boats coming back to the harbour just as we were sailing out and thought that their timetable was exactly the opposite of ours. A beautiful day with good winds and calm seas. We reached Cape Bedford after a 12 hour sail just as dusk was falling. Jameel could barely see to set the anchor.

September 3, Cape Bedford to Ninion Bay, 72 miles

A repeat of yesterday. Woke very early, had breakfast and raised the anchor. Two other sailboats left at the same time but they were heading back to Cairns. I felt envious. Again the wind was moderate and the sea calm. If sailing could always be like this…

All day we did not see another sailboat even when we passed Lizard Island which is a popular resort. Because we were sailing in an area with lots of reefs, we had to keep a constant look out which meant many hours in the sun. We are both very tanned. Arrived at Ninion Bay at 7 p.m. and had another nerve wracking time setting the anchor in the dark. A very rough rolly night but the anchor held.

September 4, Ninion Bay to Flinders Islands, 35 miles

Woke up to 18 knot winds this a.m. Jameel had a hard time retrieving the anchor which was very snugly embedded in the sand bottom. Hope tonight's anchorage is peaceful. Arrived at Stanley Island, one of the Flinders group, and anchored in Stokes Bay before 1 p.m. What a peaceful beautiful place with white sand beaches and dolphins swimming around Baraka A *and the 7 other boats at anchor in the lagoon. Almost immediately we were visited by a fellow named Doug who invited us to a pot luck barbecue on shore that evening. This gathering of strangers, who quickly became friends, will always stand out as a high point of our voyage. After stuffing ourselves to bursting point, we sat around the campfire, joked, laughed and sang songs. Now we know all the verses of 'Waltzing Matilda'! These Australians were so open and made us feel so welcome that we decided to stay another day and enjoy their company.*

The next morning we slept late. While we were enjoying a leisurely breakfast, Doug and his wife Sheena and another couple, Murray and Christina, rowed over and invited us to check out some of the nearby islands on Doug's trimaran *Crossbow*. Sherry immediately accepted while I decided to stay behind and tend to boat chores. As Sherry slipped on her life jacket and waved goodbye, I marvelled at how much my wife and first mate had changed during the last ten months. Here she was boarding a sailboat, joyfully, eagerly, for a few hours of recreation and exploration! What had happened to the anxious fearful Sherry whose idea of fun had never included going for a sail just for the heck of it. Still around, I concluded, but only during storms and dicey moments. I realised again that she would never embrace the challenge of pitting herself against the elements and coming out on top. But she got top marks for enduring the nasty bits and enjoying the nice ones, as she was doing today. As I watched her through the binoculars sheeting in the jib then throwing back her head and laughing while her long brown hair swirled around her face, a curious sense of contentment crept over me.

Later that afternoon we walked the beaches, staying clear of the sting rays swimming in the shallow water. We found some more beautiful shells to add to our collection. Our last night at Stokes Bay Doug and Sheena invited us for dinner aboard *Crossbow* and then gave us a farewell gift, a beautiful wooden mask carved by Australian aborigines.

The following morning we rose before the sun, planning to slip quietly out of the anchorage while the other sailors were still sleeping. Not to be! As we raised the anchor a cacophony of sounds – air horns, sirens, whistles, bells, and human voices rose in a chorus to wish us goodbye and safe journey. We answered with a blast from our own air horn as we waved goodbye.

"Those were some of the nicest and friendliest people we've met," I told Sherry as I sheeted in the main.

"Think about it, Jameel," she said. "Have you ever met an Aussie you didn't like?"

The answer to that was clearly no!

Sherry's Journal, Sept. 6, Stokes Bay to Hannah Island, 40 miles

We reached Hannah Island at 2 p.m. and were disappointed to find no other boats there. Although the island was a beautiful spot, with lots of vegetation and a picturesque lighthouse perched at the western end, we both felt lonely for the friends we'd left behind at Stokes Bay. Decided to call them on the radio and when we got no response our spirits dipped even lower.

***Baraka A* Log – September 7**

Today we sailed from Hannah Island to Night Island – 42 miles. Sky was grey and it rained. We passed several huge reefs and saw two freighters. We were safely anchored by 2.30 and again we were alone, just us and the birds.

September 8, Night Island to Portland Road, 40 miles

Again, an early start. Another gloomy day with rain and squalls but we made good time, arriving at our destination by mid-afternoon. On entering the harbour we spied several fishing boats and another sailboat, Coxinga. *But of even greater interest was a supply barge,* Shell 5, *where we were able to purchase diesel fuel and some bread and eggs. I also spent a lot of time petting the owners' Siamese cat which made me miss my cats even more. An invitation out to dinner aboard* Coxinga *was more than welcome after two lonely nights. I insisted on providing the main course – shrimps, which I bought from one of the fishing boats. Later we adjourned to* Baraka A *for coffee and learned that* Coxinga *was bound for the Philippines. A nice relaxed evening.*

September 9, Portland Road to Shelburne Bay, 56 miles

It rained all night and by morning the weather had not improved much. Sooty black clouds hung on the horizon as we left the anchorage. Soon the drizzle became heavy, heavy rain with accompanying squalls which did not let up all day. Very nerve-wracking to battle 28 knot winds and keep away from the reefs. Arrived at Shelburne at 5 p.m. very tired and wet and not a bit upset that we were the only ones there. Had an early dinner, thought about Essam whose birthday was today and went to bed early. We decided to stay put if the weather hadn't improved by morning. Luckily the anchorage was well protected so we had a quiet night.

September 11, Shelburne Bay to Escape River, 62 miles

Stayed put yesterday because of the weather. Today was more of the same but we decided to move on anyway. Got a really early start because we wanted to arrive in daylight. The blustery winds pushed us along at a good speed. Jameel managed to catch a yellowfin tuna and then made an awful mess in the cockpit cleaning it. How do you clean a fish without making a mess, that is what Jameel wants to know. The head, tail and other inedible pieces go overboard and the guts and blood get washed down the scuppers. The captain and first mate often need a bath afterwards, but all the work is worth it.

***Baraka A* Log - September 11**

Arrived at Escape River at 4 p.m. after which the wind really began to blow. The weather was too miserable to explore the anchorage which was dotted with pearl barges.

September 12 began badly. As we were leaving the harbour, Sherry suddenly screamed that the depth sounder was recording only 3 feet of water.

"Impossible," I screamed back. "We're in the middle of the channel."

And then I remembered another time near Rangiroa in the South Pacific when I'd almost ignored Sherry's warning and we'd nearly ended up on the rocks. I didn't know it then but the radar had gone haywire. I had insisted that I was headed out into open water but

Sherry knew something was very wrong because she could hear the waves clashing on a nearby shore.

I prayed that our present problems could be chalked up to gear failure. Otherwise we were in big trouble. There was no place to turn, no way to escape to deeper water from the narrow channel. The wind was blowing 'like stink', churning up the water into a heavy chop. As *Baraka A* plunged through one wave after another, I could do little but pray that there really was more than 3 feet of water beneath our keel.

"Keep your eyes on the depth sounder and tell me the reading," I told Sherry.

"Okay," she shouted. "Still 3 feet."

A few moments later she gave me the same bad news. "3 feet."

Then suddenly I saw her smile as she raised her arms above her head in a victory salute.

"36 feet, Jameel."

I allowed myself to relax my grip on the tiller as Sherry relayed the water depth to me,

"36 feet, 42 feet, 54 feet." And then, another shriek.

"It's reading 4 feet, Jameel."

There was nothing to do but continue on through the channel hoping that my charts were correct and the depth sounder was having an off day. Eventually we reached open water, our nerves worn to a frazzle.

"Why did the depth sounder do that?" Sherry asked me. "Look, now it's working just fine."

Something was niggling at the corners of my mind, some sailor talk I remembered from one of our anchorages. Sometimes the combination of a sandy bottom and a churning sea will cause the depth sounder to read the resulting bubbles as if those were the bottom. 'That must be it,' I concluded and explained it all to Sherry. I also apologised for screaming.

Sherry smiled.

"That's okay, Jameel. It's all part of the captain's job."

September 12, Escape River to Adaulphus Light, 20 miles

A short ferocious sail today with the wind velocity again at 28 knots and a depth sounder that scared us out of our wits. We arrived at our destination by early afternoon, and only waved at the one other sailboat in the anchorage. Too tired, wet and scared to do anything but hole up inside the boat and relax. That proved a bit difficult. The wind continued to shriek through the rigging, making for an almost sleepless night. I wondered if this was the 'easy sailing' Jameel had been talking about!

September 13, Adaulphus Light to Horn Island, 30 miles

After a miserable night of rolling and rounding up, we decided to leave Aldaulphus early and hope for better weather at Horn Island. The weather forecast did not sound good - heavy winds, rain - but luck was with us and we ended up having a beautiful sail under partly cloudy skies. Upon arrival we found lots of sailboats anchored here. Our friends at Stokes Bay had told us to keep an eye out for a boat named Socorro *owned by Dorothy and John, a Canadian couple who planned to sail via the Red Sea to the Mediterranean. Jameel motored around the anchorage on the off chance they might be here and to our delight we found them.*

Horn Island was our last stop before tackling the first long leg to Christmas Island, a distance of 2160 miles, almost similar to the Atlantic crossing which must have happened a few lifetimes ago. I remembered how apprehensive I'd been facing my first ocean though I had put on a good act for Sherry whose apprehension had grown into stony fear. Now here we were, our biggest concern provisions, not the long voyage ahead.

We soon became good friends with Dorothy and John aboard *Socorro* and decided to go with them by ferry to Thursday Island which was reputed to have better shopping facilities than Horn. After viewing the harbour from the deck of the ferry, I concluded that we had made the right decision to stay at Horn Island. This anchorage offered little protection as the blustery wind agitated the water into rolling turbulent swells, compounded, one local told me, by a strong current.

A relentless wind was blowing sand and dirt in all directions. While Sherry went to the grocery store with John and Dorothy, I found the customs shed and presented a wrinkled scrap of paper which was the receipt for my Walthers PKU 9mm pistol. The man behind the counter asked me to sign it, which I did, then he handed me my gun. Amazing! Why do some countries expend so much time and energy and money in the snarl of red tape while others don't bother? By the end of our shopping expedition, we were all worn to a frazzle. At 4 p.m. we boarded the return ferry with all the schoolchildren returning home to Horn Island.

The next morning I discovered that the butane bottles I had bought in Cairns didn't fit properly into the existing lockers. I took our old bottles to shore to get them filled. We hoped to leave the following day with *Socorro* so there was no time to have the lockers rebuilt or other hardware fabricated. Perhaps at another port.

The wind did not let up all day. As Sherry went about her last minute tasks of stowing the food and visiting the laundromat, she kept casting her eyes to the grey skies overhead, no doubt hoping that tomorrow would find us with clear skies and gentle breezes.

Did she realise that I was hoping for the same things? Although I would always enjoy challenging the sea in all her varied moods, a few hazy, lazy days were okay with me too.

Chapter Sixteen

The weather forecast at 7 a.m. on September 16 predicted winds of up to 15 knots which prompted Dorothy and John from *Socorro* and Sherry, first mate aboard *Baraka A*, to give the thumbs up sign. By 7.30 a.m. we had hoisted the anchors and were headed for the passage between Horn and Thursday Islands, the same route we'd covered by ferry on shopping day.

Unfortunately, as soon as we reached the open ocean, the 15 knot winds petered out to 3-4 so we turned on the engine. In the distance we could see the sails on *Socorro* hanging like limp washing on a clothes line and a few moments later we heard their diesel roar to life. Because their LOA was greater than ours, 40 feet to our 31, we knew their hull speed would be greater so, as they disappeared over the horizon, we made arrangements to keep in touch by radio every six hours. This was the first time we had made plans to travel any distance in tandem with another boat. Sherry found the prospect of being in contact with another vessel on a regular basis, very comforting.

***Baraka A* Log – September 16**

A tired bird arrived and settled himself on top of the hatch. I assumed he was hitching a ride. He took off and came back three times as if he could not make up his mind but then came back for good, probably because of the warm reception he received. He allowed me to take him in my hand and hold him. Sherry tried feeding him but he refused. He was probably accustomed to a diet of fish which was something I could not provide. The bird stayed with us all night, preening his feathers and sleeping almost as if we were not even there. The next morning he flew away, probably to

satisfy his appetite. I hope he returns. When we talked with *Socorro* they reported that a bird had visited them too. Same one? I doubt it.

Sherry's Journal, September 16

At sea again! Getting into the routine, learning to live with the constant motion and staying awake at night while on watch will, I realised, take a couple of days. But tonight, our first night at sea, I realised something else. This first day out, I felt so free. The peace, the quiet, and the freedom to roam the oceans are things I am beginning to cherish.

***Baraka A* Log – September 16**

A group of pilot whales, 30 or more, approached *Baraka A*. They looked a lot like dolphins but they were bigger, ranging from 10-30 feet long, and had round heads. They stayed with us for almost an hour, a welcome diversion.

Sherry commented that most of my log notes were about the birds and animals and fish we'd met along the way and that the details of our forward progress had evolved from a narrative into scribbles and numbers. True, I agreed but the 'scribbles' told a story of their own. At a glance I could tell the wind speed, the compass heading and which sails were up.

But Sherry had piqued my curiosity, so while she was on watch this afternoon I sat down with the log book and read it, almost a year's worth of entries. I had to agree that Sherry was right. For example, eleven months before, it had taken me an entire page to describe becoming disabled in the English Channel and my subsequent rescue by the Royal National Lifeboat Institute. And I recorded not only the bare facts but also my feelings and impressions: 'I rate the Lifeboat Institute services as excellent. They were a bunch of great men.' Or this entry as we attempted to sail to Falmouth: 'Making no real forward progress on either tack. The boat is very dry and comfortable for the conditions we have here. We are now considering diverting to Plymouth which is upwind, which is all right, I guess. The moon is chasing through the clouds.' Or this one from Tenerife: 'Los Cristianos is nice and full of tourists, mainly British and Scandinavians. Real blond hair. Food is plentiful but there are no showers. Had to rent a room in a hotel to shower.'

My nautical shorthand had probably come to be for a number of reasons. First, while sailing *Baraka A* would never become old hat, the problems I experienced during the first days at sea had never occurred again. Like the sail getting stuck in the slot or the boom parting from the mast or a line getting tangled around the prop. Second, the storms we'd endured on both the Atlantic and Pacific crossings could now, in terms of log notes, be consigned to the category of 'been there, done that', and a small notation was all that was necessary to keep the record accurate. But the third reason was probably the most relevant. I was aware that Sherry put time aside each day to write in her journal but it wasn't until I read some of her entries that I realised what a complete record she had compiled: weather conditions; wind speed; hull speed; distance travelled; recountings of sun-filled days and the storm-filled ones too; memories of places we'd visited and the people we'd met. Even photos and sketches of our various ports of call, the animal and marine life we'd seen and the stars in the sky. The highs and lows of all our days, whether on land or sea, had been committed to paper in smoothly flowing prose with an honesty and accuracy I could never duplicate. Another bravo for Sherry.

Sherry's Journal, September 17

The wind picked up a bit today so we shut the engine down and put up the sails and managed to make 4-5 knots. What a difference a clean bottom makes. As we near the equator it is getting hotter. We haven't seen Socorro *for a couple of days but they answered our radio call so we know they are not too far ahead of us. Maybe we'll see their mast light tonight. On my watch tonight the wind picked up and we had a beautiful sail. Maybe I'm getting more used to these night shifts. They don't bother me as much as they used to. Except tonight I smelled that horrible fish stench again. We can't figure out what is causing it.*

September 18

Woke up to a red sky this morning and thought we were in for a horrid day. But the wind blew a steady 9-11 knots until the afternoon when it picked up to 17. So far the days are going by nicely. Hope the weather stays this good. We still have two more weeks at sea until we reach Christmas Island.

By September 19 we had covered over 400 miles. Not bad considering the flukey winds that came and went. Sherry passed the time cleaning and cooking and reading, and talking on the radio to John and Dorothy on *Socorro*. The next day the wind dropped to nothing and we put on the engine once more and managed to catch up with *Socorro*.

After sitting in the hot sun all day, a cool saltwater shower in the late afternoon restored our good humour. Then suddenly the wind came back so it was off with the engine and up with the sails. In short order *Baraka A* was slicing through the water at 7 knots. Not bad!

***Baraka A* Log – September 20**

Again no wind today so we are back to motoring. Did some calculations. Was there enough fuel to reach Christmas Island if the present weather conditions persisted? Unfortunately the numbers came up short so we might have to make a short detour to Bali to purchase diesel and while there stock up on some fresh produce.

The continuing light winds prompted me to hoist the spinnaker. *Baraka A* responded like a race horse after the starting pistol. With only a 7 knot wind, we were making 5 knots and leaving *Socorro*, which didn't have a spinnaker, behind. By my calculations we had completed almost half the distance to Christmas Island but the question of fuel still bothered me.

Darkness brought a wind shift which meant a scramble to get the spinnaker down and stowed and the genoa up. Then the wind died and we motored all night.

The next three days brought no change in the weather. Wind one moment, none the next which meant that we were continually raising and lowering sails. Sherry commented that people who think sailing is nothing more than sitting in the cockpit enjoying the sun and watching the dolphins swim by should take a shift or two aboard *Baraka A* and learn the truth: sailing is hard work.

We could barely hear John and Dorothy when we called them on the 22nd. Apparently the weather conditions, hot sun and no wind had taken its toll and they had decided to anchor a night or two behind Ashmore Reef for some R&R. We decided to push ahead. If we had to divert to Bali that would chew up some precious days.

The wind continued to come and go but it never worked itself up into a really good blow which would move us along to our destination. I never thought that I would see Sherry hanging over the radio listening to the weather forecast, expressing in the strongest terms our need for some wind.

"How much would you like to order," I asked.

"Oh 18-20 knots. That would be great."

***Baraka A* Log – September 24**

Early this morning the sea was dead calm. Suddenly we saw two huge fins. It turned out to be two whales travelling in the opposite direction. Then this afternoon some dolphins came to visit and play around the boat.

Sherry's Journal, September 25

Today the wind was a steady 10 knots and the current gave us a 1.5 knot push which boosted our speed to 6 knots. Terrific! When we passed the Ashmore Reef we did not see Socorro *there. To my surprise this has been a lonely leg. I am learning again that sailing in tandem is really not possible or practical at sea, which is what Jameel tried to explain to me back at Horn Island. But I was so excited by the prospect of some company that he didn't press the point. Experience really is the best teacher. The only other sailboat we have seen is* Socorro *and it now appears we've lost her. No radio contact for a few days now.*

Before setting out on this leg, I had heard many horrifying stories about the Indian Ocean with its huge waves and fierce storms. So far the weather has been fine except that we haven't had enough wind. But I've decided that, if I had to choose, I'd pick no wind over rough seas and gales.

Tonight the wind picked up and we had a beautiful sail, just flying across the water with only the moon and stars to show us the way.

I pray to God to help us achieve our dream safely, all the way home with good weather and fair winds. Inshallah.

On September 27 we made the decision to stop in Bali. We probably had enough fuel to reach Christmas Island but why take the chance? We had never visited Bali, which is considered to be one of the most beautiful islands in Indonesia. A bonus for us was that the Indonesian archipelago is Muslim. Both Sherry and I were looking forward to hearing the call to prayer from the minaret, which was something we'd missed at sea.

As we headed towards Bali, Sherry began cleaning the interior of the boat in preparation for the customs officials who might or might not board *Baraka A* for a quick look around. I bet the customs officials must see some grungy, dirty boats during their day's work. We'd seen plenty ourselves. But never *Baraka A*. Not with Sherry in charge.

We arrived at Bali on the morning of September 29. Bucking a 4 knot current, we inched our way into the harbour at Benoa. Once inside the harbour, we anchored in the sweltering 90 degree heat and awaited the arrival of customs. To our surprise, they not only boarded us but took a good look around. Nothing obnoxious but a new experience for us. Sherry was, of course, relieved that the boat's interior was spotless.

I suspected that not having a visa was going to be a hassle after customs explained that we must get permits from the harbour master, immigration and the Navy. They suggested that I come with them in a taxi to complete the paperwork. Two gruff guys took me to a mean-looking dirty building where they shuffled papers back and forth and then got down to business, the baksheesh. No words were exchanged but I knew the drill. Since I had a nice boat with nice equipment, I must have money, at least enough to pass some their way. Then I could have the visas. A different scene than Australia.

When I got back to the boat, Sherry was sticky with heat and anxiety. I quickly changed my clothes, pumped up the dinghy and we left *Baraka A* baking in the sun.

The following morning, Budi and Goani (two Balanese gentlemen, not thugs like the customs officials) delivered the fuel and water as promised then presented us with a bill for $30. In other places we had paid up to $80 just for the fuel. Unbelievable! Then I remembered that Indonesia was an OPEC country just like Saudi Arabia. Fuel prices are unbelievably cheap there too.

Sherry's Journal, Bali, Indonesia

A beautiful place which wasn't immediately evident in the vicinity of the harbour. Jameel reminded me that this is true of most harbours except maybe Rotuma with palm trees growing out of the rocks.

So cheap here. We had a gourmet lunch for under $7 and then proceeded to the market where I bought all kinds of souvenirs for practically nothing.

We were surprised to find only one mosque on our trip to town. In Jeddah you find a mosque on every other corner. Then we learned that Bali is mostly Hindu with only a small percentage of Muslims. The Indonesian archipelago is made up of 13000 islands. How ironic that we managed to find the only non-Muslim island in the whole lot!

That afternoon we boarded a minibus and took a short tour of the island. Really gorgeous with white sand beaches and flowers growing everywhere. Such friendly, happy people, especially the children. Eager faces smiling at us, showering us with hellos. Went to the market again and bought fresh produce, bananas and small sweet pineapples, papayas and mangoes.

It began to rain later in the afternoon so we went back to the boat. We met a Dutch couple who were also sailing home via the Red Sea. Who could tell if we would see them again? The same went for John and Dorothy. Keeping track of people at sea was an impossible task, a fact which Sherry had come to appreciate. Just keeping track of ourselves was a full-time job. As I told Sherry, meeting up with friends from previous anchorages should always be viewed as a bonus, never an expectation. I thought back to our friend John from *Mr John IV*. We never made plans to sail together or rendezvous at any given spot. But when we arrived at an anchorage, the first thing we did was grab the binoculars and scan the boats looking for John. If he didn't see him we were disappointed. If he was already at anchor or subsequently appeared, we immediately and happily took up the threads of our friendship once more until it was time to say goodbye again.

The beginning of a new month, October, and the beginning of a new leg of our voyage, Benoa Bali to Christmas Island, 570 miles to the north-west. It was raining as we motored out of the harbour, the sky cloudy but not threatening. We immediately encountered head winds which meandered around to the east and then came back to hit us straight in the face. On with the motor to give us a boost. We were both relieved that the question of fuel conservation was now moot. If necessary, we had enough fuel to motor all the way to Christmas Island.

***Baraka A* Log – October 4**

Both Sherry and I were in the cockpit when we heard a noise which sounded like something huge breathing. And almost suffocating us was that horrible fish stench that we had endured so many time over the past months. I looked to the starboard side and saw a killer whale not more than 6 feet from the side of the boat. His eye was as big as a dinner plate. He dived under the boat and surfaced again on the port side where he looked Sherry right in the eye. He swam away from the boat and then dived again, surfacing off our stern before continuing on his way. This whale was bigger

than any I'd seen in any marine aquarium, at least as big as *Baraka A*. That fish stink had certainly come from whales sounding as they swam by us and around us as we sailed across two oceans. I wondered how many sailboats had gone to the bottom after being hit by a killer whale?

Sherry's Journal, en route to Christmas Island

The weather has been perfect, wind now behind us at a steady 8-12 knots and the temperature more moderate, sometimes even chilly enough for a sweater on night watch. Lovely sailing at night under a full moon and the stars and the planets. If the sky is clear again tomorrow night we might be able to enter the harbour immediately instead of waiting for morning. That would be a first for us.

We arrived at Christmas Island at 3 a.m. on October 5, the moon like a neon light in the sky. But we couldn't find the harbour entrance so we had to hove to till morning. As luck would have it, the wind chose these hours to pipe up to 22 knots which made for a sleepless uncomfortable night.

Later that morning, after completing the customs formalities, we returned to the boat and fell into a deep uninterrupted sleep. We'd earned it. When we woke up that afternoon, we found that John and Dorothy had arrived!

Sherry's Journal, Christmas Island

The people here, who are a mix of Malay, Chinese and Australian, are among the friendliest we've met. So helpful, so genuinely interested in who we are and where we're going. This morning, while Dorothy and I were walking to the laundromat with huge piles of laundry, a police car drew up beside us. In another place we might have thought that we'd broken the law. But this kind man only wanted to give us a ride to the laundromat because he hated to see visitors to his island working so hard.

Then he invited the four of us to go on a tour of the island tomorrow after lunch.

The next day began early with the sunrise call to prayer echoing around the harbour. I sat bolt upright wondering if I'd been dreaming that I was already back in Jeddah. From the cockpit I noticed the minaret of a small mosque hidden among the trees. I should have listened to Sherry when she told me that the Malay population of Christmas Island was Muslim.

After breakfast Sherry motored over to *Socorro* to borrow Dorothy's sewing machine and sew up the raggedy edges of our British flag. Then she motored back to *Baraka A*, secured the dinghy to the stern and stepped aboard. Out of nowhere a gust of wind swept through the anchorage and flipped the dinghy upside down, soaking our motor in the process. I spent some futile minutes drying the spark plugs but like it's predecessor, this motor too refused to start. What about the salesman in American Samoa who'd promised, "No worry, it get wet and still go."

We rowed to shore right after lunch in hopes of finding a repair man before our scheduled tour with the police chief.

"No problem, good as new when you get back," the mechanic promised. Which was a promise he kept.

Sherry had the knack of meeting the most interesting people in the most unlikely places. Which is how two Arabs and two Canadians and one police chief spent an unforgettable afternoon exploring Christmas Island. We visited the inland swamps and marshes, home to every kind of bird imaginable: egrets, falcons, boobies, parrots and even fruit bats hanging upside down in the cherry trees. Ugly things but they kept the mosquito population under control. We learned that crabs were the chief inhabitants of the island: red crabs, blue crabs and a variety known as rubber crabs which were the best ones to eat. Later we explored some caves filled with red crabs where freshwater streams flowed into the sea. Climbed a hill and visited a Buddhist temple which was called a stupa.

Christmas Island was our first island paradise with an industry other than agriculture. Evidence of phosphate mining was everywhere and, the police chief explained, even though some of the deposits had been mined out, this mineral was vital to the economy.

This island was one of the few with an abundant supply of freshwater. On every spare patch of earth the inhabitants (mainly the Chinese) cultivated vegetables. We had a chance to sample some of these vegetables when we went out for a Chinese dinner that evening with Dorothy and John. Afterwards we sat on the beach and watched the sunset. In short, it was a wonderful day we would never forget.

Sherry's Journal, Christmas Island

The people here on Christmas island are the perfect example of how human beings should treat each other all around the world – friendly, kind, helpful and always smiling. If life was as peaceful for everyone, it would be heaven.

Chapter Seventeen

We had designated October 9 as departure day from Christmas Island. Our destination was the Cocos Islands, a convenient stopping place on our westward thrust towards the Red Sea and home.

Rain hissed at us all morning. Delaying our departure would, I knew, make me Sherry's best friend, so I agreed to wait until early afternoon in hopes that the weather would clear. Sherry always hated leaving port especially when that meant saying goodbye to good friends like John and Dorothy. I pointed out that this was not a final goodbye but just a 'till we meet again' as we'd made plans to meet up with *Socorro* in Aden, South Yemen.

Sherry spent the morning scouring the shops for last minute provisions and saying farewell to our friends and thanking the police chief for his kindness and hospitality. She also visited the postmaster and picked up some mail for a Norwegian yacht named *Svanhild* which might or might not be at the Cocos when we arrived. Mail delivery at sea carried no guarantees.

We had barely cleared the harbour and raised the sails when a flock of boobies visited us. After swooping through the rigging, one chose the wind indicator on top of the mast as a resting place. It came as no surprise that he bent it. In the bird world, boobies are considered substantial.

No big deal. This would mean a trip up the mast for me at our next anchorage. How confidently I tossed that off, almost bordering on the nonchalant. But I could still remember my first trip up the mast. Remembered too Sherry's frightened eyes and the ghostly pallor under her tan as she watched me put on my safety harness and climb up the ladder like protrusions on either side of the mast. Although I had pretended otherwise, I wasn't completely comfortable hanging on to a swaying mast several feet above a hard fibreglass deck. My 'Frank Mulville Inspection' (the 'in port' variety only), would never be considered complete without a trip to the mast head to check the halyard fittings. Over the months going up the ladder had become routine but I never forgot to put on my harness.

Baraka A **Log - October 9**

Today we heard a call on VHF channel 16 for all traffic in the area to keep a look out for a dinghy with fishermen on board. Their motor had broken down and they had been pulled out to sea. We searched the horizon at regular intervals and saw nothing.

By late afternoon the steady following breeze we had enjoyed for a few hours increased to 22 knots. Reefed both the main and genoa in hopes of reducing the rolling, rounding up which always made Sherry seasick. A choppy uncomfortable night but we were making 6 knots and a full moon was shining down on us.

Morning greeted us with grey mottled skies and stiff winds which probably meant that we were in for another uncomfortable day.

"But," as I told Sherry, "that's the price you pay if you want to tick the miles off quickly. Yesterday we clocked in 142, almost a record for us."

Sherry gave a quick nod before ducking into the cabin for her Stugeron.

Baraka A **Log -October 12**

Heard on the VHF that the fishermen had been picked up by some Aussies in a sailboat. Wonder if we'll meet them?

By Monday, the 13th, we figured that we had only 130 miles to go. The weather remained the same - strong winds, high rolling seas which translated into a an uncomfortable ride.

Though I always approached landfalls with caution, the Cocos deserved special attention. Three low-lying islands situated in the middle of the Indian Ocean, 1100 miles west of Indonesia, really no more than a string of reefs and atolls, would be impossible to spot at night, yet so easy to run into. So again we reefed the sails to slow our speed and kept a careful watch until dawn revealed a row of palm trees far away on the horizon.

"Land ahoy," Sherry shouted. "I can't wait to get off this boat."

Which didn't happen for over four hours. As we neared the anchorage at Direction Island, Sherry posted herself on the bow to keep a sharp eye out for reefs lurking below the placid surface of the water. We were delighted to find six other sailboats at anchor, one of them *Svanhild*. Did I have a postman's cap somewhere on board?

Knowing how anxious we would have been for mail, we made delivering the precious cargo of letters to *Svanhild* our first priority. As soon as we were anchored, we motored over and met the captain and crew, which numbered seventeen, fourteen adults and three children. *Svanhild* was, by nautical standards, a grand old dowager of one hundred years, a classic wooden sailing vessel celebrating her centennial with a round the world voyage.

Sherry's Journal, Cocos Islands

We're still in Australia. Yes, these remote tiny specks, like Christmas Island, belong to one of our favourite countries. There are three main islands. Discovery, where we are anchored, has no residents except us yachties. West Island is populated mostly by Australians while the Malays have settled on Home Island. Probably a smart move as the two cultures are so different.

This afternoon we accepted an invitation from Svanhild *to go to West Island in their large sturdy dinghy. I learned that 4 1/2 miles can seem like forever on a choppy sea, especially on the way back, burdened down with 6 jerry cans of diesel and several sacks of groceries.*

That night we were invited to a fish barbecue ashore, hosted by the crew of Svanhild *who had caught a huge fish, estimated at over 100 kilos, on their voyage to the Cocos. Tasty, succulent, delicious. How can I describe this fish, which was barbecued to perfection over a fire of coconut shells?*

> *A wonderful evening. But we were exhausted after a busy day and hardly any sleep the previous night. We said good night and escaped to* Baraka A *where we collapsed on to our bunks. I was asleep before my head hit the pillow.*

The next morning we woke up to rain. We heard the whistling and moaning of the wind as it churned the ocean into an angry froth and were grateful that we were safe in a protected anchorage.

On top of our list of things to do was 'clean the hull'. My inclination was to wait for the weather to clear but Sherry decided that wet was wet, whether it be from rain or seawater. In short order she was over the side with a brush, scrubbing the algae from the waterline. Later we donned our snorkelling gear and spent a couple of hours diving under the boat taking swipes at the bottom. Never again would we allow the barnacles to build up and slow us down.

By the time we were finished the sun was blazing. Later in the afternoon we treated ourselves to some beach time. Lying on the white sand while Sherry searched for shells, I revelled in the tranquillity of this place. Palm trees bending in the wind, waves lapping against the shore, birds circling overhead. Who could ask for more?

That evening we were invited to dinner on *Svanhild*. As always, the talk drifted to 'where are you going next?' and to my delight I discovered that *Svanhilds*' sail plan was almost identical to ours in that their course would take them through the Red Sea to the Mediterranean. *Svanhild* would stop at Diego Garcia, the last British outpost in the Indian Ocean, then continue on to the Seychelles situated off the east coast of Africa. *Baraka A*'s next port of call would be the Maldives, then Oman, Yemen and on to Egypt with a stop in Jeddah.

At a break in the conversation I heard Sherry laughing. She looked up at me, her brown eyes bright with merriment.

"The same destination, Jameel, but hardly the same course since we're not going to any of the same islands."

We hoped to leave the Cocos on Friday, October 16. But before we could leave, we had to arrive officially by clearing customs and immigration. Finally on October 15, forty-eight hours after dropping anchor, the customs launch puttered out to our anchorage, thrust some papers at us, which we signed, and then with a grin and a wave, slowly puttered away.

With the customs formalities past tense, we decided to motor to Home Island in the dinghy in search of provisions. Crossing the lagoon, I heard an ominous clunk after which the motor sputtered to a stop. A cursory inspection revealed that I had sheared a pin, easy to fix as I had lots of spare pins back on *Baraka A*. But it soon became apparent that we had more to worry about than a broken pin. Even though I put all my muscles into rowing the dinghy back to the boat, it was a losing battle from the start. My strength was no match for the current which was ripping through the lagoon and rapidly pulling us out to sea. Just like those Australian fishermen. Sherry found the air horn among the jerry cans and let off five ear-shattering blasts which alerted *Svanhild*. They immediately sped over in their dinghy and towed us back home, then offered to take us to Home Island. Was there no end to the kindness, congeniality and the spirit of sharing which, I had come to believe, set members of the nautical community apart from all others?

A few hours later, with the shopping completed and the provisions stowed away, I decided to spend some time on the motor with no clear conviction that this attempt would be more successful than any previous ones. Give me a huge diesel engine and I could cope, but these little outboards appeared to be my nemesis. But, for once, my predictions proved to be true. Changing a shear pin was no big deal and soon the outboard roared back to life.

We spent our final evening on the Cocos Islands, visiting with our new friends on *Svanhild* and *Lady Rose* which was bound for Sri Lanka and then to the Mediterranean via the Red Sea. I remembered an entry from *Sherry's Journal* in which she despaired that sailors seemed to shun the beautiful Red Sea in favour of the Cape of Good Hope at South Africa's tip. Well, not the bunch we'd met recently. We issued invitations that they stop to visit us en route. Not the standard and obligatory, 'Do drop by if you're in the neighbourhood', but real ones from our hearts.

"Goodbye land and back to sea again," Sherry said as the Cocos Islands disappeared from view the following morning.

I set the sails wing to wing and with a steady following breeze the speed indicator showed that we were slicing through the waves at 6 knots. Our next landfall, the Maldives, more ink spots in the ocean, lay 1800 miles to the north-west. These islands had, in recent years, become a popular holiday destination for residents of the Kingdom. Only a six hour journey by jet, the Maldives offered all the ingredients necessary for a tropical paradise getaway: white sand beaches, crystal water, palm trees and superb scuba diving. Except that we weren't travelling there by jet at 500 mph but on *Baraka A* whose top recorded speed was around 9 knots and whose average daily speed fell far short of that mark.

***Baraka A* Log – October 16**

During the evening hours I discovered water leaking into the bilge. I pumped it dry twice. Hope to discover the source when daylight comes.

October 17

Discovered leak around propeller shaft. Tightened the Teflon nut and the leak stopped. Thank God.

Sherry's Journal, October 19-20

Two days of steady winds followed by two with hardly any wind at all. Yesterday we made only 100 miles, even flying the spinnaker. The dolphins who visit us every day help keep our morale up.

Today a boobie landed on our whisker pole and, instead of flying away after a few moments, just settled down there. At night he preened his feathers and stuck his head under his wing. How could he sleep balanced on the whisker pole, poor little fellow? I wanted to pick him up and bring him inside, out of the rain which began to fall at dusk.

The next morning he was still with us. So were 'the calms'. The sea is like glass. We can motor one more day in search of wind. After that it's shut off the motor and drift. Once we cross the equator, we will hit the real doldrums where sometimes there is no wind for weeks so we must conserve our diesel. I think we're in the doldrums already.

The boobie seemed unconcerned, still sitting on the whisker pole. When he got hungry I wondered if he would have to fly all the way back to the Cocos.

This afternoon he took off and we thought that he had left us for good, but he returned after a half an hour. Jameel said he'd gone looking for his dinner.

***Baraka A* Log – October 20**

Is *Baraka A* a bird sanctuary? The boobie keeps us entertained. I think he's taking advantage of a free ride. Today the weather was very hot so he just flew away, took a dip in the ocean and returned. While he was still our guest, a lovely little bird (don't know what kind) landed in the cockpit, flew around then settled down on the shampoo bottle in the head. He spent the night then flew away. The boobie is still with us.

On October 22, I calculated we still had 1000 miles to go before reaching the Maldives. The sometimes steady winds appeared to have departed for good and we were plagued with the shifting capricious variety which escalated and then dropped to nothing. In order to squeeze every bit of forward speed possible, I put up the spinnaker. During the early morning hours on October 23, we were slammed broadside by a violent squall that appeared out of nowhere. The thrashing of the sails and the lurching of the boat as she fought to stay upright woke Sherry who bolted topside.

"Grab the tiller and turn her into the wind," I shouted as the bow slammed into the waves sending spray cascading into the cockpit. "I have to get the sails down," I continued, hoping the wind hadn't carried my words away.

But Sherry knew what to do. She shoved the tiller over hard until *Baraka A* was in irons. I scooted forward, grabbing the shrouds for support and bagged the spinnaker after a ferocious struggle. Then I crawled back to the mast and managed to reef the main down to the fourth reefing point. That accomplished, I scrambled into the cockpit and eased the genoa out a notch.

"Thanks Sherry," I shouted over the roar of the wind as I gave her hand a squeeze. "You really were those extra pair of hands today."

We sagged on to the cockpit seats, wet and exhausted. Then, as suddenly as it had appeared, the squall was gone and the waves flattened out to mere ripples.

Sherry's Journal, October 23-25

The weather has been awful. When the wind is behind us, it dies. What wind we get comes in the form of squalls and hits us head on. A steady diet of 'the calms', squalls and rain and more squalls hitting us at 26-30 knots.

Because of the constantly shifting wind, the windvane and autohelm are not much use so we have been taking turns at the tiller. We are both tired and depressed, especially since we have only covered 756 miles in 7 days. We had hoped to make at least 120 a day. Even the dolphins have disappeared.

On the afternoon of the 23rd, our morale got a huge boost when we spotted another sailboat on the horizon. It turned out to be Lady Rose *from the Cocos en route to Galle, Sri Lanka. They sailed over close to us and we shouted at each other across the water. Wonderful to see and hear some other humans!*

To compound my misery, I hurt my neck. Can't remember when or how but it is very sore and makes sleeping difficult.

We had our first break from the stormy weather on October 26 when the wind dropped to 10 knots. We wondered for how long as we watched an army of huge black clouds marching across the sky to a drum roll of thunder.

Sherry finally decided to try a folk remedy for her sore neck after aspirin, Panadol and Tylenol had failed to ease the pain. Back in American Samoa she had purchased a tea with the herbs ' good for muscles'. This morning she boiled some water and made a tea with the herbs. The good news was that, like magic, the pain eased. The bad news was that the wind followed suit, easing back to near zero. It was as hot as an oven aboard *Baraka A* with the equatorial sun blazing down on us.

Sherry's Journal, October 27

In the last 24 hours we covered less than 70 miles. Very depressing. We are still being hit with several squalls a day, some of them quite fierce with gusting winds up to 40 knots. The wind is coming straight at us, paralysing our progress. We still have 560 miles to go and right now have no idea when we will reach the Maldives. Our supply of fresh produce is gone as well as all the soft drinks so we are down to water, tea and coffee but we must watch the water. Also the diesel.

This trip has been terribly tiring, wind from the wrong direction, waves slamming us, no wind at all then squalls with lots of rain, then 'the calms' again. It's been like this every day, all day for one week. We are exhausted.

***Baraka A* Log – October 28-29**

Changing course to Galle, Sri Lanka because of continuous north-westerly winds and a tremendous number of squalls with winds reaching Force 8 and a 2 knot current which is also against us.

After changing course, I noticed the barometer falling. I am afraid some cyclone or tropical storm is building. I hope we make it to Galle, 300 miles away, before the worst hits.

Later the barometer began to rise and the wind eased to 14-15 knots. Weather looks better. Hope to make Galle tomorrow. Bad news. Our refrigerator is not working.

Sherry's Journal, October 29

Bad weather never stayed with us so long in the past. Stormy weather, bad seas and the constant motion of the ship have made this leg something I will never forget. Everything on the boat, including us, is covered with a sticky salt residue. Can't wait to get to Galle. Jameel looks so tired but he is pleased about the boat's performance during all the horrible weather. Although I hate stormy weather, I'm not so scared any more because Jameel is so confident.

Approaching Galle in the early morning hours of October 1, we ran into a terrible storm. The sky was blanketed with dark menacing clouds which produced pounding rain and the usual accompaniment, blustery squally winds. The heavy winds whipped the sea into a frenzy of rolling breakers which crashed over the boat and slowed our speed to 3 knots. But the end was in sight – we hoped. At 10 miles out we could see nothing. At 6, there was a faint indication that land lay ahead of us. Unfortunately, 'land' also meant freighters entering and leaving the harbour at Galle. Through the wind blown mist I could see one of these monsters heading directly for us. I called on the VHF asking them to alter course as there was no way we could get out of the way in time. The freighter refused! Then another ship in the area warned the freighter to obey the rules of the road, which it did, much to our relief. Three long, brutal hours later we entered the harbour at Galle and anchored behind a protective breakwater without the aid of charts. This lack of charts had worried me more than I let on. Was it possible to find our way to the anchorage with only a book from our library on cruising the Indian Ocean for reference? Apparently yes, which was a good thing because we'd run out of options.

As soon as the customs officials appeared and departed, we headed for a hot shower and then into town for a good meal. We'd earned it!

The next morning we met a fellow named Don Windsor, a Sri Lankan businessman who, with the help of his family, catered to the needs of visiting sailors with enthusiasm and charm. The 'business' part of him was rarely evident.

"Anything you need, I have," he announced, smiling broadly. "Laundry, showers, supermarket, gem shop, restaurant, tour guides, all are here."

There were sailors from every part of the world in the small harbour: Australians, Canadians, French, Germans and us, the only Arabs. Don Windsor confirmed that we were the first Arabs to visit

Galle and insisted on taking our picture standing beneath the Saudi and Egyptian flags.

That evening after dinner we gathered together, as sailors always do, to exchange ideas and information. The head winds which had forced us to make a detour to Galle would not become favourable for at least a month. To say we were discouraged was the understatement of the year. So close to home, yet so many miles away and now this delay. What should we do? Stay put in Galle waiting for the wind to shift around or head out and take our chances?

"Or," I asked Sherry, presenting a third possibility, "jump on Saudia Air and fly to Jeddah and wait for the favourable winds there?"

"Yes," Sherry replied. "Most definitely, yes."

Sherry, I knew, could handle living aboard *Baraka A* for a month. Even though 31 feet was a tiny space for two people, even though Galle was a commercial harbour and not a tropical paradise, Sherry could keep herself occupied. Visiting sailors from other boats, reading and shopping would fill her days.

But how would I fill mine?

"Harbours rot ships and men," I told her again. "I can't sit here for a month having nothing to do but scrub the deck."

Don Windsor's son drove us to Colombo in his mini-van where we caught the plane to Jeddah on November 6. On our frugal budget we were naturally flying economy but then some of the flight crew recognised us and we were whisked to first class where we were treated to a sumptuous meal and enjoyed a visit with the captain.

The following weeks were crammed full of visiting, shopping and media interviews. The major newspapers in Saudi Arabia carried full page features on our trip. Sherry was interviewed on two radio stations. Most of the questions dealt with a woman's perspective of life at sea. Sherry's responses focused on the positive. All the bad parts – the storms and boredom and seasickness – were downplayed to the ordinary and expected and were more than offset by the pluses: tropical islands, glorious sunsets, and the people we'd met. But that's human nature. Bad memories fade away while the good ones thrive and grow and get even better.

A high point for me was a visit with His Royal Highness Prince Majed bin Abdulaziz who wished us continued success.

But even higher was the warm reception I received from my parents. Gone were the gloom and doom predictions about our foundering at sea. Instead, my father dragged me around to visit his friends, talking proudly about my exploits. He insisted on donating a few dollars to our dwindling cash supply so that we could buy the replacement parts we needed. I did not refuse.

Recreational sailing in the Kingdom was almost non-existent, a situation I hoped to change when I returned. But in the here and now, no sailing translated into non-existent or poorly equipped chandleries. And we needed replacement parts for the autopilot, depth sounder and refrigerator, new navigational lights for the bow and an additional whisker pole to replace the one that was surely going to break somewhere between Galle and Jeddah.

And so we flew to Paris, where we found everything we needed except the parts for the refrigerator so we would have to sail home without one. We'd forgotten that winter in Europe could be brutal, especially since the last cold weather we'd experienced had been in the English Channel a lifetime ago. Had it really only been twelve months?

Sherry's Journal, Jeddah

I have been thinking about the poverty in the world since we came back here where there is hardly any. We have seen so many people on this sailing trip who live on nothing. They stare at the yachties as we come ashore to spend our money. But they are not envious. Their good nature conquers those feelings and instead they are kind and generous. They know nothing of the world, of jet planes or big cities. There is an ache in my heart that they will live and die knowing nothing but the sea and sand and the place where they live. I am more fortunate. I know both their world and mine.

Before returning to Galle I flew to Turkey to visit a favourite aunt who was very ill. Sherry stayed in Jeddah with my parents and finished her shopping which included a tiny red oriental carpet for the boat, not the flying variety I hoped.

When I returned, she showed me her list of things to do:

1) Throw out all the old junk we don't need – charts, flags, books and clothes
2) Make new drapes for the hatch
3) Wash all the cabin drapes
4) Replace oven. The old one's all rusty
5) Clean bilge
6) Clean all the lockers and get rid of the old food
7) Put dining table back
8) Fix whisker pole

Like husbands everywhere, I propped my chin in my hand and murmured, 'hmm'. If I believed that harbours rot men and ships, then I had to acknowledge that being away from 'home', even a 31 foot one, made a woman ache with the need to return to her own turf.

Don Windsor's son was waiting at the Columbo airport when the plane landed at 7 a.m. on December 4. On the way back to Galle we stopped at a supermarket to pick up some basic supplies to tide us over for a couple of days.

Arriving back at the harbour, all thoughts of sleeping off our jet-lag vanished. Bobbing gently at anchor were *Socorro* and *Svanhild*. We were overjoyed to see our friends and over coffee at Don's restaurant we learned that they had also been forced to take a detour to Galle to wait for a change in the wind direction. Finally fatigue, compounded by the simple need to climb back aboard the only home we'd known for the last year propelled us out of the restaurant and on to the jetty.

"Later," we promised. "We'll get together for dinner."

Baraka A had clearly not enjoyed her month alone. The stench of mildew and rotting eggs greeted us as we opened the hatch boards. Sherry groaned as she viewed the cabin's interior, then changed into her jeans and T-shirt and began the clean-up.

Sherry's Journal, Galle Sri Lanka

Mildew everywhere: on my clothes, the sheets, blankets, pillows and towels. First job was to get our beds ready. We hadn't slept a wink since yesterday. Made many trips to the laundromat this afternoon. By 6 p.m. I was so tired that I fell on to my bunk and was asleep instantly. No dinner on shore for us. Woke at midnight and scrubbed and cleaned until 4 a.m. Every square centimetre of the boat had a film of mildew clinging to the surface. The deck is filthy too, dusty and splotchy with dried sea spray. Ditto for the kayak which Jameel has not used once since he bought it in Australia, a fact I pointed out to him while he scrubbed it. Jameel, of course, decided that a paddle around the anchorage would be a great way to relax after a hard day's work. Why was I not surprised!

Sherry continued her fantastic job of cleaning the interior of *Baraka A* in the 90 degree heat while I busied myself buying diesel and ferrying it back to the boat. Ditto for water. Then I changed the oil in the diesel engine, repaired the forecabin storage lockers and found a local lad to clean the hull.

Our second night back, we did make it to shore for dinner and met our sailing friends at Don Windsor's restaurant. The cuisine was uninspiring unlike the company, which was great. We learned that when *Svanhild* had run into head winds they began to motor and almost immediately had ran out of fuel. Luckily their call for help was heard by a Norwegian freighter which sold them enough fuel to reach Galle.

The following evening there was a bon voyage party aboard *Svanhild* for three crew members who were returning to Norway. After a delicious dinner they entertained us, strumming their guitars and singing Norwegian sea ballads.

Sherry's Journal, Galle, Sri Lanka, December 7

There are 30 other sailboats anchored here with us, all on hold till the wind changes direction. After 3 days of hard work, Baraka A is in good shape and ready to go. But the wind is not co-operating. There is very little of it and it is coming from the wrong direction. Everyone here plans to stay until after Christmas or later. Jameel wants to leave in a couple days' time and for once I agree with him. It is so hot here and there is not much to do but sit around and complain about the lack of wind. Jameel has been looking at some charts he bought in Paris and he thinks we have a good chance of finding wind out there. So we've decided to go for it.

We spent our last night in port with John and Dorothy, treating ourselves to a luscious dinner at the New Oriental Hotel. The next morning we made a last run to the shops for some fresh produce and said goodbye to everyone again. By 2.30 we were ready to go. As we motored past the sailors who had become our friends over the last months, we felt a wave of sadness wash over us.

"Do you think we'll ever see any of these people again?" I asked Sherry. "Cruising around the world, we've made so many friends. Some have been as close as family. But, when the voyage is done and we're all back to living regular lives, it won't be the same somehow. I think these are special friendships that came to be because of..." I smiled as I groped for the right words.

"A time and a place and a need," Sherry suggested.

"Exactly. Maybe this type of friendship needs saltwater to survive."

Sherry grinned.

"Maybe, but I hope not. So many special people, so many happy memories. I want to hold on to them for ever."

Chapter Eighteen

Sherry's Journal, December 9, leaving Galle, Sri Lanka for Salalah, Oman

I spent this morning cooking cabbage and rice dishes in case I am too seasick to do anything tonight. Jameel said there was not enough wind to make the sea rough but sometimes, even when it's calm, the boat wallows in the swells. Jameel counts it as a good sign that another boat from here, Fam, *is also heading out, bound for Oman. We're not the only crazy ones!*

The first two days out, the engine worked overtime due to the continuing light winds. I hoped that once we entered the Arabian Sea we'd find favourable winds from the north-east to give us a push. Sherry said that she didn't mind 'the calms' for a couple of days as she needed some lazy time to recuperate from her marathon cleaning session in Galle.

"I've earned a holiday," she said. "Nothing to do but read and sunbathe and write in my journal."

"And keep a wary eye out for ships," I reminded her.

Wind or no wind, we were once again in the shipping lanes, a fact which was slammed home to us after sighting twelve freighters and tankers in one twenty-four hour period. Lazy days would also have to be vigilant ones!

***Baraka A* Log - December 11**

While Sherry was on watch she saw a huge freighter which seemed to be heading straight for us. I called on Channel 16 – no response. Looking through the binoculars, I saw the ship's navigational lights, and no anchor light which

indicated they were underway. Changed course immediately to avoid a collision. Soon realised that the ship was stationary. We passed so close that we could see the cranes on the decks. Two minutes later, the anchor light went out. Called them again on the VHF and got no response.

Sherry's Journal, December 12-13

Last year on this day I was somewhere on the Atlantic Ocean waiting for wind. One year later the situation is identical. Jameel and I are growing impatient with 'the calms' – no wind for 4 days plus a current that is setting us by 1-2 knots and slowing our speed. We hope that when we pass the island of Minicoy and enter the Arabian Sea, we will find wind. Boats are forbidden to stop at this island. Too bad, as it would have been a convenient place to top up our diesel. Today I played a cassette of Turkish music which I bought in Jeddah. It sounded a lot like Arabic music but I didn't understand a word. Sounded good though.

Today, December 13, when we entered the Arabian Sea, I felt close to home even though we had 1125 miles to go before reaching the port of Salalah in Oman. I calculated that we had enough diesel to get us half-way. Somehow we would have to find the wind to take us the remaining miles.

That afternoon, as we were wallowing on the flat seas under motor, suddenly, as if by magic, a beautiful 12 knot wind appeared and blew steadily for five hours before it petered out.

That night the wind returned with a vengeance, a storm from nowhere almost identical to the one we had encountered after leaving the Cocos. I was lazing in the cockpit letting the autohelm do the work and watching the sails flutter in the breeze. Suddenly a fierce wind slammed into *Baraka A*, causing her to heel over so far that I thought the spreaders surely must be underwater. I leapt to my feet and released the autohelm and both the main and genoa sheets which allowed *Baraka A* to right herself and come around into the wind.

"Sherry," I yelled. "Come take the tiller while I get the sails down."

Sherry was in the cockpit in double-quick time, still rubbing the sleep from her eyes. Grasping the tiller in both hands, she held the boat into the wind while I took down the main and winched the genoa in until just a sliver remained. If ever I was grateful for a roller furling jib, it was that night.

This time the wind did not disappear but howled around us for the rest of the night. I stayed topside while Sherry sat cross-legged on her bunk, her eyes cloudy with fear. Dawn found us exhausted and grateful when the wind finally moderated to 10 knots. A clear blue sky decorated with cotton candy clouds and the sun dancing on the waves made me wonder if the storm had just been a dream.

Baraka A **Log - December 15**

Discovered the boat was taking on water, requiring about 40 pumps every 24 hours. Same problem as before. Tightened the Teflon nut again and the leak stopped. Then I discovered oil leaking from the oil filter. I changed the filter which stopped the leak. I checked the oil level with the dipstick and discovered that I had already lost half my engine oil. And it appears I don't have any in reserve. I thought I had some in the parts locker but it has disappeared. I consider the situation critical. We are low on fuel, low on oil and there is no wind. We are still 1000 miles from Oman.

Well, in spite of the oil disaster some good things happened today. Around 3 p.m. a beautiful breeze from the north-east blew in at about 17 knots, which helped us to put some miles under the keel. Then a delegation of pilot whales paid us a visit. We recognised them immediately because of their flat noses, which distinguish them from the pointed-nosed dolphins. They swam along beside us long enough for me to get some good video footage. Sherry wondered if they were showing us the way to Oman.

The pilot whales cheered us up enough to try piecing together what might have happened to the missing oil. I remembered a green trash bag full of empty cans in Galle. Sherry remembered adding more trash to a green sack before heaving it into the dumpster. I also recalled that the engine oil was stored in a green plastic bag. The answer seemed obvious. Somehow the engine oil had been thrown out with the trash. Sherry was convinced that the mistake was hers while I was equally convinced that I was to blame. After a few volleys of 'your fault – my fault', we ended up laughing hysterically. If one of us were proven guilty, what appropriate sentence should be meted out? Walking the plank? Keel-hauling? A diet of bread and water until we reached Salalah? I treated Sherry to one of my favourite quotes – 'Water under the bridge can never flow upstream' – which, for some reason, sent her into another round of laughter. We agreed that the oil was gone and there was nothing to do about it except make solemn promises to always inspect the trash before heaving it, and pray for wind so we wouldn't have to use the engine.

The next two days brought us the answer to our prayers. Winds blowing 17-24 knots moved us along at a steady 5-6 knots, sometimes reaching 7 knots during the evening hours. But we paid a price for the wind – high rolling seas and a rough ride which made Sherry dive for her Stugeron once more. Sailing a beam reach translated into lots of water in the cockpit when rogue waves slammed us broadside, drenching everything.

Sherry's Journal, December 16

I was lying on my bunk this afternoon reading a book when a big wave hit the side of the boat. Water came through the hatch soaking me, the book and the sheets. I had to change the bed, change my clothes and wipe the floor dry. Things like this make your day, don't they?

December 17

We have closed the hatch and I have been sitting inside as it is too wet and windy to be topside. It's been 6 days now since we've sighted a ship. We're all alone out here with only the sky and the sea as companions, just like so many other times.

Jameel caught a big yellowfin tuna today but by the time he got it on board a shark had eaten everything but the head. But we managed to scrape enough flesh from the head to make a meal. We have both lost weight. After all the good food we ate in Paris and Jeddah it's hard to go back to eating rice and spaghetti. Maybe that's why we were so excited about a fish head!

For the next few days the boat ploughed through the water at a steady 5-6 knots thanks to a steady consistent wind from the north-east. I enjoyed the freedom of being able to set the sails, put the boat on autopilot and basically relax, a rare experience for me. Also, the temperature moderated to a pleasant 80 degrees during the day, even dipping down to 'sweatshirt weather' at night, restoring our energy in the process.

***Baraka A* Log – December 22**

180 miles from Salalah. A lucky day as I caught a dorado which Sherry cooked for lunch. That night I sighted 4 ships, the first we'd seen in days. I called on the VHF Channel 16 to notify them of our presence. Two responded, two did not, but I figured that was because they saw us and altered course.

Sherry's Journal, approaching Oman

Oman will be our first Arabic port in over a year. It seems like a dream that we are so close now. I still remember the days when we were in the Caribbean heading for the Panama Canal with the whole Pacific, Australia and the Indian Ocean ahead of us. So much is behind us now, thanks to a lot of effort and a strong will. And, thanks to God's care, we are almost home. For the first time our parents and friends will see the boat. We're counting the hours now till we reach Oman. We are dreaming of cold drinks with lots of ice.

During the morning hours of December 23, I alerted the harbour-master at Salalah of our impending arrival. Sherry, of course, followed her usual routine and went on a cleaning binge until the boat sparkled.

We were surprised and pleased when an official welcoming committee in the form of a coastguard cutter met us at the harbour's entrance around 2.30 in the afternoon and escorted us to a prime anchorage near the customs dock. I presented them with a tuna I had just caught thinking that our dinner plans did not include cooking a fish and eating it aboard *Baraka A*. As always, after a long sea passage, our first thought was to get off the boat, have a shower and find a restaurant. This time we'd decided on a special treat, a night in a hotel with lots of hot water and a bed that didn't move.

"So sorry," the coastguard officer explained. "You cannot leave your boat until you clear customs and immigration, in the morning, some time after 8 a.m. During the day you may go where you like but by 6 p.m. you must be back at the harbour. It is the rule here."

Even this bad news failed to dampen my buoyant spirits. For so many months we'd been the first Arabs anyone had ever met. What fun it was to turn the tables on the coastguard officers and tell them *they* were the first Arabs we'd seen in over a year, at least while at sea. Obviously I wasn't counting our two trips home to Jeddah.

Jabbering in Arabic made me feel that I was already back in my world. Almost home! We'd done it, Sherry and I, sailed a 31 foot boat across the world's oceans and survived and also enjoyed most of the moments. A feeling of contentment and inner peace crept over me. Who cared if we couldn't go to town that evening? And sleeping aboard *Baraka A* was no big deal. We'd done it hundreds of times.

Later, when Sherry presented me with a plate of scrambled eggs and melba toast and called it dinner, I regretted ever giving the tuna away. The thought of some barbecued tuna filets sizzling on the grill made my mouth water.

As promised, the customs and immigration officials and the Ministry of Health arrived at 8.30 a.m. and boarded a clean and tidy *Baraka A*. Once the official inspection was completed and the papers signed, Sherry made coffee. As we sat in the cockpit fielding questions, we realised again that we really were unique. No other couple from the Arab world had ever attempted a circumnavigation. In fact we were the first Arabs to have ever sailed into this harbour. What impressed them most was the size of the boat. How did we live in such a small space for so many months? Sherry's lips curved into a slow mischievous smile. I shrugged and grinned back at her. I marvelled again that Sherry and I, like many married couples, were so in tune that we could send messages without saying a word. No, we would not tell *all* our secrets: of how we argued sometimes and longed for privacy, how we got sick of each other's company and learned to carve out our own space.

I cleared my throat before answering.

"Yes, this boat is not very big, only 31 feet. Very cosy and compact but that's what we like about it. A bigger boat means a lot more work and we have all we could handle with our 31 feet."

After the officials left, a journalist with a photographer in tow paid us a visit. Could they interview us? We never said no to the media. We spent another couple of hours talking to them about our voyage.

"We still have a long way to go, all the way back to Casablanca," I explained.

"Do you wish your voyage was going to end in Jeddah?" the interviewer asked.

Sherry fielded that one.

"Yes and no. We've been at sea for over a year now and I miss the comforts of home. I can't deny that. But after we finish the circumnavigation our lives will never be the same. I think we will miss the freedom of the sea."

The harbour-master had arranged for a local official, who turned out to be a police officer, to show us around Salalah and help us in any way he could. The first stop was the Holiday Inn where we gorged ourselves on a sumptuous buffet lunch which included cold drinks with lots of ice. Afterwards we visited the produce market, then the supermarket where we stocked up on enough food to see us all the way home to Jeddah.

My last task for the day was to buy enough diesel oil to fill up the engine and still have plenty in reserve in the event of another oil leak.

Christmas Day, December 25

A German couple we met on our first day here picked us up in the morning and took us to their home where we had tea. In the afternoon we went to the beach for a barbecue with some members of the ex-pat community who worked for the British Air Force in Salalah. Good food and great company but the wind blowing in from the sea was brisk and cool, which made everyone grab for their sweaters and complain about the weather.

But not us. By any standard, this Christmas Day was 'over the top' compared to last year's. Would we ever forget rolling around the Atlantic swells hoping Antigua would magically appear on the horizon. For dinner we'd shared a can of fruit!

Sherry's Journal, Salalah, Oman

The town of Salalah is clean, charming and filled with gardens and palm trees. Outside the city there are farms where bananas and apples and olives are grown. Our police guide told us that the soil is very fertile here. The harbour is one of the best we've been in, also very clean with every facility and a harbour-master who reminds us of Mohammed back in Casablanca. Knows everything and everybody and is so helpful and friendly. When we leave Oman it will be with a good impression of the people and the place.

Today we called our families. They are anxious to see us and see the boat and keep asking us when we will get there. I know Jameel wants to get there quickly. One reason is to see Essam, whom we missed in November because he was in England taking his end of the year exams. His term break lasts until mid-January. We are determined not to miss him again.

We had decided on December 26 as our departure day so early in the morning we pulled up our anchor and motored to the dock where we picked up nine jerry cans of fuel. The soldier on duty kindly hosed down the deck and filled our water tanks and would take no payment for either the diesel or the water.

Then a commander in the Omani Navy appeared, boarded *Baraka A* and presented us with the Sultan of Oman's navy emblem and two beautiful books to add to our library, one on the maritime history of Oman and the other on the voyages of Sindbad the Sailor. As I leafed through the pages, I felt transported back in time to when I was a young boy. I could see myself curled up in a corner avidly reading about the voyages of this legendary adventurer. Perhaps Sindbad as much as Adam Troy and his boat *Tiki* had challenged me to take up sailing.

Sherry made coffee and we sat for more than a few moments talking to this interesting Navy commander who had a few stories of his own to tell about his years aboard the Omani ship *Sahur*. Then he invited us to join him for lunch aboard an Omani cargo ship where we met the captain and crew.

Sherry and I were overwhelmed with the hospitality and kindness which, we came to understand, had been extended to honour our achievements as the first Arabs to attempt a circumnavigation. There was no adequate response to such warm-hearted generosity except the customary thank yous, which barely conveyed our appreciation.

At 2 p.m. we said our final farewells and headed out to sea where we found favourable 15 knot winds. Destination Jeddah, 1300 miles away. I told my mother who conveyed the message to my father that we would arrive about Jan 5th. My mother replied that my father didn't like the 'about' part. He wanted to arrange a huge welcome for us, the press, official welcoming committee, the whole nine yards and for those kind of festivities he needed an exact date.

Was this the same father who fourteen months previously had admonished family members to not lend me one cent to finance our voyage? I remembered his exact words:

"You are sending him to his death."

Now, here I was returning home to Jeddah. Just seeing him waiting on the dock for me to arrive would make all the months at sea worthwhile.

Chapter Nineteen

Our course from Salalah, Oman took us westward along the bottom of the Arabian Peninsula. Our destination – Bab Al Mandab, 400 miles away in the Gulf of Aden off the coast of South Yemen. We had abandoned the idea of stopping at the port of Aden, which was a rendezvous point we'd discussed with John and Dorothy aboard *Socorro*. An unstable political climate and, according to the sailor's grapevine, not much to buy in the way of provisions had prompted us to change our plans and sail straight on to Jeddah. Supplies were not the problem. We'd stocked *Baraka A* with enough food in Salalah to sail around the world again (my opinion, not Sherry's). But what about John and Dorothy patiently waiting for us in Aden?

"All sailors accept the fact that plans made in a moonlit cockpit at one anchorage must never be cast in cement," I told Sherry who was fretting about missing our friends.

"Life at sea is not predictable. There are too many variables," I continued, "Weather, gear failure, even illness. Don't worry. If we're lucky we'll make radio contact with them. In any event, they'll catch up with us."

Sherry's Journal, December 28

Today the sea is much smoother than yesterday, probably because we are not fighting the wind and current, both of which are going our way, at least for now. The knot metre is reading 6, a respectable number but another knot or two would be terrific.

I am finding it hard to stay awake on my night watches. How good it will be to get to Jeddah and sleep the whole night through with no worries. About 10 more days at sea and this dream will come true.

Had a saltwater shower this morning. Brrr! So cold. Of course we are north of the equator and it is winter. To starboard lies the coast of Yemen, 20 miles away. I can barely see it because of the haze.

Today, December 29, I decided to catch a fish for lunch. I baited my hook and threw my line into the water with my usual, 'well, here goes nothing' attitude. Imagine my surprise when a powerful fish quickly took the bait, almost pulling me into the sea. Bracing myself against the stern pulpit, I finally managed to land my prize, which turned out to be a baby white tip shark. Many people say shark is delicious but I'm not one of them. So I threw it back into the sea and Sherry made us foul medames instead.

The area around Bab Al Mandab was notorious for its erratic shifting winds. Those I could deal with but the current tried my patience and endurance to the limit. We either bounded along at 6-7 knots when the current was with us or inched forward at a mere 3-4 when the current turned against us. The reversing currents made the sea choppy, even in light winds. I hoped for favourable conditions, i.e. the wind and current on our side, when we passed Bab Al Mandab and entered the Red Sea. I agreed with Sherry that the Red Sea was beautiful, but I also appreciated that it was a tricky piece of water to navigate.

First there was the marine traffic. An average of two hundred freighters-and oil tankers use the Red Sea as a corridor from the Mediterranean to the Indian Ocean each day. Secondly, the Red Sea is narrow, only one hundred miles wide and dotted with coral reefs. And thirdly, the prevailing winds are from the north-west which meant that we would be sailing into the teeth of it, making us choose whether to tack in the channels between the reefs while dodging freighters or turn on the engine. Luckily we had a more than adequate supply of diesel.

Sherry's Journal, December 31

At 6.30 p.m. we entered the Red Sea accompanied by 7 big ships. While Jameel kept track of the marine traffic, I watched schools of tuna swimming around Baraka A. *Suddenly a flying-fish sprang from the water with a tuna in pursuit. Flying-fish actually live up to their name and 'fly' through the air, but I'd never seen a tuna doing it. Quite a sight.*

Tonight rain and thunder! The Arabian Peninsula receives very little rainfall, especially the west coast. How could we be so lucky?

Happy New Year to everyone. May it be a good year for all of us.

***Baraka A* Log – December 31**

I called all the ships in the area on the VHF Channel 16 and sent a message from the captain and first mate of *Baraka A*: "Happy New Year. May God give us another beautiful year." Got two responses!

January 1.

The beginning of another year. After being at sea for over a year I came to the conclusion that long distance sailors, especially those who tackled the Pacific, were the most adventuresome and interesting people I had ever met.

The winds remained capricious, falling, shifting and rising and so we motored most of the time. It was a full-time job keeping track of the freighters and tankers. I compared us to a child's bicycle on a highway clogged with huge monster trucks barrelling along at top speed. There seemed to be a never-ending chain of these huge ships bearing down on us. We continued with the watch schedule that had worked so well for us – six hours during the day, three hours at night.

This afternoon a small white bird tried to land on the boat but he fell back into the water. He looked so thin and tired and sick. Just as we were contemplating turning around to pick him up, he gathered his strength and flew toward us and landed in the cockpit with a barely perceptible thump. I noticed that he had a broken leg. We tried to feed him but no luck. Finally Sherry made a bed for him out of a towel and put him in a protected spot in the V-berth.

During the night the wind picked up to 20 knots so we set the sails wing to wing and sped through the water.

We paid a price for the frisky winds the next morning. The sea rolled and churned around the boat, tossing us from side to side while I fought the tiller to keep us on course. Then suddenly there was a ship bearing down on us fast. Sherry got on the radio while I let off a white flare, hoping someone would see us and get the message:

"Hey, big freighter, I'm just a little guy and you're about to demolish me!"

The flare did the job and the boat changed course. Our next encounter was with a Portuguese vessel which I managed to raise on channel 16. It was possible that I misunderstood the fractured English but my best guess was,

"You change course. We don't like sailboats."

Sherry's Journal, January 2

At sea you see death with your eyes. I was never more scared than I was today watching those huge monsters coming straight at us. I was shaking and trembling uncontrollably from fear. Even the dolphins who came to visit failed to cheer me up. Only the bird made me forget those ships. He looked more energetic today and is trying to stand on one leg.

***Baraka A* Log –January 3**

I called Jeddah and confirmed we would arrive on the 5th, Inshallah. Sherry also called her family in Egypt and they were overjoyed and relieved that we are almost home. The bird looks stronger today.

The bird managed to eat some fish I'd caught. Maybe, we thought, just maybe he'd continue to grow stronger and fly away to live a normal life. As I held him in my hand, I noticed that he was infested with ticks and mites. Apparently his injury had weakened him to the point that he was unable to do a proper job of preening his feathers. So I decided to help. I soaked a tissue in insect repellent and gently rubbed his feathers. Five minutes later we noticed that the bird was no longer able to stand. Sherry brought him out to the cockpit for some fresh air but in a few short minutes he collapsed and died. Trying to help the poor thing, I killed him.

Sherry's Journal

Jameel feels so bad about killing the bird. We are both choked with sorrow. We told ourselves that maybe it was for the best that he died. How could he live a normal life crippled like that with only one leg? How could he fly or catch food? Neither of us believed a word.

Tomorrow we will arrive in Jeddah on time thanks to the good winds and a reliable engine which kept us on schedule. But this leg had taken its toll on both of us. We were tense, nervous, yes, downright scared of the monster ships plying the waters of the Red Sea. *Baraka A* was so tiny in comparison and so underpowered if we needed to get out of someone's way in a hurry. Never, not even for a moment could we let our attention lag. No afternoon naps in the cockpit letting the autohelm do the work while Sherry puttered in the galley.

Night-time was the scariest time. Off watch, I'd been sleeping with one ear cocked toward the helm in case Sherry needed help to avoid a collision. But Sherry had managed her watches like a pro and hadn't called me even once. I continued to marvel at her growing competence, energy and skill at handling even the most difficult tasks, like bundling a sail into a bag during a blow. Gone was the terrified, apprehensive woman whom I'd coaxed aboard the boat in Casablanca. In her place was a first-class first mate!

Today, January 5, *Baraka A* approached the Jeddah Islamic Port at 12.00 noon right on schedule. For the first time since we had left Gosport we removed the Union Jack from the stern staff and replaced it with the national flag of Saudi Arabia. The boat was scrubbed and rubbed till it almost shone. Also the captain and crew. We'd endured a cold saltwater bath and donned fresh clothes that Sherry had secreted away for just such an occasion – trousers without rips, shirts with all the buttons and even shoes!

As we approached the entrance to the harbour, four pilot boats surrounded us and escorted us to the dock where our family waited, waving, smiling and shouting greetings. Hard to believe that we'd seen them all just a month before. Everyone, that is, except Essam who was shouting the loudest of all. Waiting too were hordes of journalists and photographers anxious to record our homecoming for the evening news and the morning newspapers.

After exchanging greetings with our family, we decided that sooner rather than later *vis-à-vis* the media made the most sense. When they swarmed aboard, Sherry retreated into the cabin.

Sherry's Journal, Jeddah, January 5

It seems strange that I am sitting inside Baraka A while Jameel talks to the reporters. But I remind myself that I am back in Saudi Arabia now where women keep themselves in the background. I know that I will be asked if this bothers me. Not really. I have learned from visiting so many countries that each one has its own traditions and customs. And I have also learned to respect those differences. How dull the world would be if everybody and every country was the same.

True to his word, my father had invited a throng of friends to join us for a 'Welcome Home Lunch'. Between bites we posed for pictures and answered questions. Top on the list was how had we managed to live for so long aboard such a small boat.

"It's cosy," Sherry replied. "Easy and quick to clean, which was important because I had to do the work."

Another hot one – how did we get so tanned?

"There's really not much shade on a sailboat," I replied.

The lunch festivities over, I treated myself to a hot, freshwater shower, then donned the official Saudi garb for men, a white thobe and red and white checked gutra, for my meeting with the Ministry Of Youth and his advisers. Over tea, I told them of my dream to teach the youth of my country the joys of sailing.

I was overwhelmed when the Minister presented me with a silver plate with the Saudi national emblem engraved on it. What a moment! The lump in my throat threatened to choke me as I rose to thank the audience for the honour. I thought back to the day we'd left Casablanca. Everyone had thought we were crazy to attempt a circumnavigation in a 31 foot boat captained by an skipper with no experience in ocean sailing and assisted by a first mate who knew even less. Only Mohammed had smiled and said:

'You'll come back and I'll be here.'

I reminded the audience that we hadn't made it, not yet. Ahead lay the rest of the Red Sea, the Suez Canal, the Mediterranean, the Straits of Gibraltar and the Atlantic Ocean until we reached our final destination, Casablanca. We had to make the circle complete before we could say we'd done it - which in sailor's lingo meant 'tying the knot'.

I arrived back from my tea party exhilarated and exhausted and grateful that the hordes of well-wishers had departed. We spent the evening visiting with the family and talking to Essam. Somehow, in our absence, he had changed from an awkward youth into a handsome young man of fifteen who was almost as tall as his father.

That night we fell exhausted into a bed with crisp clean sheets and fluffed feather pillows, a bed that would stay in one place, a bed that would not dump us out on to the floor. We would sleep without fear of capsizing or running into a freighter.

"There are only a few really important days in the life of any man," I told Sherry. "For me they are the day my son was born, the day you became my wife and today. To be welcomed home with such exuberance and genuine kindness is a tribute to everything I am or hope to be. I will remember this day always."

Chapter Twenty

Jeddah is the most beautiful of all the cities in the Kingdom. At least that's what its residents claim. Known as 'The City of Lights', 'Bride of the Red Sea', and 'Gateway to Mecca', Jeddah is all those things and much more. To the west is the Red Sea, home to some of the most spectacular coral reefs in the world. Along the coast, which is known as 'the Corniche', are magnificent villas, royal palaces, first-class hotels and the city's finest restaurants, strung out one after another like a necklace of precious gems. In the evenings families gather at the water's edge, to sit on carpets and gaze out at the sea, to eat their evening meal and sip strong sweet coffee while the children play on the swings and slides or run across the sand. To the east the Hijaz mountains rise from the desert floor, their stark peaks creating a backdrop for the shifting desert sands that surround the city on three sides.

Every time we returned to Jeddah we marvelled at the villas popping up all over the desert, the clean wide streets, the elegant shopping malls and were always delighted to call this beautiful place home. But this time we were home just for a visit, a concept many found difficult to grasp.

We spent nearly ten weeks in Jeddah, a time which was both too long and too short. On the one hand there was *Baraka A* sitting like a disgruntled and exiled family mc4mber at her anchorage in Obhur Creek, which is an inlet off the Red Sea. She seemed to sag at her moorings as if to say,

'Come on, folks, enough of this city living. It's time we headed out. Lots of exciting adventures are waiting for us just beyond the horizon – people to meet and places to visit and sunsets to enjoy.'

On the other hand, my family did not want us to leave.

"But surely you've proved your point," my father argued. "No one would blame you if you stopped here and got back to some regular living."

Maybe no one but the two people who counted most, me and Sherry. And 'regular living' was the last thing on our minds.

"A circumnavigation means you have to make a circle and return to your point of embarkation," I told my father again.

"But you've done the hard part already," he continued. "Why waste the time by going on?"

It wasn't just my father who believed that 'the hard part was over.' But I knew that the Red Sea, the Mediterranean and the Strait of Gibraltar were not 'a piece of cake' in nautical parlance. Also the Atlantic between Gibraltar and Casablanca could be downright nasty, a first-hand experience I was happy to share with anyone who asked.

We divided our time between *Baraka A* and 'other things'. Top on that list was, of course, the family and all the relatives and friends we hadn't seen in months. My father held another reception in my honour at the Sands Hotel, inviting everyone we knew which included the media. An old friend from the University of Miami, Abdullah Magellid, who was chief engineer at the Department of Civil Aviation, invited me to be guest of honour at a banquet at the Hyatt Regency where I was presented with a gold medallion by Sheik Nasser Al Assaf, President of Civil Aviation. Again, I was deeply moved.

But, at the same time, I almost felt like a fraud. Here I was accepting honours for a job I hadn't finished. I was determined to prove to all those who had supported and honoured me that I was not about to rest on my laurels. Sherry and I would become the first persons from the Arab world to *attempt and complete* a circumnavigation.

Our happiest moments of those ten weeks were spent aboard our boat, giving her the TLC she deserved after carrying us safely across three oceans. Sherry did a massive housecleaning, throwing out all the junk we'd accumulated over the past year – old charts, books we'd read, clothes that had seen better days but not the carton of diesel oil, which I'd clearly marked with a black grease pencil.

I gave the standing rigging a thorough check-over and to my surprise found that the shrouds and stays were still in good shape. So far we'd only had to replace one piece of the original standing rigging, a frayed lower shroud, which had snapped as we sailed up the Grafton Passage to Cairns, a testament to the superb quality of the 'Nick 31'.

Frayed halyards and sheets were either spliced or replaced. I pulled up the floorboards and gave the bilges a thorough muck out which was a hot, dirty job, then greased the winches and blocks and polished all the stanchions and pulpits until they looked like new.

The weather was glorious. Some people think that Saudi Arabia is always unbearably hot. In the summer yes, but the winter weather is superb - warm crisp days with minimum humidity followed by clear cool nights. Occasionally there is a thunderstorm, like the one we'd experienced en route. The rain is brief and heavy and clears out quickly. And sometimes there are sandstorms when the wind blows sandy grit into every crevice and crack. We had one of those too with the wind velocity clocked at 51 knots, which meant another round of boat cleaning. But somehow we didn't mind. *Baraka A* was our home and our refuge. When the rounds of visiting, family meals and media interviews threatened to suffocate us, we would escape to the peace of our boat. There, with the gentle waters of Obhur Creek lapping against the hull, we found some peaceable moments which restored our minds and bodies for the next round of socialising.

Our repair list was not extensive and we managed to complete it quickly. We counted ourselves lucky to find replacement parts for the refrigerator, autohelm and depth sounder. And then we found out the SatNav wasn't working - again! I did my usual fiddling and jiggling and shouting to no avail. With no repair facilities in Jeddah, I decided to take the SatNav and fly to England and find out once and for all what ailed it.

Sherry's Journal, Jeddah

While Jameel was in London seeing to the SatNav, I stayed behind in Jeddah with my in-laws and spent the time buying the last items on our list for the next leg of the trip, the fresh produce, eggs, bread, cheese and meat. We'd already made the other major purchases, everything from new clothes to basic provisions to the 'goodies' we liked so much on night watch: dates, raisins and nuts. I made sure that we had enough foul medames to see us through to Casablanca. These hearty beans were the mainstay of our diet at sea. Shopping in Jeddah was so easy compared to other places because everything was available in the huge shopping centres. By the time Jameel returned from London with a new SatNav antenna, all the shopping was done and we were ready to go except for one last minute chore, rounding up Jameel's diving equipment and oxygen tanks. We would be sailing near some spectacular reefs where Jameel hoped to enjoy the sport he loves. There's no better diving anywhere than in the Red Sea.

On Saturday March 18th, I undid the mooring lines, turned on the engine and motored out of Obhur Creek, headed for the Jeddah Islamic Port which meant back tracking 30 kilometres. Sherry sat in the cockpit where I serenaded her with 'Happy Birthday'. Exactly one year before we'd done the same thing, celebrated Sherry's birthday while casting off the lines as we said goodbye to Taboga and set sail for the Galapagos. It seemed like a lifetime ago.

A gentle breeze that barely rippled the surface of the sea invited us to raise the sails and we spent a pleasant few hours drifting along and enjoying our last glimpses of Jeddah for who knew how many months.

The Jeddah Islamic Port is a commercial harbour filled with freighters and oil tankers, huge container ships and, on March 18, one small 31 foot sailboat. Soon after we arrived we discovered that no one really knew what they were supposed to do with us and so we were shuffled from one official to the next, each one as confused as his predecessor about the correct protocol for a sailboat. Finally, I stumbled upon an official who knew about us from the TV and radio coverage and he promised to cut through the red tape and get the departure documents ready and stamped, which was a promise he kept.

I knew what we were *supposed* to do next. The rule is that after the exit visa is stamped, you must leave the country *at once*. Setting off in the dark into a body of water infested with freighters and oil tankers was at the bottom of the list of ways to spend an evening. Better to leave in the morning. Was there a way to circumvent the rules? While dusk fell I puttered around the boat as if we were getting ready to leave. If anyone asked me why we were still tied to the dock I had a ready excuse – engine problems.

Meanwhile Sherry remained below cooking a delicious dinner to celebrate her birthday. I wished that I had been competent to take over the galley just this once. I could throw a meal together in a pinch but 'delicious' was not part of my vocabulary.

Baraka A **Log – March 19**

Left Jeddah harbour at 5 a.m. with no one the wiser that we'd spent the night there. Sea was rough. Wind started at 10 knots and increased to 20 knots which gave us a very rough ride.

Sherry's Journal, March 19,
en route to Hurghada Egypt, 465 miles

The sky was grim and the waves high. We put the sails up but the motion was very uncomfortable, waves crashing over the bow, getting us and the cockpit wet. I started feeling seasick immediately even though I took some Stugeron last night and again this morning. I couldn't stay inside at all. We put the awning up and I found some shelter under it. The wind was blowing from the north and it was cold.

After tacking for a few hours then plotting our position, we found that we were going backwards toward Port Sudan. Impossible to sail with the wind and current against us so we motored at about 3 knots. An awful day.

Back at sea! I should have been overjoyed but, if the truth be known, I was more than frustrated by the weather conditions.

Given the choice, we probably would have stayed put in Jeddah until the weather improved but, once our papers had been stamped with an exit visa, we had to leave, like it or not, or face an awful bureaucratic tangle. Maybe the next time around I wouldn't be lucky enough to find an official willing to take us in hand.

With the wind coming straight at us, the boat ploughed over the swells and troughs, and crashed through the breakers. Cold saltwater cascaded over the foredeck, right back to the cockpit drenching our bodies and spirits.

I had never seen Sherry so seasick. Even with Stugeron to ward off the nausea, she found it impossible to stay below out of the wind and the weather. Huddled under the awning shivering, I could only suppose that she wished she were any place else.

In an attempt to lessen the motion and hopefully increase our speed, I decided to try tacking instead of heading straight into the wind. Not a successful manoeuvre, as it turned out. Off the port rail lay the continent of Africa. On a starboard tack the current seemed to lift us up and carry us towards the coast. Forced on to a starboard tack, we basically sailed back across the same stretch of water, losing a bit of ground each time.

"No headway, no good," I concluded and abandoned tacking until the current lessened, disappeared or turned in our favour.

Baraka A Log – March 19

Lots of marine traffic. Sherry called it a 'highway of ships'. We came across one anchored in the middle of the Red Sea flying a Russian flag. I contacted it by VHF radio, thinking perhaps that the radio operator might have an up-to-date weather forecast. For once we got an immediate response but his English and my Russian were about equal. We exchanged pleasantries for a few moments and then said goodbye.

To really make my day, the autohelm and tiller parted company which meant that I had to drill new holes for the screws, an easy enough job under normal circumstances but horrendous with the boat pounding through the water, drenching me with spray.

Bad weather was bearable, I'd found, if the price paid meant some solid miles under the keel. But our forward progress was dismal. We checked the knot metre constantly hoping the needle would edge up from the 1-3 mark to at least 5 or 6. Once or twice we managed 5 but 6 was a dream.

Sherry's Journal, March 21

This is the first day we were able to make some progress. We motor sailed averaging 5 knots, which is excellent compared to the usual 1-2 knots. Saw only five ships today and passed by Zaborgad Island. Good weather didn't last long. Around 8 p.m. the wind shifted back to the north and picked up to 20 knots. Then the sea got rough again which made me feel sick. We had hoped to reach Hurghada by March 23. Impossible in this weather. Where is the beautiful Red Sea I wrote about in my journal.

***Baraka A* Log - March 23**

Weather is still bad. Barometer is rising to 1027. The sky is cloudy and red. It has been rough since the beginning.

Sherry's Journal, March 23

Last night we took such a beating - rough seas, huge waves, 27 knot winds. So today we decided to head for the closest anchorage, which turned out to be Marsa Tarifa on the Egyptian side of the Red Sea. After anchoring we looked around and discovered that we'd found not only a safe secure anchorage, but a truly beautiful place. The water was so clear that we could see the fish darting through the coral reefs. From the pristine sand beach, the desert stretched as far as the eye could see to the low-lying, almost flat, mountains in the distance. In the haze of late afternoon they appeared to be bluish-grey. Reminded me of a giant sleeping caterpillar.

Soon after we anchored, the coastguard came to visit and check our documents. Then the two officers invited us for tea and we whiled away the afternoon hours talking to them about our trip. Later Sherry went shell hunting while I shot video footage and bought some freshly-caught fish from one of the locals on the beach. That night we enjoyed char-broiled fish on our new portable barbecue.

I placed a call to my aunt in Egypt just to say hello and tell her that we were okay. She said that she was glad to hear from me because my cousin Magrid and other family members had planned a huge reception for us at the Suez Yacht Club in Suez City on Monday, March 28.

I explained that we'd made plans to meet up with some sailing friends from our Indian Ocean days in Hurghada.

"The reception cannot be changed," said my aunt. "There will be all sorts of officials present to honour you and Sherry."

What could I do but promise that we would be there and ponder what might have happened had I not, just on a whim, decided to make that call. Next I contacted *Svanhild* and *Lady Rose* who were waiting for us in Hurghada and told them about the reception.

"A slight change of plans," I said. "Can we meet in Suez City instead?"

Svanhild and *Lady Rose* replied that not coming to Hurghada was probably the wisest thing we could do. They were more than anxious to leave. Apparently the wind around Hurghada followed a predictable cycle. For eight to ten days there would be fierce winds, up to 50 knots, followed by three days of decent weather when we could make some headway. The nice weather was due to begin the next day.

We awoke on the morning of the 24th and found that the good weather days had indeed kicked in. The wind had dropped and the sea appeared calm so we raised the anchor and set off again, our new destination Suez City.

After so many weeks of living with landlubbers, talking with our sailing friends the previous evening was just the tonic Sherry and I needed. As we sailed along enjoying the fair winds and moderate seas, some dolphins dropped by to show off the new additions to the family. We had never seen such tiny babies.

The next morning the congenial weather was still with us. Through the morning haze we could see the outline of Hurghada in the distance, but we just waved as we continued pushing ahead at a respectable 5.3 knots. We saw some pilot whales but as usual, by the time I got the video camera out, they had disappeared.

Well, all good things must end. Around 8 p.m. that evening I knew that we were in for it when the wind picked up to 20, then 30, then 40 knots. With the wind blowing like crazy, the sea soon became very agitated. Huge breakers, their crests decorated with foam, tossed us around like a plastic toy. Every time the bow met an oncoming wave, *Baraka A* became a submarine, burying her nose in it while tons of water washed over us. A lot of it found its way to the bilges via the anchor locker in the bow.

I wished Roy Mullender could have seen 'the two pairs of hands' working in concert that night. Because the autohelm could not hold a course, one of us had to stay on the tiller while the other pumped water out of the bilges at ten minute intervals. Then the SatNav quit and the whisker pole broke in two and flew overboard. I could survive without the whisker pole but the SatNav was crucial! What a time not to know our position, with ship traffic and oil rigs all around us and the visibility down to nothing. I grabbed the flare gun, hoping that a ship bearing down on us might see us and change course.

To make my bad problems even worse, the depth sounder began to register zero. I made a mental list of why I had to assume the depth sounder was playing the same trick it had played on me before, picking up water bubbles and translating that into water under the keel. One, the channel was very narrow with land on both sides. Two, the number of oil tankers taking on crude at the numerous oil rigs was too frightening to contemplate. Three, I didn't know my position and even if I had there was nowhere to go.

"This storm makes the one I went through on the way to Casablanca seem like a walk in the park," I told Sherry.

"Well, I'm glad you never told me the whole truth about that storm or I never would have signed on," she replied.

To sum it up – a harrowing night, our worst ever.

Sherry's Journal, March 26

The storm lasted all night and continued on today as well. The boat was hit by very big waves; one filled the whole cockpit, another went through the companionway into the cabin, soaking our bunks. I remembered other storms in the Atlantic and Pacific when we just hove to, went inside, closed the hatch and waited it out. Impossible this time because of the ships in the vicinity and the narrow channel. Jameel said that if he could find a stretch of beach he'd run Baraka A aground and call it quits.

Before dawn we contacted our Norwegian friends aboard *Svanhild* who now had *Lady Rose* in tow because of engine problems they had failed to resolve in Hurghada. While we were exchanging information about our respective difficulties during this terrible storm, which was still with us, a radio operator aboard one of the oil tankers broke in.

"We have you on our radar. I'll give you a compass bearing for Ras Gharib and guide you in."

"Thank you. We appreciate your help," I replied, which seemed like an inadequate response under the circumstances.

True to his word, the radio operator gave me the bearing and stayed with us until we entered the harbour. We dropped anchor at 8 a.m. exhausted, grateful and happy to have made it safe and sound.

Svanhild and *Lady Rose* soon joined us and after a round or two of 'Wasn't that an awful night?' we headed for our bunks which by then were stripped bare as Sherry had hung all our wet bedding on the lifelines to dry.

By late afternoon we felt rested enough to have lunch and reassess the weather conditions. Since the wind had definitely died down, we decided to head out and try our luck. Again, that old enemy time was snapping at our heels. In two days we had to be in Suez City.

Sherry's Journal, March 27

The weather was kind to us all last night and today, flat calms which meant that we had to motor but we made good speed, averaging 6 knots. 'Svanhild' with 'Lady Rose' in tow, was just ahead of us and we were able to keep them in sight all day.

Around midday we motored into Masaiia Anchor, one after another like ducks in a row. Tomorrow is our big day when our family and friends and the local officials will welcome us to Egypt with a reception in our honour. 'Svanhild' has promised to take video footage.

Once we were anchored, Jameel called the harbour officers and asked them to process the immigration and customs papers for our friends and ourselves as expediently as possible. They came immediately, picked up the passports and crew lists and promised that all formalities would be completed so we could leave early tomorrow morning for the Suez Yacht Club. Hope everything goes well. Inshallah.

Chapter Twenty-One

Sherry's Journal, March 28

Woke early and gave the boat a final cleaning. Jameel contacted the Suez Yacht Club and was advised to leave Masaiia Anchor around 11.15 a.m. This time Baraka A *was the lead duck with* Svanhild *and* Lady Rose *bringing up the rear. About half-way to Suez City we were met by two power boats. Through the binoculars I could see our friends and relatives waving and smiling from one of the boats. What a moment!*

It wasn't until we reached the Suez Yacht Club and were formally introduced that we learned the identity of the two people on the other boat. We were past impressed to overwhelmed. Ahmed Al Desouki was not only the Deputy Minister of Defence but a consultant to the Suez Planning and Development Board. Fathi Socar was the head of the biggest marine services company in Suez. His business was booming due to the number of recreational boats now entering the Mediterranean via the Red Sea.

Once on the jetty, we were received by the Governor of Suez, the Secretary to the Minister of Youth, and the usual media circus of journalists and TV crews. And, of course, our families. I had expected all my Egyptian relatives to be present but my mother and father?!

"You never mentioned one word about coming to Egypt," I said, kissing my mother on the cheek.

"Then it wouldn't have been a surprise," she replied.

After a welcoming speech by the Governor, we adjourned to the Yacht Club for lunch, which was just the beginning. More speeches, television interviews and entertainment by a troupe of folk singers and dancers filled the afternoon hours. We were presented with the Emblem of the Suez Canal, one of Egypt's most prestigious awards. Later, when Sherry was presented with a beautiful floral tribute, I saw her fighting hard to hold back the tears. My emotions were riding pretty close to the surface too. Although Sherry and I had both been born and raised in Egypt, we had not lived as permanent residents of that country for many years and never imagined that we would be welcomed home with such enthusiasm and genuine affection.

The afternoon was just a wind-up for another party at the Yacht Club which continued through the evening. Our host was the Governor of Suez, who had issued a blanket invitation to all foreign sailors in port to join us. What a night renewing the acquaintance of dozens of people we'd met at various anchorages during the past fourteen months at sea! Sailors from Sweden, America, Australia and, of course, Norway. Somewhere in the crowd were *Lady Rose* and *Svanhild*. I hoped the video camera was still rolling.

The only ones missing were John and Dorothy from *Socorro*. But from other sailing friends we learned that they were in the Sudan and planning on coming to Suez to meet us. That bit of news, made the day perfect.

As we walked back to *Baraka A* that evening I gazed out over the harbour at all the boats flying the Egyptian flag.

"Another first for us," I told Sherry. "Usually we stand out because we're the *only* ones with an Egyptian flag."

"We still stand out," Sherry retorted. "Look at our flag, so faded and frayed. It's a disgrace. All the others look so new."

"Well, a lot of them probably are new," I replied. "They're courtesy flags. Remember when we got to Australia, the first thing I did was buy an Australian flag and put it on the lanyard with the others as a courtesy to our host country."

"I remember," Sherry replied. "But I still think we should get a new one."

"Agreed. I'll put it at the top of the shopping list."

Sherry's Journal, March 29

Yesterday was a day that will stay with me for ever. We held on till after midnight before saying goodnight to all the yachties and collapsing into our bunks. My legs ached from all the standing, something I'm not used to doing aboard a boat.

This morning we visited with the Governor of Suez and discussed how his country could encourage sailors to take the Red Sea route instead of sailing south to the Cape of Good Hope. We showed him some pages we had photocopied from a book by Alan Lucas, none of it very complimentary.

"We don't agree with much of this," I explained, placing the papers on his desk. "But other people who read it are going to take it as the truth. I think the biggest concern people have about this part of the world is the tangle of paperwork they face and the fear of getting held up because of inadequate documents. From my own experience, sailors don't mind paying a fair price for services or even offering a small tip for a job well done. But when nothing gets done without the baksheesh, then sailors become wary."

The minister sighed.

"Such a difficult problem. We have become more determined to deal with it and have seen results."

"That's what I heard from other sailors at the dock here. The situation is much improved. Realise, I am only reporting what I have heard and read. From my own experience over the past couple days, I would say this is one of the most hospitable and friendly places we've visited."

Next on the agenda was lunch with Fathi Socar, head of marine services for Suez, who asked for our input on how to make Suez more 'sailor friendly'. After the welcome we had received, the temptation to say that everything was just fine was the easy way out. But then I reasoned that he wouldn't be asking our advice if all he wanted was a rubber stamp. So again, we gave as honest an answer as we could. Make it easy and safe for sailors to come and go and they will stop and visit you.

We also visited the Ministry of Tourism where I floated an idea which had been percolating in my head for months past several officials. What if I made a single-handed trip by kayak from the Aswan High Dam to Cairo? A distance of only 800 miles but a gruelling trip. Going with the current, I figured it would take me seven days. It came as no surprise that Sherry was as frosty about the idea as she had been about the purchase of the kayak so many months ago in Cairns.

"Please, Jameel, let's finish this adventure before you can start dreaming up another one."

The Minister of Tourism himself backed her up.

"Far too dangerous. There are long stretches of the Nile where you would be totally cut off for days. We could not be responsible for you. Imagine the consequences for our office. We welcome you home as a hero one day and send you into danger the next."

Sherry flashed me a triumphant smile then grabbed the Minister of Tourism by the hand and said thank you at least three times.

At least she didn't leap into the air and shout 'Yea!'

In the afternoon we anchored *Baraka A* away from the docks, off-loaded the diving gear and two oxygen tanks which I had not used once on our Red Sea journey. That miscalculation would be something to laugh about somewhere down the road. I also reluctantly unlashed that other bone of contention from its place on the bow. I had to give Sherry credit. She hadn't niggled me too many times about my kayak purchase but, oh, how she hated the way it cluttered up the foredeck. Now my brilliant idea had been broadsided. But, just for the present, I reminded myself as I loaded all our gear into the taxi. New days and new challenges lay just over the horizon.

When we reached the apartment which we call home while in Cairo, we decided on an early night. After dinner we watched ourselves on the 9 o'clock TV news then tumbled into bed.

Sherry's Journal, At Home in Cairo

This is the first time Jameel and I have had so much fun playing tour guide. Our friends from Svanhild *and* Lady Rose *make us see our country through a newcomer's eyes. They are enchanted with this city and its history and its fine food. We've had some memorable evenings at our favourite restaurants. To save them from driving back to their boats each night after a full day of sightseeing and shopping, we found an apartment for them in Cairo.*

Will the surprises never end? We have been invited by the Ministry of Tourism to spend 3 days as their guests in Luxor and Aswan. Even though we called Egypt home for years, neither of us have ever visited these historic sights. There's a small catch. We have to hold a press conference at the Ministry of Youth before departing. It should be interesting. We have so much to share.

We arrived at the Ministry of Youth at 12 noon, the appointed hour, well ahead of the reporters and journalists. When everyone was assembled, we were ushered into a conference room, served tea and then Sherry and I began answering questions with the aid of a map of the world on the wall behind us.

The questions were the same ones we'd answered over and over many times before. Whose idea was it? How did Sherry feel about it? What countries had we visited? Where did we sleep? What did we eat? How did we spend our days at sea? What about dangerous storms?

When the press conference concluded, the minister closed with a brief speech, the gist of which will remain with me forever. He lauded our courage and persistence in face of a mountain of disapproval, both official and familial. He also admired our pluck to undertake such a journey without one cent of commercial sponsorship.

"You are the first but you will not be the last," he said. "Your circumnavigation will rekindle the spirit of adventure and daring which is part of your culture just like a man who went before you, Prince Sultan bin Salman bin Abdulaziz, the first Arab in space."

"That's what I've been saying all along," I whispered to Sherry as we left the minister's office.

"I know, Jameel, but somehow it sounds different coming from him."

Sherry's Journal, Luxor

We left Cairo after our press conference and were met by a guide at the Luxor airport who took us to our five star hotel, The Isis. That first evening we visited the Luxor Museum and the Karnak Temple where we enjoyed a 'light and sound' show.

Splendid. In the temple everything around us was magnificent, the statues, the walls, the pillars.

Our room was lovely, overlooking a garden and swimming pool. But we didn't get to sleep in. Our guide was there by 8 a.m. Our second day, we visited the 'Valley of the Kings and the Valley of the Queens', took a ferry ride on the Nile and visited an alabaster workshop. Bought a beautiful alabaster vase and will carry it in my hands all the way back to Cairo.

The next morning we were supposed to take a plane to Aswan but the flight was cancelled due to mechanical problems. The alternative was a 4 hour journey by bus in the heat. So we decided to stay on in Luxor. Good thing. Right after lunch Jameel began to feel very sick, with an upset stomach and a high temperature which was probably food poisoning. He went to bed and stayed there. Tomorrow we will fly back to Cairo.

When we arrived back in Cairo, we found that quite a few articles about our voyage had appeared in various newspapers and magazines. We also found that John and Dorothy from *Socorro* had made it safely to Suez and had already hooked up with our Norwegian friends. We invited John and Dorothy to stay with us in our apartment so that all the yachties would be in one place. Then Sherry and I resumed our job as tour guides taking our friends everywhere – to the pyramids, museums, the sphinx, the ancient mosques, the gold souk and through the twisting alleys that made up the old city. Would I admit that some of these places were as new to us as our guests?

In our spare moments we gave follow-up interviews to the media, posed for photographs and answered hundreds of questions. Did we ever grow tired of the constant barrage of publicity? Not really. We wanted the world to know what we were doing and why and there was no way to accomplish that by keeping quiet.

By mid-April we had made the decision not to sail on to the Mediterranean with our friends but to stay on in Cairo through Ramadan. Last year we'd been at sea during Ramadan. This holy month of fasting is a special time for Muslims to get in touch with their spiritual selves. To accomplish this, the faithful fast from dawn till sunset when the fast is broken with dates and sweet drinks. The evenings are spent renewing family ties, visiting friends, exchanging presents and attending family dinners.

There were pragmatic reasons to delay our departure as well. Like boat repairs. Luckily, Obeon, our friend on *Svanhild* who was a mechanical genius, was able to solve my most critical problem, the SatNav. But there was the new oven to bolt in place and the refrigerator to repair (again).

Also we'd decided that cruising the Mediterranean would not degenerate into something we had to do to complete the circumnavigation. No, we would take the opportunity to explore this beautiful body of water with all its varied and interesting ports of call. Weatherwise, it only made sense for hot weather people like Sherry and myself to wait for the breezes to become balmy.

The middle of May seemed appropriate, right after Eid Al Fitr, which is the holiday week following Ramadan when the population tries to get the days and nights back in their proper place.

Sherry's Journal, April 30

While we waited for the weather to warm up, Jameel spent many hours working on the boat which was anchored at Suez City. Driving home on the night of April 30th, a car came out of the desert on the wrong side of the road and ploughed into our Mazda. Our driver was at the wheel, Jameel in what we call the 'gun shot' seat. At 1.30 a.m. I got a call from Jameel telling me that he'd been in an accident and was at a friend's house with a broken nose and elbow. I agreed to meet him at the hospital. The next morning at 8 a.m. they took him to surgery. He looked terrible. When he came out of surgery he looked even worse with his nose so stuffed with packing that he couldn't breathe. Also his elbow was very painful.

What Jameel said was so true.

"After spending all those months at sea where nothing happened to us, I come back to land and get into a car accident."

As soon as the anaesthetic wore off, I spoke to the doctor who gave me not very encouraging news. This was no simple break. The doctor had pinned my shattered arm in several places. I would be in a cast for three weeks. Then it would be removed so the stitches could be taken out after which my arm would be put in another cast for two more weeks. Prognosis: after the removal of the second cast, I would need a minimum of three months of physical therapy before I could expect the arm to function anywhere near normal. That made a total of over four months!

Sherry's concern was my broken arm and nose while mine centred on whether we would be able to sail the Mediterranean as planned during the summer months. The worst case scenario was having to delay our trip till the following summer. The media seemed more than ready to seize on that possibility.

"I can't tell you whether we will go on or abandon our plans till next year," I explained. "It all depends on how quickly my arm responds to therapy."

To my doctor's dismay I was not a patient patient. The second cast was supposed to stay in place for two weeks but I grew depressed over the spectre of a non-functioning arm and removed the cast myself after ten days so I could begin the exercises. What I saw depressed me even more: a thin shrivelled appendage, so atrophied that I could not straighten it out or make a fist. I had faced adversity with fortitude and optimism many times in my life but this withered arm brought me close to tears.

What to do? Sherry prodded me to get a second opinion. We asked ourselves the obvious questions - who and where? And then like someone lifted a curtain, we had our answer. Our physician and friend in Palo Alto was a man we trusted implicitly. He would refer us to a top orthopaedic surgeon and hopefully lay my fears to rest.

On May 28 we had planned on basking in the sun somewhere in the Mediterranean. Instead we were flying over oceans and continents to America. Two days after our arrival, I found myself consulting with an orthopaedic specialist in Menlo Park, California.

"The X-rays show your arm is healing very well," he said. "Now we have to get you started on a vigorous physical therapy programme."

"Will it take three months before my arm is back to normal?"

"Not if you work hard and consistently. But you won't have full mobility until the pins are removed."

"Will I be able to move it enough to sail a boat?"

"Let's see how the therapy goes, but I anticipate food results."

No patient ever followed his doctor's orders so diligently. Every day I worked on strengthening my arm, going through all the prescribed exercises no matter how much it hurt. At first my arm seemed as weak and useless as ever but I persisted and soon the strength began to return. I was never able to straighten my arm until the pins were removed some months later after I returned to Jeddah. Just as the American doctor had predicted.

Sherry's Journal, Menlo Park, California

This accident caused an abrupt change in our lives. Having to leave the boat in Suez City and fly to the States has not been all bad. We rented an apartment and a car and have been enjoying the California lifestyle. There are so many channels on the TV, so many restaurants to check out. There will be some real adjustments when we go back to sea after living on land for two and a half months. We will have to learn to discipline ourselves all over again.

Menlo Park is as beautiful as ever. If there is a place on land where I could choose to live, it would be here in California, where we lived for five years. The hills and valleys are covered with evergreen trees. The sun is shining and the birds singing. The only problem is the price of real estate – sky high. It will be expensive to find a good piece of land.

Jameel's therapy continues to go well. But my biggest worry is what happens if he hurts his elbow while we're at sea and ends up with a useless right arm. On a 31 foot boat you bang your elbows a lot on winch handles or on anything at all when the boat rocks. Jameel might need a permanent elastic padded cover to protect his elbow. He is considering wearing his life harness at all times as an extra safety measure.

With time on my hands between physical therapy sessions, I decided to look for a new SatNav, a Magnavox with an interface card instead of an antenna. I always believed the SatNav itself to be a superb piece of equipment. I believed the problems I'd encountered were caused by incorrect installation of the antennae which sometimes I'd been able to overcome, and sometimes not. Just my luck. The Magnavox had to be ordered and wouldn't be ready for a month - too long. In a month we hoped to be back at sea. So we would make do with our old SatNav and keep our fingers crossed.

On July 2nd we boarded a plane and flew back to Cairo, just six weeks after the accident. The doctor okayed the continuation of the voyage but warned me to be careful and advised me, in no-nonsense terms, to wear the padded elbow cover while at sea. With Sherry on the doctor's side, what could I do but agree.

We spent ten days in Cairo visiting the family and attempting to persuade them that my arm was okay. Hadn't I had been pronounced fit and ready to go by our American doctor? Well, maybe, but why had the doctor in Cairo been so adamant about a three month course of physiotherapy? I fielded the questions as best I could and then escaped with Sherry to buy provisions. Never had shopping seemed like so much fun.

Sherry also tried to get a visa for Gibraltar through the British Consulate. For some reason this is a requirement for Egyptians but not Saudis. She filled out the forms and sent the bank draft as instructed. We waited and waited, but no visa. The Consulate advised patience. But our patience was running out. Should we wait around for it to arrive or sort the problem out when we reached Gibraltar. Sherry, who was as anxious as I was to get underway, agreed that we should take the latter course.

Sherry's Journal, July 13 Cairo

After spending 10 days in Cairo we returned to Suez City to get the boat ready. We plan to leave here on the 15th. Bad news awaited us at Suez City. Someone had stolen all our dock lines, two fenders, our generator, and a plastic box with bits and pieces - junk to anyone else but for Jameel irreplaceable. The valise for the life raft had been opened so we knew that they had thought about taking that too.

This act of vandalism and thievery could not be the work of the locals. We were too well known. No, it was probably another sailor who had helped himself to our things before departing.

I was more disappointed than angry. I had always thought that sailors lived by a unique set of rules where honesty and camaraderie and helping one another were considered an inviolable code of ethics.

Sherry shrugged off my philosophical mutterings. She was as angry as a hornet and spent more than a few moments fantasising what she would do to the thieves if she ever found them.

In the end we went to a marine supply store in Suez City and replaced the missing items.

Chapter Twenty-Two

We left Suez City on July 15, bound for Ismailia which is the southern terminus of the Suez Canal. What a feeling to be back at sea after three and a half months' incarceration on land. Too much time ashore and the walls started to close in, making me feel like I really was in a prison. Only at sea did I experience a feeling of complete freedom. I could go where the winds took me, following a timetable that was my own. Being in charge of my life was what counted most. I could take a break from the 'must do's' that clutter up everyone's agenda. Family obligations and social necessities were just the tip of the iceberg. At sea there were no bills arriving in the mail, no leaking roofs to be fixed or gardens that needed cultivating.

I knew that Sherry would argue with me: 'Give me a break, Jameel. This freedom you're talking about doesn't exist aboard *Baraka A*. There's always something or other that *must* be done. Not tomorrow but right now! And your timetable doesn't leave *me* with much freedom to relax. We're always leaving one anchorage so we can hurry to the next one.'

I replayed this imaginary retort a few times and conceded that Sherry had a point. Maybe freedom was the wrong word. But a phrase like 'the opportunity to challenge my sense of adventure' was too cumbersome to make much sense.

On board *Baraka A* was our pilot and, per the marine regulations in this crowded and difficult stretch of water, he kept his hand on the tiller for the entire 70 mile trip. Yes, I conceded, even at sea there were rules which must be followed.

We arrived at our destination, Ismailia, by 11 a.m. which left the whole day yawning in front of us. We started off with lunch at the yacht club where we were the only patrons. No fun at all. Nothing to do but head back to the boat and wait for morning, when we would make the passage through the Suez Canal into the Mediterranean.

Late that afternoon two sailboats arrived from Port Said, which is the northern terminus of the Suez Canal. They were heading for Australia. We spent the afternoon talking, like sailors always do, exchanging information on the good places to anchor and the ones to avoid, the weather and wind conditions and the availability of provisions which always meant diesel. Man can live off canned food, even bread and water, but an engine must have a proper diet of fuel!

The next morning, our pilot who had promised to arrive at 5 a.m., finally showed up at 8. Then there was another delay while we waited for a monster Esso tanker, which took up the entire canal, to get out of our way. Finally at 9 a.m., with fog hanging in the shrouds like a giant spider's web, we set off. As we puttered along I thought back to our other canal crossing eighteen months before and marvelled at the contrast. During the trip through the Panama Canal we'd travelled lashed together with two other boats through a cut in a tropical jungle. This time we were a solo act with just our pilot for company and the barren desert on either side of the canal was as far away from a jungle as you could get.

Known as 'the Big Ditch', the Suez Canal, 190 kilometres in length stretches north and south across the Isthmus of Suez. Because there is no difference in the level of the Red and Mediterranean Seas, there are no locks.

Sherry, as usual, had all the facts about the Suez Canal at her fingertips.

"Just imagine this, Jameel. When this canal was opened in 1869 it shortened the distance between England and India by 9700 kilometres." She paused. "That's a lot of kilometres."

"Not as long a trip as crossing the Pacific. That was 8000 miles, not kilometres."

Sherry turned back to her book.

"This canal was only 8 metres deep when it was built, 22 metres wide at the bottom and 70 metres wide on the surface. That seems really small. How did ships get through it?"

"Ships were smaller," I replied. "Our size and a bit bigger."

"It says here that the canal has been enlarged several times and is now 19 metres deep and 226 metres across. I think the Panama Canal was much more picturesque."

"That's a simple matter of geography," I replied. "Think of the historical significance. Imagine how much time and revenue have been saved because ships can pass through these canals and not go the long way around. Before they were built, ocean voyages must have been horrendous, a real test of skill and endurance."

By midday the fog had burned off and a blistery sun sent us scurrying for cover under the canopy. Then, as the afternoon progressed, the winds picked up to 18 knots, hitting us right on the nose which naturally slowed our progress.

We arrived in Port Said at 5 p.m. after a tedious journey that had taken us eight hours. Although the pilot had been at the helm the entire distance, we were exhausted and my elbow ached.

Sherry's Journal, Port Said

After dropping the pilot, we headed for the Port Said Yacht Club, thinking it would be as low-key and deserted as the one in Ismailia. A very different reception awaited 'those two Arabs going around the world'. The yacht club staff and members had read about our adventures in the Egyptian newspapers and had seen us on TV and we were given a rousing welcome. We felt like real celebrities when we were introduced to the Commodore and invited to be his guests at dinner. That evening we met a group of sea scouts who had come to the yacht club for their regular weekly meeting. Evidently they had been tracking our progress and were so excited to meet us and hear about our trip. They asked us dozens of questions. At the end of the evening they sang us a song they had composed about Baraka A. *As usual, I had to fight back the tears. What a touching tribute.*

The sea scouts kept us entertained all evening. Their enthusiasm was contagious. How I hoped to carry some of that back with me to Jeddah and infect the young men of my country with the itch to raise the sails and follow the wind.

The next morning we hoped for an early start but when the Commodore invited us to be his guests at lunch we could not say no. Nor could we refuse his offer to show us around Port Said and to stay over another night and meet the Past Commodore of the yacht club and some other officials.

Sherry was delighted about this delay, having heard from some arriving sailors about the 25 knot winds, 'out there'. Sherry never liked leaving port unless the wind and weather conditions were ideal, meaning no chop and light breezes not exceeding 15 knots - a rare event.

"You've been through 40 knot blows and you know the boat can take it," I reminded her. "Even you have learned to take it."

"But never by choice," Sherry reminded me. "Doesn't it make sense to wait for the winds to drop a bit?"

"Okay, one more day. But I'm anxious to get moving."

That evening after a sumptuous buffet dinner we sat in the yacht club lounge enjoying a panoramic view of the harbour from the wide windows of the club house. Again everyone was interested in the whys and wherefores of our voyage. We could predict the parade of questions and the answers we knew by heart. But that evening the talk drifted to another topic, not a new one for us - what could be done to encourage sailors to sail through the canal to the Med?

"I think if you acknowledge a problem exists, you are halfway to finding a solution," I replied.

Several men nodded their heads in agreement.

"I've heard that some ship agents charge as much as four hundred dollars to cross the canal," I continued. "That's a lot of money. Some people think if you own a boat you must be rich but the truth is that most sailors are very short of cash. As I told the authorities in Suez City, no one objects to paying a reasonable price for services. But a man who pits himself against the seas has earned and deserves fair treatment which translates into good value for money. If this route costs more than is affordable or equitable, the word goes out on the sailor's grapevine.

***Baraka A* Log - July 18th**

Left Port Said at 9 a.m. headed for Cyprus, 237 miles to the west. Wind gusting 15-22 knots, sea choppy. Sherry was not used to the motion and got very seasick. Even Stugeron didn't help. Average speed was 6 knots in spite of the rolling and lurching and rounding up. First time at the tiller and my arm seemed okay. Decided to forego elbow pad which

made my arm feel like it was in a vice. Sherry fussed (and continued to do so for the rest of the voyage) but the elbow pad remained in the V-berth in its box, undisturbed!

Sherry's Journal, July 18

A horrible first day. I threw up all morning, I rested this afternoon but when I woke up I felt too sick to cook so we managed with sandwiches, mangoes and sweets.

***Baraka A* Log – July 19**

Sighted a destroyer this morning at dawn. It looked like a ghost ship through the fog. Later a low flying aircraft made two passes over the boat. I wondered who was checking us out and then saw the markings on the fuselage. It was an Israeli fighter jet. We got out the video camera and took some footage. Before heading home he passed over us once again and did a couple of flips, then waggled his wings before disappearing.

Like a fool I stood in the cockpit shouting, "Say hello to our friends Claude and Emilia Allouch and tell them we remember all the fun we had with them anchored in Cook's Bay in Mooréa." I wondered if they were still at sea.

We sailed through the fog towards Cyprus on the morning of July 20. Having no charts for the area made me nervous but I'd worked out a plan. Once we sighted land, I'd sail parallel to it along the coast until we spotted the harbour. Luckily the fog burned off and we were able to see the breakwater and enter the harbour at Larnaca, which was crowded with sailboats. Five minutes after tying *Baraka A* to the dock, the customs and immigration officials appeared, signed the forms and officially welcomed us to Cyprus.

Imagine our surprise and delight to find *Socorro* with our dear friends John and Dorothy on board, tied up to one of the docks. We'd last seen them in Cairo before the accident. Already they'd been in Cyprus for two months and planned to stay put until the weather improved and they could make a dash for Gibraltar. We celebrated our arrival at our first Mediterranean port having dinner on shore with John and Dorothy. A great beginning to this last leg of our voyage.

Sherry's Journal, Larnaca, Cyprus

I love it here. The town is clean and the people are so polite and friendly. We have tried a few restaurants in town and rate the fried calamari and Greek salad as excellent. The facilities at the marina are wonderful – showers, laundry, grocery store, plus a welding shop and a carpentry shop, all right here. The marina is very safe and well-guarded. But best of all we have water and electricity hook ups right here on the dock. Almost like a luxury resort. We called my family today and learned that 8 of our friends are flying to Limassol which is about 40 kilometres down the road from here. They have rented an apartment so now we cannot leave immediately but must stay and visit with them! We met another boat in the harbour, Lady Catherine, *which we hadn't seen since Cairns. They have been here for over two months just like John and Dorothy. It seems that we are the only ones who rush to leave harbours.*

Seeing John and Dorothy made Sherry's spirit soar. Although I was anxious to get back to sea, I knew that I was consigned to spending a few extra days in Cyprus to visit with our friends. In my spare moments I took care of the boat chores, filled the diesel tanks and tightened the belt on the engine. Also put water in the batteries.

Sherry's Journal, Larnaca and Limassol

This is the first time in all these months at sea that friends have come to visit us. We spent 3 days with them in their apartment in Limassol and then we invited them back to the boat. Baraka A *had not experienced so many people aboard at one time since her commissioning. A wonderful 6 days of partying and eating and having a lot of fun.*

As I told Sherry, Crete was waiting for us, just 400 miles away. Nevertheless it was with a heavy heart that she bade goodbye to our Egyptian friends and John and Dorothy. We were up before the sun on July 27, our departure day, so that Sherry and Dorothy could go to the fruit and vegetable market and say goodbye to each other one last time.

By 8 a.m. we had cleared customs. Just before our planned 9 a.m. departure, a power boat with a weather fax told us that the wind was blowing 22 knots.

"I really want to get going," I told Sherry. "We've managed 22 knots lots of times. A sailboat can take the wind better than a power boat. Besides you know me, too many days in harbour drives me nuts."

"It's really not the weather," Sherry replied. "It's just so hard saying goodbye to John and Dorothy.

Sherry looked unhappy but, as always, agreed to follow my lead.

Once out of the harbour, I raised the sails and we sailed westward towards Crete on a beam reach, a point of sail which often made Sherry seasick. That day was no exception. By midday the wind had shifted further to the west, forcing us to sail close-hauled which was always a wet, rough ride. By nightfall the wind had kicked up a notch. By 4 a.m., cold wet and tired, I figured out that it had taken us fifteen hours to sail 85 miles which was just a nibble out of the pie. If the bad weather persisted we'd be out here another four days trying to chew up the remaining miles. Sherry's face was grey with fatigue and nausea. I was also dead on my feet and my arm throbbed. And so I pushed the tiller over hard, executed a 'chicken jibe' and headed back to Cyprus. This time we decided to try the harbour at Limassol.

Sherry's Journal, July 24

Why is it that wherever we go we have the wind coming right at us? This time the wind won the battle. At 4 a.m. we turned around and 10 hours later reached Cyprus. What a day and night! Awful try. We covered 85 miles back and forth in vain.

Limassol Harbour turned out to be home to nothing but fishermen, with no full service marina like we'd enjoyed in Larnaca. We were advised to sail on to the Sheraton Hotel and harbour 6 miles down the coast. On the way out of Limassol, we ran aground, a first for us, but luckily we were able to use our engine to power us out of the muck.

The Sheraton Marina was upscale compared to Larnaca. The huge and fancy sail and power yachts made our small unpretentious boat look like a poor country cousin. The marina had every facility imaginable and was very clean and very pricey so I hoped that our stay would be a short one. The wind howled all day so that even the water inside the harbour was rough. According to my readings, the barometer had been falling steadily for two days. I promised Sherry that we would not budge until the wind blew itself out. Although I was adventuresome, I was not foolhardy!

Sherry's Journal, Sheraton Marina, Cyprus, July 29

Funny weather in the Med. Yesterday, strong winds. Flat calm this morning and no breeze all day. We decided to stay here and leave tomorrow since the barometer is rising.

An American couple on a 38 footer came to see our boat and talk to us about the circumnavigation. They invited us to their boat this evening where we met a couple from Iceland who own a 70 foot power boat. Wherever we go there are always interesting people to meet.

Tomorrow we will try again to sail to Crete.

Chapter Twenty-Three

This morning, July 30, as we motored out of the harbour, there appeared to be no wind at all. The sea was mirror flat even though the marine weather forecast had predicted gale force winds to the south of Crete. What to believe? Just in case, we decided to take the northern route in the hope of missing the worst of the nasty weather, should it appear. I turned on the engine and let the autohelm do the work. Sherry, who was feeling much better, concocted a delicious lunch.

An interesting day with lots of sailboats, too many to count, heading off in every direction. I remembered on the big oceans how seeing another boat was a major event and often rated a log note.

Sherry sat, fascinated, watching a sea snake swim around the boat with its head out of the water as if checking us over. Most sea snakes are poisonous. In the Red Sea I always gave them a wide berth.

***Baraka A* Log – July 30**

The weather in the Med is unpredictable. This morning no wind so we motored. By early afternoon the wind had picked up enough for us to raise the sails. By nightfall we were enjoying a 10 knot breeze which was pushing us along at 4-5 knots. Good speed, considering we were fighting the current.

Sherry's Journal, July 31

This morning the wind was perfect, 10-12 knots with a flat sea. We made good progress until noon when the wind picked up to 22 knots and changed direction, coming straight at us again.

We didn't want a repeat of oulast attempt to reach Crete so we decided to change course and by-pass Crete altogether. Our new destination was the Greek island of Kastellorizon, just off the coast of Southern Turkey. All afternoon we beat into the wind, which had veered the moment we changed course. Just knowing that we would reach a nice anchorage tomorrow morning made it bearable.

Kastellorizon reminded me of Rotuma in the South Pacific. Both were places we never intended to visit. And both turned out to be places that would always evoke wonderful memories of our time there. Was it luck, fate, pure chance or a dogged determination to get out of the weather that sent us scurrying to Kastellorizon. A tiny dot of an island, less than ten square miles in area, located just two miles off the coast of south-west Turkey, it was definitely off the tourist beat, unlike Rhodes which was only one or two days' sail away.

We discovered that we could tie up to the dock in the harbour near the fishing fleet or anchor out in one of two bays. Naturally we chose the solitude and privacy of an anchorage. To our surprise there were no customs and immigration formalities to complete. Unlike Rotuma, this place was too small to support an office!

That afternoon, after a swim which ended up as a hull scrubbing exercise, we inflated the dinghy and rowed to shore to explore the tiny fishing village. We discovered a wonderful cosy taverna and enjoyed a lunch which included a plate of sea urchins, which is one of my favourite treats. Just like the Arabs, the Greeks prefer these delicacies with a squeeze of lemon to bring out the flavour.

Sherry's Journal, Kastellorizon, August 1

We stayed in this charming place for one perfect afternoon and evening. Meandering along the twisting cobblestone streets of the village, we drank in the scenery – tiny whitewashed houses with brightly coloured doors and windows, mountain peaks rising from the centre of the island, weathered stony beaches where water as clear as crystal lapped the shore. On the edge of the village we explored some ruins; I'm guessing that they were from the Byzantine era. Before returning to Baraka A, *we filled our jerry cans with diesel in preparation for our departure tomorrow.*

The following morning at 8 a.m., we waved goodbye to Kastellorizon and set our course for Rhodes, completely abandoning our plans to head straight for Crete. If Kastellorizon was a sample of the beauty of the Greek islands, then we wanted to see more!

"I love this kind of sailing," said Sherry. "It's just like our trip along the Great Barrier Reef. You sail a few hours, stop and relax and then sleep at night instead of standing watch. Even if the weather turns bad, there are so many places to run and hide and most of them are pretty close."

As we sailed along the rugged Turkish coast, Sherry dived for her travel books and gave me a geography lesson.

"There are six thousand Greek islands," she informed me, then stopped for a moment letting the book fall open on her lap. "That's a lot of islands when you think about it. I wonder how many we'll visit."

"Half a dozen, give or take a few."

"It says here that they are divided into eight major groups. Rhodes is one of the Dodecanese Islands."

I managed an appropriate comment now and then while Sherry continued with her reading. Researching the places we hoped to visit was clearly Sherry's job aboard *Baraka A*. My interest was every bit as keen as hers but, as I often reminded myself, it's the wise man who realises his limitations and lets the better qualified individual get on with it. Whenever we arrived at a given port, Sherry was as well informed as a tour guide and, knowing what might interest us, steered us toward it.

The day was glorious, a sapphire sky dotted with white cloud puffs. Likewise the scenery. Craggy mountain peaks rising to meet the sky, leaving behind their reflections in the still blue water.

Sherry's Journal, Anchored in Iblis Bay
en route to Rhodes, August 2

If someone asked me today how I liked sailing around the world in a 31 foot sailboat, I would say, 'I love it!' Why can't the weather always be like this? Drifting along this afternoon, we spotted a tranquil bay and decided to stop and check it out. Jameel dropped a stern anchor and, with the help of a young man named Shaker, tied the bow to a tree on shore. Don't know the name of this place as it isn't on any of our charts or maps. It appears to be a remote camping spot on the Turkish mainland. Again, no customs!

The decision was unanimous. This place was so perfect and so pretty that we decided to stay overnight. We spent the afternoon swimming and scrubbing the hull, which is something we seem to do every time we go over the side. Later we found a friendly taverna ashore where we had a delicious dinner and learned that the name of this beautiful spot is Iblis Bay. Later we watched a belly dancer dancing to Egyptian music! Before we left, the owner gave us a watermelon and some peaches. How is it possible to find two perfect stopping places two nights in a row as if by accident? Jameel said it reminded him of looking in the drawer for some paper clips and finding instead a couple of emeralds.

***Baraka A* Log, Iblis Bay – August 2**

Again, no customs here which is a good thing because we do not have visas for Turkey. Took down our Saudi and Egyptian flags, leaving only the Union Jack in place, thinking that there might not be a visa requirement for British visitors.

We untied ourselves from the tree and lifted our anchor at 6 a.m. Rhodes was still 45 miles away. We hoped to arrive there by early afternoon. Inside the bay, the wind had picked up so we were not surprised to encounter 25 knots once we left protected waters. The first half of the trip brought back all the bad memories of our first days on the Mediterranean: winds howling, the boat crashing through the waves while Sherry hung over the rail wracked with seasickness.

By the time we arrived at the bustling harbour on Rhodes, the fickle weather we were beginning to know so well had changed from her dungarees into a party dress. As we fought our way through a tangle of ferry boats, charter yachts and private yachts, only a light breeze rippled the surface of the water and a warm sun blazed down on us from a cloudless sky.

Sherry's Journal, Rhodes, Greece, August 3-4

A crowded place with no facilities in the harbour for private yachts, even the necessities like toilets and showers. Water and electricity are available only for charters. We are tied to a quay near the main street, very noisy both day and night.

After finishing with customs we took a walk in the town. Rhodes is not a new place for us. We flew here for a vacation five years ago. Nothing has changed much. It is still very crowded and touristy. Some people thrive on the hustle and bustle but we prefer quiet places. Our last two anchorages spoiled us! Tied up right beside us was a Camper Nicholson 35. We met the people and they invited us aboard. A nice boat, but I was surprised that the four extra feet made so little difference.

We stayed put in Rhodes Harbour for one more day to restock the boat with fresh fruit and vegetables and soft drinks and to top up the diesel and refill our jerry cans. Diesel always topped the list of things to buy in port and wherever and whenever we found it, we bought as much as we could carry. In the Mediterranean we were never that far from a port but... ? I had no answer except that old habits die hard. We had run short of fuel so many times over the past year that having full tanks and jerry cans gave us peace of mind.

We were so crammed into the harbour that we wondered how we would get out the following morning. Squeezed between two big power boats, we watched in horror and disbelief when another, bigger, boat stopped right in front of us and dropped his anchor, in all probability, right on top of ours. I mentioned our 6 a.m. departure and suggested to the skipper that he move his boat. He waved me away like a pesky fly.

Even though the marine weather forecast predicted Force 4-5 for the following morning Sherry said okay which told me that, just like me, she was more than anxious to leave this crowded noisy harbour.

Our destination was Tilos, a Greek island only 20 miles away.

Sherry's Journal, Rhodes to Siskle, 21 miles, August 5

Well, as we suspected, when the guy in front of us dropped his anchor, it got tangled up with ours. Jameel did not even feel sorry about waking him up and asking him to hoist his anchor, which he did, all the while mumbling and grumbling. It took us an hour to get unhooked.

Out of the harbour the wind was blowing 15-18 knots and the sea was very agitated. We abandoned our original plans to sail westward to Tilos and changed course to the NW for a tiny island called Siskle.

When we arrived, we saw only 1 sailboat and 2 power boats. By 5 p.m., everyone had left and we were all alone to enjoy a swim in water so clear that it almost sparkled. The island was supposed to be uninhabited. Who owned the goat and the cat and the donkey we saw on shore?

Around 7 p.m., a luxurious 86 ft sailboat anchored near us. We recognised the skipper whom we'd met in American Samoa the year before. He was no longer sailing his own boat but working as a charter skipper for Camper Nicholson.

A beautiful place. Another emerald in the drawer with the paper clips. Our decision to explore these beautiful islands was the right one.

***Baraka A* Log - August 5**

We left Siskle bound for Tilos – 21 miles away – at 5 a.m. The sea was flat calm until 9 a.m. when it started to blow, right in our face. The Greek islands are charming but getting from one to another is often difficult.

Wind blowing 25 knots, the sea choppy with short, steep breakers. Autohelm useless in these conditions so I'm at the tiller.

The continuing fickle weather was sapping our strength and humour. Some sailors we met in Rhodes thought that August was the worst month to sail the Med, the prime months being May and June when the winds were moderate and consistent. None of my pilot books gave this argument much credence and we had no first-hand knowledge to say yea or nay. My accident had delayed our trip through the Med. If we'd missed the best weather we'd enjoyed more than adequate compensation. While ducking high winds and seas we'd discovered a succession of delightful anchorages. If we'd made it to Crete on the first attempt we would have missed the emeralds.

We dropped anchor in Megalo Bay on Tilos at 11 a.m., and, to our amazement, realised that we were the only people anchored there. Except for Rhodes, we'd had exceptional luck in missing the crowds.

The beach, however, was not deserted. We watched a volleyball game in progress in which all the players appeared to be nude. Nude sunbathing and swimming was common in Greece but volleyball? Saudi Arabia's customs concerning proper attire couldn't have been more different. While men are required to cover their bodies from the waist to the knees, women are expected to cover up completely, with only their hands and face visible. Many choose to keep their face hidden from view behind a veil. So many people we'd met during our months at sea were fascinated by the traditional clothing that most Saudis wear and asked the inevitable question: "Do you wear it too?" I usually wore Western clothes as did Sherry, the only difference being that when Sherry went out of the house she put on a long black cloak known as an abeya over her clothes and she covered her head with a scarf.

Sherry's Journal, Tilos Island, Greece, August 6

We met a Swedish couple this afternoon when we went to shore in search of a restaurant. They showed us the way to a house where a lady served meals to visitors. We enjoyed a meal of stuffed tomatoes and macaroni and found it interesting and amusing that the food storage area also served as a bedroom.

Later we invited the Swedish couple to Baraka A *for coffee. A pleasant interesting day.*

At 8 a.m. the following morning we were underway again, this time headed for Crete, the same destination we'd tried to reach so many times before. We immediately encountered stiff winds and a rough sea and just as immediately abandoned the idea of enduring 200 miles of bad weather. Another failed attempt! We changed course for Nissos Iyoannis island, just 36 miles away.

We found a comfortable anchorage next to a rock cliff. I tied the bow to a rock, threw out a stern anchor and pulled us off the shore. It blew 25 knots plus all afternoon and we were very thankful that we weren't 'out there'.

Sherry's Journal, Nissos Iyoannis Island, Greece, August 7-9

The island appeared to be deserted. We didn't see anyone on shore but in the late afternoon a herd of goats with bells around their necks came down the mountain and with them was a black and white cat! We watched them until they disappeared.

At 3.30 a.m., we were awakened by the wind, which was howling around Baraka A. *By morning it was still blowing hard so we decided to stay put. We enjoyed a relaxing day. I cooked a nice lunch with some frozen chicken we had bought a few days ago, cleaned the inside of the boat, had a shower and hoped for better weather tomorrow. I thought back to my shower at home in Jeddah, a stall with glass doors and a pulsating shower head, pelting lovely warm water at me. That was a dream. Reality: a bucket of cold seawater dumped over my head while standing in the cockpit.*

The following morning two fishing boats entered the bay seeking shelter from the wind, which was still blowing like fury. From our anchorage the sea looked like a huge bowl of frothy egg whites.

After breakfast, the goats came back, a larger herd this time. Where there were goats there must be a goat herder and possibly people, at least one. We decided to climb the rocky cliff and find out what was on the other side but we gave up. Too steep, too rocky and too dangerous, especially since my arm was still aching and weak.

At 7 p.m., the wind was still howling around *Baraka A* in even stronger gusts. Strangely the anchor chain captured the vibration of the wind, creating a strange mournful whistle. I took it as a warning and secured the bow with another line around another rock on shore.

At 7 a.m. on August 9 we were awakened by the sound of bells as the goats came down to the shore for a breakfast of shrubs and weeds which grew in the crevices between the rocks. Good news - the weather appeared to have settled down enough for us to make a dash for Crete, 140 miles away. We decided not to waste one moment in case the wind returned. We pulled the dinghy aboard and deflated it, untied the bow lines, and pulled up the anchor in a matter of minutes. We would eat breakfast underway.

Outside the bay, the wind was blowing a lovely, gentle 14 knots. In the afternoon it went up to 22 knots but then settled back to 14. An enjoyable sail with an average speed of 5 knots, which meant a long slog to Crete.

A night at sea brought us back to the reality of night watches and looking out for passing freighters. We saw four. Luck stayed with us and the winds remained steady at 14 knots. There was a part of me that hated to leave the charming, secluded anchorages on those tiny Greek islands. But another part was saying, 'Let's get on with it. We've got some miles to cover before we can call ourselves 'circumnavigators' and the first Arabs to have ever attempted and accomplished such a feat.'

At 2 a.m. we were still 40 miles from Crete but I could say with certainty that this time we really were going to make it. Crete would be the jumping-off point for the rest of the Mediterranean, first the long haul to Sardinia and then several shorter hops to the south of France and Spain until we reached Gibraltar.

Sherry's Journal, Khania Harbour, Crete, August 10

Arrived at 11 a.m. and tied the boat stern in to the dock. This place was like Rhodes, with lots of power cruisers and charters but thankfully not so crowded and hectic. And no one dropped their anchor on top of ours!

A fellow from the immigration office named Pavlos was fascinated that we had come such a long distance in such a small boat. We were, he said, the first Arabs he'd ever encountered in all his years as an immigration officer.

"We hope that will change," Jameel told him. "Once we've done it, others may follow."

Then Jameel got our scrapbook, which Pavlos studied with interest. He said his wife would be very interested in meeting us. Could we come and have coffee in her coffee shop that afternoon?

We had picked August 12 as departure day from Khania harbour, destination Sardinia, 814 miles to the west. Since this would be our first long leg in many weeks, we immediately set off for town in search of provisions after bidding farewell to the immigration officer. We found plenty of well-provisioned shops and were able to find all the items on our shopping list, even a new tea kettle as the old one had completely rusted through.

As we stood in the check-out line, I turned to Sherry.

"We don't have to wait till the 12th. If the weather's good, let's head out tomorrow."

She nodded.

"The diesel truck's due this afternoon. Then the only job left is to fill the water tanks. We can do that in the morning."

After lunch we met Pavlos at his wife's coffee shop and spent a delightful few hours talking with them and hopefully dispelling the myths that all Arabs are terrorists. Sure, we've got some bad apples in our barrel but so does every other culture. People should be accepted as individuals not judged by the behaviour of others. I hoped that was able to convey these thoughts without sounding like a pompous jerk.

That evening we went to town for a delicious Greek meal and later phoned our families. Tomorrow we faced another challenge: sailing across the Mediterranean to Italy. If the weather got rough, we would have to tough it out as there were no hideaway anchorages offering a safe haven like we'd experienced in Greece. 'It's just like crossing the Atlantic and long stretches of the Pacific,' I reminded myself. I didn't say 'no big deal'. Only a fool would ever underestimate the power of the sea.

Chapter Twenty-Four

We awoke the morning of August 11 to flat seas, perfect conditions for Sherry to leave the harbour in a positive frame of mind. Too often we'd left port to the accompaniment of screeching wind and pounding seas with Sherry sitting stone-faced in the cockpit as if she'd just received a death sentence. Once underway, I hoped the winds would kick up enough to give us some speed.

We puttered around port during the morning hours buying ice, some fresh fish for our first dinner out and topping up our supply of bottled water. No matter how often we cleaned our water tanks, the water always had a funny taste. After lunch Sherry went to pick up our laundry while I signed the necessary customs forms and said goodbye to the three Swedish sailors on the boat next to us.

Sherry's Journal, Crete

We enjoyed our stay here even though the harbour was bustling and congested like Rhodes. And, like Rhodes, the dining out was excellent. But it was the supermarkets that got my attention, the best we'd found anywhere which guaranteed that we'd eat well on the way to Sardinia. For the first time since our voyage began, we did not find many people who spoke English so communication was a bit difficult. Amazing what I managed to say with my hands.

Our first afternoon en route to Sardinia, the wind was non-existent so I cranked on the engine and we skimmed effortlessly across the glassy water. That evening the wind kicked up to 15 knots and we were able to raise the main and genoa. Again we kept a wary eye out for ships and during the night sighted five. By morning the wind was blowing 18 but, as I reminded Sherry, good stiff winds meant steady forward progress. First day out we clocked 136 miles. Very encouraging.

Sitting in the cockpit our second evening out, having enjoyed another of Sherry's gourmet meals, we got to talking about the various harbours we'd visited. While I insisted that we had never been in a really bad place, I had to admit that some spots received a better mark than others.

We both agreed that we preferred quiet anchorages to crowded noisy ones but quiet did not have to mean all alone.

Sherry was quite firm on that point.

"After being on this boat with you for days I needed to see other people. The first thing I always wanted to do was look around for any familiar boats and most times I spotted at least one. If I didn't I knew there was a great way to meet new people – just throw a pail full of books into the dinghy and row around asking if anyone would like to exchange. Someone always did."

"I liked anchorages where we could eat out." I pointed to my plate which only sported a few breadcrumbs. "You needed a break from the galley."

Sherry smiled.

"Not all our meals were as good as this one, especially if we'd been at sea for a month. Remember Tahiti, where we lived on tomatoes and rice until our money came through?"

"Don't forget the fresh fruit. We used to hike into the hills and pick anything we wanted right off the tree."

Sherry gazed at the horizon, her chin cupped in her hands and then turned back to me.

"Hiking and walking were my favourite ways to pass the time after being cooped up on the boat for days or weeks. I liked anchorages where we could go ashore and explore the town and go shopping."

"And I liked the ones with a repair shop or at least a handyman who could fix things."

Sherry hid a giggle behind her fist. "Like outboard motors?"

"Let's not forget the SatNav," I said, peering into the cabin. "But keep your voice down. It's been on its best behaviour lately and I don't want to upset it."

"Okay," she whispered.

"People were always important for me," she said, resuming a normal tone. "Friendly people like the ones we met in the South

Pacific. I never understood how they could be so happy to see us when they didn't even know us. Here in the Med, harbours aren't the same. Neither are the people, both the natives and the sailors form other boats."

"I keep thinking about Australia," I replied.

"Don't forget Australia," I replied. "Never met people who were so congenial and outgoing and so much fun. We had a great time in Cairns. Remember the barbecue on the beach?"

Sherry nodded.

"Every place was unique. Every place left us with some good memories. Like the Galapagos. I'll always remember the turtles. Who cares that the shopping wasn't so great."

"I've been sitting here thinking about Crete," she continued, "and wondering what good things we'll remember about that place. I know what's at the top of my list, even before the supermarkets. Getting the water and diesel on board was so easy at Khania harbour. The fuel truck came right to the dock and the water pipe was just a few feet away. Remember the places where we had to load the jerry cans and water bottles into the dinghy and make all those trips back and forth to the boat? Once you had to hitch hike to find diesel. Where was that?"

"Aitutaki. We were in the anchorage with just one other boat, from Denmark, I think. I remember the rain never stopped."

"Rotuma was one of my favourite stopping places," said Sherry. "So quiet, so perfect."

"How could I ever forget Rotuma?" I replied. "When I think of that place I will always remember falling out of the papaya tree." I pointed to a scar on my leg. "Here's the reminder."

Sherry laughed. "How I wish I'd had my camera that day."

The sun hung low in the sky like a burnished disc as *Baraka A* sliced through the waves with a saucy confidence. Sherry made us a second cup of coffee. We sat in companionable silence in the cockpit watching the sun disappear over the edge of the horizon.

"Speaking of memories," I said, "how about tonight? What could be more perfect than this? I feel at peace with myself and with the world."

I thought I heard a whispered, "Me too," from Sherry's corner but, when I looked over, I saw that her eyes were closed and her chin had fallen on to her chest.

Sherry's Journal, August 14

Early this morning while I was sitting in the cockpit, a tiny yellow bird landed on the windvane. He looked like a land bird and was so small. I approached him and took him in my hand and he didn't object at all. I woke Jameel up and showed him our new guest. God knows how he flew so far as we were at least 70 miles from the nearest land - Sicily. We took some pictures of him standing on Jameel's head. He liked his hair - maybe he thought it was a nest! He stayed with us for almost an hour, flying everywhere, inside the cabin and around the cockpit. Then, as suddenly as he appeared, he was gone again, flying high.

Perfect weather so far, some calm stretches but mostly steady consistent winds of about 15 knots. Pushed us along nicely at approximately 115 miles a day. At this rate we would reach Sardinia in less than a week. We were in the shipping lanes and the fishing lanes. All along the way we saw fishing markers, jerry cans, fenders, black flags tied to anchored sticks and lines. But no fish for us. We tried throwing out a line but no luck.

***Baraka A* Log - August 15**

Sighted the coast of Sicily off the starboard rail this evening. Very busy shipping lanes. So far no close calls. We have a leak, forcing us to pump the bilges every 4 hours. Probably in the propeller shaft like the other times. Will fix it in Sardinia.

Sherry's Journal, August 16

We still have 160 miles to go but hope to reach land tomorrow afternoon. Very light winds so we are motor sailing. We still have ice and cold drinks which is delightful in this hot weather. During the daytime the temperature reaches 33°C and falls to 28 degrees at night. We are getting a real nice suntan since we are in the cockpit most of the day. Tonight will be our 6th night at sea. Weatherwise we have been very lucky.

The morning of the 17th, the sea was as smooth as an oil slick, not a ripple anywhere. The engine would have to take us the remaining 55 miles. Sherry busied herself cleaning the deck and the cockpit and the interior of the boat. I knew that if she needed my help she would shout. During our months at sea I'd learned that Sherry viewed this 'final clean up' as her special province.

"I like doing it," she told me once. "It's like I'm saying thank you to the boat for getting us there safely."

I appreciated and applauded Sherry's efforts. More often than not, when we arrived at a port we would turn out to be the first Arab sailors the customs and immigration had ever met. What kind of impression would we make if *Baraka A*'s decks were streaked with grime and the galley sink stacked with greasy dishes? Not good, no matter how sweet the coffee we offered or how hospitable the skipper and first mate might be.

After lunch we lazed in the cockpit listening to the radio. We agreed that one of the nicest things about sailing these waters was the availability of so many radio stations.

We arrived at Cagliari harbour on Sardinia at 4.30 p.m. on August 17, after a six day passage. We barely had time to turn off the engine before we were boarded by customs and immigration. They did not seem interested in the fact that we carried Saudi and Egyptian passports or impressed with Sherry's cleaning efforts. Almost brusquely, they asked to see our insurance papers.

"Insurance papers?" I asked, putting on my most disarming smile. "I don't understand."

"Proof of insurance. You need it to dock here for the night."

"We have never needed these papers before in all the ports we've visited on our trip around the world. We're on our way back to Morocco where we will complete the circumnavigation," I smiled again. "We're the first Arabs to have ever attempted such a journey. We tried to get insurance but… "

"Not important," said the immigration officer as he waved his hand impatiently. Obviously he didn't care if I was an Arab or an Eskimo. The message was clear – no insurance papers, no stay.

One of them must have caught sight of Sherry sitting slump-shouldered on the hatch, looking as crestfallen as a kid whose bag of sweets has just fallen through the sewer grating.

"Please," she said, her voice near cracking. "We've been at sea for two weeks and we are very tired." She looked up at the customs officer, her brown eyes shiny with unshed tears. "Is there no way you can make an exception? "I ducked into the cabin and returned with our folder of newspaper clippings.

"I hope these articles will tell you who we are and what we are doing." I also hoped they'd pick up my subtle message. Does Sardinia *really* want to be the only place in the *entire universe* which did not put out the welcome mat for us. Now, that would make a really interesting news item.

One of them looked at his watch, then back at Sherry who was now resting her head on her knees, a portrait of despondency. After consulting his watch one more time and then whispering with his colleague, he nodded. "Okay. Since it's almost the end of our shift, we'll just pretend we never saw you. Don't go near the customs office in town. Don't get into any trouble tonight. And you've got to leave here first thing in the morning."

"Thank you," we mumbled.

Sherry even managed a tentative smile. "Yes, we will leave, even before sunrise."

"Before eight will be fine."

We watched them saunter along the dock then scrambled into the cabin in search of a pen and paper to make out our shopping list.

"Two weeks at sea?" I asked

She flashed me a grin.

"Well, it seemed that long and the immigration guy felt sorry for us."

"Sorry for you, I'm guessing. I don't think he liked me a bit!"

One quick glance around the marina told me all I needed to know: we were in an industrial area which meant no shops and no supplies. I found a taxi for hire outside the marina gates and we immediately set off on the first of several shopping expeditions to buy diesel, fresh produce, bread, cheese and ice. At 9.30 we were finished but hungry as a couple of bears. No time or inclination for gourmet dining. We decided that a quick pizza would have to do.

While waiting for our order, Sherry raised the issue that had been hovering in my mind since our visit from customs.

"I know we have no insurance, Jameel."

I nodded.

"Not one company would touch us. The conditions were impossible. We had to promise 'three competent people', and apply for a renewal each leg. I always thought I was competent. And you too. But three people? How could we have sailed this far with three people on board? And think of the mess of paperwork. I always wondered who decided what constituted a leg."

"I understand all that. It's just that I thought insurance was for being wrecked in a storm or losing a mast, you know - disasters at sea. Why would anyone need insurance in a harbour? Nothing can happen to you in a harbour."

Images of fire burning its way down a dock incinerating the yachts and cruisers in a conflagration of diesel fuel and gasoline flashed through my mind as I answered Sherry.

"Actually, most accidents happen in harbours - fires, boats colliding or ramming into the docks. Sometimes boats spring leaks and just sink to the bottom right beside the pier."

"I learn something new every day," said Sherry, attacking her pizza like a starving refugee. When we were finished we zoomed back to the boat where we fell into our bunks, too whacked to even think about getting into trouble!

Not the leisurely few days in Italy that we'd imagined but I figured the customs fellows meant business. What would they do if we didn't leave by 8 a.m. Confiscate the boat? We didn't plan to stick around and find out. The need for insurance in Sardinia would have to remain a mystery!

Chapter Twenty-Five

The morning sky was streaked with clouds as we motored out of Cagliari harbour even before the 8 a.m. deadline. Whenever the immigration and customs began their morning rounds, they would find our berth empty. Our choice would have been to stay put until the weather improved and I'd had a chance to investigate the leak. But we hadn't been given a choice!

Once outside the harbour, the full force of the wind hit us. We clocked 22 knots on our wind gauge; not a gale but not comfortable either. The boat crashed through the breakers, heeling over on a hard beat. It soon became apparent that, in spite of all the motion and commotion, *Baraka A* was making dismal forward progress. At one point Sherry told me that the knotmeter was registering only 2 knots. We raised the sails to give the engine a boost and slowly we began to inch forward with just one thought in mind – to find a safe place and hole up until the wind died down. Sherry positioned herself on the starboard rail and 36 miles later spotted two masts behind a natural outcropping of rocks. Where there are boats at anchor, there must be a cove with room for one more.

***Baraka A* Log – August 18**

Westerly wind 19–22 knots so we decided to seek shelter in a little bay on the southern coast of Sardinia and wait for a weather change.

Sherry's Journal, an unnamed bay on the south coast of Sardinia

A calm and lovely place, a big improvement over the marina. No customs! We took down our Saudi and Egyptian flags and left the Union Jace flying, hoping to avoid any further hassles with the Italian authorities in case they dropped by. After we anchored, I fixed us a beautiful lunch – two steaks that we bought last night. In the afternoon we rested for a while and enjoyed the scenery. The bay is ringed by rugged outcroppings of rock which come right down to the water's edge.

While Sherry tidied up the V-berth, I busied myself with other boat chores. First I topped up the oil in the engine, then tackled the leak. I suspected that the source was, once again, the propeller shaft which would account for the slow but steady trickle seeping into the bilges. As it turned out, getting to the problem was more of a challenge than solving it. First I had to pump the bilges dry, then clear all the items out of the hold. After wriggling head first on my back into the small confined space, I confirmed that the problem was indeed a loose screw. Anyone who has ever tried to tighten a screw situated two inches above his nose while crammed into a space no bigger than a breadbox will appreciate the difficulty I had getting my screwdriver in place and applying enough pressure to do the job. I had learned from previous screw-tightening episodes that the important part was tightening it just enough. Too much and the screw might damage the housing. Too loose and the water would continue to trickle. The weather was so peaceful, the bay so beautiful that we decided to stay the night and store up happy memories of Sardinia.

The morning of the 19th, we were underway early, slicing cleanly through a glassy sea under motor heading for the Balearic Islands, better known as Mallorca, Menorca and Ibiza. Our destination – Ibiza, the most southerly of the three islands composing the group. A contingency plan in case of renewed bad weather or overwhelming headwinds was to head for Palma on the island of Mallorca.

A ruffling breeze which barely rippled the surface of the water made me doubt that our contingency plan would ever come to be. But the capricious Mediterranean had other ideas.

Baraka A **Log – August 19**

No wind this morning. By noon it had picked up to 18 knots, coming at us from the north-west right in our faces. Our depth sounder told us that we were sailing through shallow waters. The sea is choppy and waves are slamming into the boat. Very rough and wet. By nightfall the wind had dropped and the seas became flat. The current is with us so we are making good time. Saw 3 big freighters and 1 sailboat heading east.

Sherry's Journal, August 20, En route to Ibiza

This morning the barometer was falling and the sky overcast. Long clouds which looked like cigars made us think that something was cooking. But we sailed along all day under pleasant conditions, 10-12 knot winds and gentle seas. We didn't see any other boats, just birds who flew by us, none stopping to visit. We tried fishing with no luck even though we had live bait – a squid that we found in the cockpit this morning. We haven't seen much marine life in the Mediterranean, hardly any whales or dolphins or sea lions. We saw so many of them in the Pacific and Indian oceans. Why is it different here? Wonder if the cause is pollution?

Sherry's cigar clouds turned into a nasty weather front which hit us early that evening and continued through the night with no respite. Dawn greeted us with 22 knots and huge rolling breakers which tossed the boat around like a paper boat in a puddle. I took a third reef in the main and furled in the genoa to reduce our sail area. The wind knocked us sideways, propelling us at surfing speed down into the troughs between the breaking waves. With nowhere to go, *Baraka A* buried her nose in the oncoming wall of water. As the bow rose to meet the sky, tons of spray and foam cascaded over the decks and back to the cockpit soaking the captain and his first mate.

A longer boat would have handled the breaking waves with greater ease. But I had learned, while researching a suitable boat for a circumnavigation, that every boat has its shortcomings. I remembered

Jeremy Lines advising us that we should never consider a boat which the two of us could not handle comfortably, putting great emphasis on the 'fatigue factor' which, he said, must be carefully calculated. Bigger boats might be more comfortable, might handle our current weather situation with ease. But balanced against that was the effort needed to sail a bigger boat.

I'd concluded that the Nick 31 was perfect for our needs. Big enough to take the weather but small enough for Sherry and me to manage on our own. And so well constructed that she'd taken many a pounding and come up smiling.

But, all philosophical considerations aside, our present situation, though not dangerous, was uncomfortable. Why continue when the island of Mallorca was only a day's sail away? Sherry reminded me that some of our most memorable stopping places had been the unplanned ones, the anchorages we'd found by accident or run to seeking escape from the weather.

The next morning we sighted land at 11 a.m. But the first landfall was still 23 miles away and the harbour another 26. Still, our spirits got a good boost just knowing that relief from the wind was not far off.

Farther off than we wished, however, as we did not reach our anchorage at Palma until 6 p.m. As we approached the breakwater, we saw passenger ships, fishing boats and every type of yacht, motor cruisers and sailboats, most of them big. Again we seemed to be the smallest boat there.

Sherry's Journal, Club Nautic Harbour, Palma, Mallorca

There are actually 5 marinas in one huge, beautifully made harbour. There are separate docks for the big passenger ships and fishing boats. We docked at the Club Nautic, which has everything a cruiser could want including a hotel, car rental agency, yacht club and repair facilities. But, best of all, there were no port police or health officials. We just filled out a form and paid the docking fees, then went to town for dinner.

Early the next morning I went ashore to arrange for a rental car and to phone our families, leaving Sherry to empty the jerry cans into the diesel tanks, top up our water tanks and swab the deck. Looking back, this division of labour seems hardly equitable! Though the sky was still cloudy, an improvement in the weather seemed imminent, according to the barometer, which was rising quickly.

That afternoon the town of Palma was bathed in soft sunshine as we set off on the first of our sightseeing expeditions. Sherry's first impression was 'clean and green'.

Sherry's Journal, Palma, Mallorca

The sea front is full of shops, cafes and cute hotels. Driving along the narrow twisting roads into the countryside, we found farms scattered on the hillsides and nestled in the valleys. Nicely built houses, everything so neat. We saw olive groves, fig and lemon trees everywhere.

We stayed in Palma for 3 relaxing days. We badly needed a rest. We'd been hopping from island to island, usually just staying one night. Having a car was a big bonus. We didn't have to carry everything from the store to the dock. The day before we left, it rained. I hoped that some of the sand and grit got washed off the mast, radar reflector and the sparfly at the mast head.

We made plans to leave Palma in the early *evening* on August 24. This was a clear departure from our usual schedule of before sunrise departures. We calculated that Ibiza lay fifteen hours to the west. Leaving at night meant that we would arrive some time the next afternoon. Leaving in the morning translated into an arrival after dark which, in turn, meant a night hove to waiting for the first hint of dawn. It was still daylight when we cleared the tip of the island of Mallorca, sailing along enjoying the 15 knot breeze. Later the wind dropped to around 8 and the seas became flatter. The half moon riding high in the sky gave us excellent visibility.

Sherry's Journal, en route to Ibiza

Sailing along, I started thinking again about how the sailors in the Med are so different from those we met sailing across the Pacific to Panama. Med sailors don't seem as friendly. I guess it's because there are so many boats around. In the Pacific there would be sometimes as few as 6 boats in a harbour so we would get to know each other immediately. We exchanged information and went sightseeing together and helped each other with repairs. Here it's so different. We have hardly talked to any other skippers. Everyone seems to keep to his own boat and his own business.

Sherry shared her journal entry with me and we had a lively discussion while we enjoyed our coffee in the cockpit this evening. I agreed that Med sailors and Pacific cruisers are very different. Maybe it's because people cruising the Mediterranean do just that, go from port to port and then back home. Maybe they do it every year until it's old hat. The sailors we met in the Pacific should be called seafarers in search of adventure. Most of them were like us, first-timers, not old-timers, and we were excited about what we were doing. Every day was a new challenge. Sharing information, helping each other was the glue that held us together. I knew that some of these friendships would endure long after the voyage ended.

We arrived at Ibiza on schedule at 10.30 in the morning on August 25. Again the harbour was clean, new, with every facility imaginable all at a reasonable price of $20 a night. Sherry was most impressed with the shopping centre right in the marina, which looked as if it had been completed just last week. We found a good restaurant on shore and had lunch, then rolled into our bunks for an afternoon nap.

Later that afternoon I was standing in the cockpit, emptying jerry cans of diesel into the tanks, when I heard the traditional Arabic greeting, 'Salem Aleikum'.

I lifted my head to see a man, clearly a native of the Middle East, standing on the dock. We exchanged pleasantries. He'd noticed our flags, the first Saudi and Egyptian flags he'd ever seen in this port, and felt that he must come and introduce himself. He was a businessman from Kuwait living in Ibiza in an apartment overlooking the harbour. He was astounded that we had sailed so far in such a small boat and that we were now approaching the final leg of our circumnavigation. He peppered us with questions which we happily answered.

"Please," he said, "will you be my guests at my apartment? There we can talk and take some refreshment."

We quickly agreed. I thought back to our conversation the previous evening. Here was what we'd been missing sailing the Med – someone else to talk to rather than just to each other! We spent the evening at his apartment. When we mentioned that we had to call our families he was kind enough to offer us the use of his phone. Courtesy demanded that we decline but we were very grateful when he insisted. Using the SSB radio had its drawbacks. A regular two way phone conversation was a luxury.

We weighed anchor and were underway by 8 a.m. the following morning. Our destination was Cala Bardina on the south coast of Spain, 160 miles to the west. If the winds continued to co-operate, we would arrive about 4 p.m.

Sherry's Journal, en route to Cala Bardina

Talking to the man from Kuwait last night got me thinking. I should be happy that the circumnavigation is coming to an end but I feel sad and a bit depressed too. How will it be back in the real world facing reality?

***Baraka A* Log – August 27**

We made excellent time from Ibiza to Cala Bardina with steady winds, a favourable current. At 00.05 GMT *Baraka A* crossed the Greenwich Meridian.

Dropped anchor at 5.30 p.m. in the small bay at Cala Bardina, almost on schedule. A tranquil place with beautiful villas on the shore, a large hotel and a sandy beach. There seemed to be every type of water sport available for the tourists: windsurfing, paddle boats, dinghies, surfboards. Sherry pronounced it 'very nice' then got busy in the galley cooking the chickens we had bought in Ibiza. After dinner we relaxed and enjoyed the scenery. Sherry wished that we could stay here longer and really discover this place but I was anxious to push ahead. The end of our sea odyssey was in sight and I was anxious to complete the voyage and say we'd done it. But another part of me was thinking how flat life might be when this adventure was over. What in the day to day grind could ever be as exciting as the challenge of the sea?

We left early the next morning, heading in a south-westerly direction towards Almeria on the south coast of Spain.

***Baraka A* Log – August 28**

25 knot head winds forced us to change plans and seek shelter from the weather again. Dropped anchor at Point de Carboneras where we will monitor the weather station at Monaco.

By the next morning the weather had moderated so we raised the anchor and continued on towards Almeria. It wasn't until late afternoon that the winds picked up again. As we were approaching the harbour and the end of another long day aboard *Baraka A*, the engine coughed and spluttered and stalled out. My first instinct was to check that no errant lines were trailing in the water. Since that never-to-be-forgotten incident in the English Channel when a line tangled around the propeller shaft had almost caused me to founder on Eddiston Rocks, I always made sure that all lines were aboard and secured. The Yanmar diesel engine had served us so faithfully over the intervening months that engine failure was something I never thought about and something I didn't want to think about then with land so close and night falling fast. I held my breath and turned the key. A low rumble, a sputter, then nothing. On my third try, the engine again wheezed into life, spluttered a couple of times then settled down to the rhythmic throbbing we'd come to know so well but, perhaps never fully appreciated? I suspected dirty fuel, an easy matter to check at Almeria.

Sherry's Journal, Almeria to Marbella, 113 miles

Left this charming clean place after lunch on August 30 at 3 p.m. after a one night stop-over. I bought provisions while Jameel started and stopped the engine many times and was not able to find a problem. We topped up the diesel.

Hope everything is okay. In the early evening the wind died completely and the sea was like oil. As the sun set, some dolphins came to visit us. We noticed that in the Mediterranean they are a lot smaller than the ones we saw in the big oceans. A lot of seagulls seemed to be resting on the water. They only flew away when we got close. We motored all night with no further engine problems.

At 11.30 a.m. we entered the marina in Marbella, docked and cleared customs before we realised that we were in the wrong harbour, the old harbour of Porto Deportivo, not the new one called Porto Benus, a few miles away. Sherry had read that Porto Benus was reputed to be the most sophisticated marina in the world. And probably very expensive. Even more than the 'old' harbour which made a bigger dent in my wallet than I would have liked.

Since we were only 35 miles away from Gibraltar, we decided to wait and resupply the boat there. Also we only planned to spend one night in Marbella and the time could be better spent sightseeing than shopping.

We walked into town, had an expensive lunch and did some window shopping – no buying – as the prices were very high. I guess that was to be expected in a place which catered to the rich and famous aboard their luxury yachts. Strangely, our docking fees were only $20 for the night, exactly what we'd paid in Mallorca.

The first day of September marked the beginning of a new month and another milestone – the last leg of our voyage. Exhilarating to think that we were almost there. But how difficult was it going to be to leave the cosy confines of *Baraka A* which had been our home for almost two years?

Our plan was to stop in Gibraltar for provisions and rest up for our dash through the Strait into the Atlantic. Then we would turn south for Casablanca. Gibraltar lay just 39.4 miles to the west of us.

“An easy one day hop,” I told Sherry as we left Porto Deportivo, Marbella in the early morning. As we motored through the fishing fleet there was not a breath of wind to rattle the halyards.

But again the Mediterranean turned cranky and two hours later we were battling 15-20 knot winds which in short order piped up to 30. The sea became very agitated with ridges of foam skittering across the crests of the waves.

As we neared Gibraltar, the massive rocky cliffs rising out of the sea filled me with a sense of awe and dread. From my reading I knew that rounding Europa Point at the tip of Gibraltar was a hazardous undertaking due to the strong current and jagged rocky coast. This day there was another factor, a raging wind blowing out of the south-west which would drive us right on to the rocks if we lost control of the boat.

That day all my sailor’s instincts were on red alert. ‘Screw this up now,’ I told myself, ‘and you can say goodbye to your dream. Not now, when you’re so close.’

I had a gut feeling that I should be well clear of the shore before tacking over to head into the harbour. Also niggling in the back corners of my mind was the question of the engine. True, it had stalled out only once in two years. But what if it chose this particular time and place to stall again? I recognised a potential disaster since there would be no time to take evasive action.

The main was already down and tied to the boom, the genoa furled to a sliver but that should still give us enough sail to tack away from the shore. Once out in the Strait I would start the engine and then head for the marina.

“Ready about,” I shouted to Sherry, who looked up at me in surprise.

She knew the ‘coming into port’ drill by heart, having done it hundreds of times. First you take the sails down, then you turn on the engine and proceed into the harbour. ‘Ready about’ was not part of the sequence.

“Why are we going back out there?” she asked.

“Don’t know – just have a feeling. We’re too close. If something goes wrong I have no room to manoeuvre.”

Sherry frowned. “Jameel, is there something wrong?”

She switched the genoa sheet to the starboard winch.

“Should I let the sail out?” she asked.

I shook my head. "No need. Soon as I get the engine started we'll turn back."

I turned the key, expecting to hear the familiar throaty rumble. There was nothing, not even a wheeze or a cough like we'd heard on the approach to Almeria. I swallowed hard and assessed the situation. The wind and the current were fast pushing us towards the rocky shore.

First I had to get more sail up and head for open water and then worry about the engine. If I couldn't get it going, we would have to sail into the harbour under genoa. I could count the times I'd come into a harbour under sail alone on the fingers of one hand. And I'd never tried it with a 30 knot wind at my back.

To say I felt confident that I could pull this off would be stretching the truth. A determination and commitment to meet the challenge and do my best was all I could muster. Above all, I needed to remain calm.

Sherry felt no such constraints. She turned to me, her eyes wide with fear.

"What's happening?" she shrieked.

"The engine's conked out again," I replied, through clenched teeth. "We need more sail up to give us some steerage."

I didn't have to spell out the procedure to Sherry. She'd done this job many times. She popped the sheet from the cleat and wrapped it around her hand, then let the furling line out slowly. But, as the genoa began to unfurl, a gust caught the sail with such force that the sheet was yanked from Sherry's hands. Like a snake in the wind, it whipped through the air, whacking the lower back shroud on the port side.

"Jameel," Sherry screamed. "Look at the shroud - it's broken. What can we do?"

Losing a shroud was not good news. 'Lose a shroud, lose a mast', was a phrase I'd read in one of my sailing books. This was a certainty with a deck-stepped mast, especially in these wind conditions. Again I sent a thank you to the designers of the Nick 31 who had incorporated a keel-stepped mast into the design. We would make it into port with the mast intact.

"It's okay, Sherry," I shouted in reply. "Hold tight while I try the engine again." I stood in the cockpit rubbing the key between my thumb and forefinger, almost afraid to try it. But then I thought of another problem equal to or greater than a non-functioning engine and a broken shroud. The genoa was flailing like a bedsheet in a hurricane, snapping and cracking as it captured the wind gusts. *Baraka A* ploughed through the waves, assaulted by the winds and a pounding sea. Heeling over till the rail was under water, I wondered if she would recover but she always did, rounding up with a lurch and a roll into the next wave trough. Somehow I had to get the genoa under control. But first the engine.

"I'm saying a prayer, Jameel," Sherry shouted.

"Me too," I replied, as I turned the key.

The engine roared to life without a whimper.

"Come, take the tiller Sherry," I said as I put the engine into forward gear. "I'll get the genoa sheet."

As I stood holding on to the mast while the boat careened through the seas, I thought of another time when I'd had to capture and secure a sail with the boom attached in the middle of a storm. I'd accomplished that without a reliable first mate at the tiller. This should be a piece of cake.

I soon found out that a big bulky sail was much easier to seize than an elusive piece of line thrashing in the wind but, after a few lunges, I managed to grab hold and wrap it around the winch. I decided not to furl the genoa in all the way. If the engine conked out again we'd have to convert back to sail power and very quickly.

Back at the tiller, I gazed at the parted shroud. A genoa sheet could not have inflicted so much damage. Surely metal fatigue was the root cause. The rigging must have taken a real pounding during our weeks in the Mediterranean.

Once we reached Gibraltar I'd do a thorough inspection of all the standing rigging and replace the broken shroud.

The motor continued to propel us toward the harbour with a sure and steady beat.

"I wonder what happened to the engine out there," said Sherry.

If the Yanmar had been able to answer I could imagine the reply: 'Come on folks. I was only clearing my throat!'

It was after 6 p.m. when we finally arrived at the Bayside Marina, exhausted, wet, and, above all, thankful to have made it safely to port. This day had not turned out as I'd predicted. Not the 'easy one day hop' I had talked about so cheerfully that morning but a real test of my endurance and seamanship. I remembered Roy Mullender telling me that I knew how to do everything – I just hadn't done it yet. During our years at sea, I'd done a lot and learned a lot. Especially that a sailor should always follow his gut instincts.

"I was terrified out there," Sherry said as she tackled the mess on the cabin floor. Books, magazines, charts, anything not bolted down had become airborne during our wild ride.

"You don't think I was terrified?"

"You always look so calm, like you know exactly what you're doing."

"That's not true, Sherry. Sometimes I know exactly what to do, but lots of times I don't. I've been scared most of the way around the world. But I've found that most problems can be sorted out if I use my head and don't panic. If my first plan doesn't work, I try something else. So even if I feel scared, I don't let myself think scared or act scared because, if I let the fear take over, I'd freeze up and that would mean disaster. When the crisis is over I can look back on it and appreciate how scared I really was."

Sherry propped her chin in her hand, then looked me straight in the eye.

"I've been sailing around the world with you for almost two years and there are still times when I can't figure out what goes on inside your head. Probably never will. But that's what makes you interesting! Now let's get something to eat. I'm starving."

Chapter Twenty-Six

Like Sherry, I too was starving after our battle with the elements. But before we could jump ship and find a restaurant we had to pass through the customs and immigration formalities.

Two officials boarded *Baraka A* about a half hour later. We presented our papers, then waited for the immigration officer to purse his lips, frown and then ask the question we'd been expecting:

"Your wife does not have a visa for Gibraltar. Didn't you know that one was necessary?"

Sherry smiled, though I knew she was smouldering inside.

"During the month of July I applied for a visa to this country through the British Embassy in Cairo. I was given a form which I filled out. Then I was told to send a bank draft for £180 and the completed form to the immigration authorities here. I never got the visa or any refund of my £180."

The immigration official coughed politely.

"Do you have a receipt for the bank draft?"

Sherry's smile remained plastered across her face.

"Unfortunately no. It is with my papers back in Cairo. Is there a possibility that my visa might be at the immigration office?"

Again the official hid his face behind his fist while he cleared his throat. Clearly we'd lobbed an unfamiliar ball to his side of the court. But, in a flash, his British resilience surfaced, putting him back in charge.

"If it is convenient, please come to the immigration office tonight around 9 p.m. We'll get everything sorted out then."

"In the meantime can we go ashore and get something to eat?" I asked.

"That would be acceptable. Just don't get into any trouble."

As we watched customs and immigrations depart, Sherry poked me in the ribs with her elbow.

"What kind of trouble does everyone expect us to get into'?"

I shrugged.

"Brawling in the restaurant? Lobbing hand grenades around the harbour? I heard on the radio that the IRA has been letting off bombs here and three of the troublemakers were killed by the police just a few days ago."

"Jameel, be serious. We don't look the least bit Irish. Sometimes people wonder if we're Arab terrorists. I don't like it but it makes more sense than thinking we're linked to the IRA."

"Just kidding, Sherry. Maybe staying out of trouble means we're not supposed to hang the washing on the lifelines. Who knows?"

"Well, there's nothing to worry about then. I'm treating our clothes to a trip to the laundry."

We found a small restaurant right on the wharf and enjoyed a well-earned meal. As we enjoyed our after dinner coffee we wondered what would happen regarding the visa when we visited the immigration office that evening.

"One thing I can promise you," said Sherry. "I will not agree to leave here tomorrow morning, no matter what the threats or consequences."

"I doubt this is another Cagliari, but I agree – we can't leave. There is no place to go." I paused. "I suppose we could sail around in circles until the weather clears enough for us to make a run for Casablanca."

"You can't be serious," Sherry retorted, her eyes flashing.

She stopped for a moment then let a smile play across her lips.

"You're teasing me again and I always fall for it. Then I look at your eyes and they always give you away."

I held up my hand. "Guilty as charged."

According to Sherry, I was a master at keeping a straight face – thin-lipped and serious, but my eyes could never follow suit. Slit-eyed stares, dark brooding gazes were apparently beyond me.

Later, on our way back to the boat, we chanced upon a ship repair yard with a mechanic still on duty. My biggest worry continued to be the engine. We would not and could not set out for Casablanca until it was running perfectly. Was the problem dirty fuel as I suspected, or something more ominous and more expensive? Would the engine need replacement parts? Were they available? If not, how much time were we looking at? Visions of pound notes disappearing from my wallet as we lingered in Gibraltar kept intruding into my thoughts like a fly buzzing around the remains of a picnic. Whoever said that a boat is a hole in the water into which you throw money spoke the truth.

Sherry, who often accused me of worrying unnecessarily, was also concerned. She peppered me with questions as we walked back to the boat, which all boiled down to 'how much?'

After a day of incredibly bad luck, what could we expect but the worst? But the mechanic, after examining the engine, was full of good news.

"Just a clogged fuel strainer, sir," he said, showing me a piece of metal smaller than my thumbnail. "I'll clean it and replace the filter and you should be fine."

After the mechanic went back to his shop, we sat down with our repair list and listed the essentials. The broken shroud must be replaced and any other standing rigging that needed it, repaired. The roller furling, which had become stiff after almost two years at sea, needed a thorough going over. Also, as I had suspected for some time and had confirmed that day, the winches were inadequate and needed an upgrade. At the top of my wish list was a Loran C as a back-up for the SatNav. Unlike the SatNav, which picks up directional signals from an orbiting satellite, the Loran is a navigational instrument useful when cruising coastal waters where it picks up its signal from a land-based station. Perfect for the rest of our voyage to Casablanca and the return trip to Jeddah. But first the essentials, then, if funds permitted, the luxuries.

While we waited for our 9 p.m. appointment with customs, Sherry fixed coffee, which we hoped would keep us awake. I cast longing glances at my sleeping bag and pillow. We were tired beyond belief after our battle with the elements.

At the appointed hour we presented ourselves at the immigration office, trying hard to stifle our yawns. We were told to come back the next morning.

Dutifully we followed orders and reappeared the following morning. Sherry, they declared, didn't need a visa, She could go anywhere and do anything but again was admonished not 'to get into any trouble'.

"Don't worry, sir," I said. "I'll keep an eye on her. Make sure she doesn't get out of line."

Picking up my cue, Sherry stared at her feet.

"He always watches over me very carefully," she said. " I will be on my best behaviour while I'm a guest in your country."

We managed to keep straight faces until we were clear of the immigration office then let the waves of laughter consume us. Sherry wiped her eyes with the back of her hand.

"Seems like it should be me watching over you. You're the one who always gets into trouble."

Three days later all our repairs were completed, leaving enough money in my pocket to buy the Loran C. Sherry had spent those days cleaning the boat, like a whirling dervish, scrubbing, sorting and discarding. In a 31 foot boat we'd learned there was only room for the essentials. I completed my inspection of the rigging and pronounced it sound. Then I climbed the mast to check the mast head fittings and also to scrub the radar reflector and mast head light which were crusted with sand. I checked the batteries and filled them with water, filled the diesel tanks and jerry cans. Also I topped up our water.

We bought postcards and sent them off to friends and family and members of the press who might be interested that the voyage of *Baraka A* was almost finished.

"All the way around the world I've been mailing postcards telling people where we were and what we were doing," said Sherry. "I never thought the day would come when I'd be saying that we were less than 200 miles from the end. These are probably the last postcards I'll write. I don't know whether I'm happy or sad."

She paused.

"I wonder why completing a circumnavigation is called 'tying the knot'. Or is that something you dreamed up? Tying the knot usually means that you're getting married."

I sucked on my pipe and blew smoke into the clean air.

"Agreed. But think about it. When you get married, two people join together to become one. When you begin a circumnavigation, you leave a line trailing in the water. When you return, you find that line and tie the ends together so that they are connected, just like married people are connected."

Sherry laughed.
"A very complicated explanation for a simple phrase, but it fits."

Sherry's Journal, September 4th, Gibraltar

The boat is ready to go and so are we but the weather says no. Jameel called the weather office this morning. Wind is from the west, blowing Force 5. The sky has been overcast since early morning.

There is a cat here in the marina who comes to visit us, eats some food, then falls asleep in the cockpit. Reminds me how much I miss my cats.

I picked up the laundry today. It is clean but very wrinkled.

September 5th

Weather worse today. Force 7-9 in the Strait. Winds are from the east and sea is very rough. Barometer is high. We are planning to leave early tomorrow morning and take advantage of the easterly current. I hope the wind and sea calm down.

September 6

The alarm woke us up at 5 a.m. GMT. We could hear the wind blowing inside the marina. When Jameel checked the forecast with the weather office at 7 a.m. the news was not good. Force 7, perhaps increasing to Force 8 or 9. We cancelled our plans. We hope to leave when the sea and wind are moderate. Hope it's soon. We have only 200 pounds and 100 dollars left until we reach Casablanca. And we still have to pay our marina fee here.

As anxious as I was to leave Gibraltar and get on with it, I wanted our circumnavigation to end on a high note so that Sherry could take happy memories away with her. That would not be possible in Force 7-9 winds.

Also I had vivid memories of the last time I had sailed down the coast of West Africa on the never-to-be-forgotten Vilamoura, Portugal to Casablanca leg. The wind had nearly blown me out of the water. I shuddered when I thought of my lack of experience, the gear failure when the boom and mast had parted company, and the freighter looming over me in the night. Why had I, a novice in every sense of the word, arrived in Casablanca unscathed while bigger boats with experienced skippers had suffered substantial damage? Why had I survived when others had lost their lives? Beginner's luck? In part yes. I had been frightened half out of my wits but I had no benchmark against which to measure the storm. Maybe I thought it was par for the course, part and parcel of ocean sailing. Had this motivated me to put my fear on the back burner and just keep going?

From my perspective, the answer was a simple yes, and the lessons learned during that storm had stood me in good stead all the way around the world.

But, as always, I had to come back to *Baraka A* herself. The boat had brought me through the storm. My presence at the helm had been secondary.

No, we would not leave until the wind dropped to somewhere near normal. I hoped this would be soon. September 9th was Essam's birthday. Last year we'd called him from Shelburne Bay on the Great Barrier Reef with birthday wishes. This year we hoped to send him the same message from Casablanca and then tell him that we'd done it – tied the knot. A perfect way to end our journey.

I was impressed with the marine facilities in Gibraltar. The boatyards seemed to be busy and efficient. One day I asked about the possibility of hauling the boat and learned there was a long waiting list. *Baraka A* was badly in need of bottom scraping and repainting. Maybe I could arrange to have that done on the way back. Or perhaps Malta would be a better choice.

When I talked to my family yesterday they could not understand why I was 'wasting' money on expensive repairs when we were so close to the end.

"Yes, the end is very close," I agreed. "But the journey is not over. We have to sail the boat all the way back to Jeddah. And the first leg will be tough, beating into the wind until we enter the Med. If we take good care of the boat, she will take good care of us. Look what a good job she's done so far."

I took the mumbled reply as assent.

While the wind howled through the marina, Sherry spent some of her spare time reading up on Gibraltar and passing on snippets of information to me. I learned that the limestone cliffs rise from the sea to a height of 1480 feet and the Strait which separates the Rock from Africa is only fourteen and a half miles wide. But it wasn't until she started to tell me about the origin of the name Gibraltar that she really tweaked my interest. Originally it was known as Djeb el Tariq, or The Hill of Tariq, named after the Muslim leader by that name who had crossed the Strait from North Africa in 711 AD to begin the conquest of Spain. Over the years the Spanish and English had adapted and readapted the name. The final product is Gibraltar.

This short history lesson really got me thinking. Here I was, an Arab and a Muslim, anchored in a place named after another Arab and Muslim who'd sailed these waters thirteen hundred years before. Our agendas could not have been more different. For Tariq - the conquest of Spain. For me - some good weather and a peaceful journey to Casablanca.

Sherry's Journal, September 7

It was cloudy in the morning and blew hard. But this afternoon the wind died. The cat is now almost a family member. She stays with us night and day. I guess she likes the food. She is very sweet and loveable and I will miss her.

Though we are anxious to leave, our stay in this marina has been enjoyable. People are friendly and it is quiet at night although there are restaurants right here on the wharf. The wind was quiet all night. Maybe tomorrow?

Chapter Twenty-Seven

The morning of September 8, I called the marine weather office and, for the first time in days, heard some good news. The winds on the north side of the Strait would be light, on the south Force 5. Good enough. We sailed out of the harbour and hugged the Spanish coast until we reached Tarifa. As we turned south across the Strait, heading for Tangier, the wind picked up to 20 knots and the sea became rough.

Tangier, at the northernmost tip of Africa, greeted us with steep seas and frisky winds. Nothing we couldn't handle but, oh, how I wished for a gentle following breeze. We headed out into the Atlantic before setting our course south for Casablanca. A wise move to get offshore into deeper water as the winds dropped to 12 knots and the chop flattened out to a smooth roll. We were on our way!

That night neither of us slept much. Fulfilling my childhood dream of sailing around the world was no more a 'maybe' but just a few short miles of becoming a reality. We were too excited to sleep. And perhaps a little apprehensive that some unidentified thing might stop us during these final hours.

The sea had become flat calm, with huge rolling breakers which slowed our speed. *Baraka A* wallowed sluggishly as though she were expressing all our unsaid thoughts.

'Hey, guys, it's almost over, this journey of ours. I don't think I'm ready for it to end just yet.'

We could have put the boat on autopilot and passed this last night as we had all others. But somehow we both wanted to be in the cockpit with our hands on the tiller. This would be our last night at sea, just me and Sherry and *Baraka A* alone under the stars. We wanted to savour every last moment of it.

We motor sailed through the night with fishing boats, as always making sure we were well clear of them. We were mellow, happy and focused only on our objective.

Around 2 a.m. we encountered head winds of 11 knots. I wondered why the wind always blew straight in our faces, no matter what direction we were heading. At dawn the wind dropped to nothing. I cranked up the diesel to full throttle. We still had 80 miles to go to reach Casablanca.

We passed through patches of fog and mist suspended just inches above the water. Shivering, we dived for sweaters, then huddled in the cockpit. Even more disconcerting was our visibility, which was cut to less than half a mile. Fog was one element we had not encountered too many times during our circumnavigation. I was unfamiliar with it and feared the possibility of some vessel or obstruction looming out of the water in front of us. Above all, I hated feeling closed in. Fortunately the fog was intermittent. One moment we were surrounded by white swirling mist, the next we emerged into bright sunshine.

At 5 p.m. we sighted the buoy marking the entrance to Casablanca harbour. That day there were no straggling disabled vessels seeking shelter from a storm. Just us coming back to the beginning. Our journey had taken us one year, ten months and eleven days.

A customs boat came out to greet us as we motored down the channel. The crew stood on the deck with arms raised above their heads in a victory salute.

"Welcome back," they shouted. "Welcome home!"

I felt like laughing and crying at the same time. This was one day I would never forget. I was exhilarated that I had completed what I'd set out to do. But mingled with my joy was a bittersweet sadness. How much would I miss the life of a seafaring wanderer? I feared it would be a lot.

We tied to the customs dock and completed the formalities. I would not go to jail that evening, like I'd done on my first night in this port, but instead would sit with Sherry aboard *Baraka A* and revel in the good wishes showering down upon us. And later we would call Essam and wish him Happy Birthday.

I noticed a young man standing back from the others, waving and smiling. Could it be Mohammed, the young lad who had been so helpful and friendly during our first visit here, the one who'd stood on the point of land outside the harbour the day we left, waving at us until *Baraka A* disappeared over the horizon?

"When you come back, I'll be here," he'd promised.

This really made the circumnavigation complete, I thought as I jumped from the cockpit on to the pier and held out my hand in greeting.

"Hello Mohammed. We made it."

"Yes, Mr Jameel, you did."

***Baraka A* Log – September 9**

The circumnavigation is over. Now we will look at new horizons!

Sherry's Journal, Casablanca

It was a great feeling tying the knot in Casablança. We have been to many harbours but this one was very special for us. I remember the day I left the marina here at 6 a.m. on November 20th. I was so scared about the days ahead, so worried. Now my views about sailing and living on board a boat are so different. It is a beautiful lifestyle if you have the time and the experience and the money. I have so much more confidence today in the boat and in myself but there is still so much more to learn. The bad moments were only the spices that created the feeling of adventure and the great sense of accomplishment.

I do not ever regret joining Jameel in this fulfilling trip. I hope my sailing life will not cease. I do not want this to be the end. When I am old, I will remember our days aboard Baraka A. So many beautiful memories. Like they say, an old day is a good day.

Next time I dream of going around the world in a bigger boat and at a much slower pace, making it a way of living for at least 4 years. We could spend the hurricane season in Australia or New Zealand, spend a couple of years exploring the Pacific, a year in the Caribbean and Venezuela. I would love to see ALL the islands in the Marquesas.

On the morning of September 10, a representative from the Ministry of Youth came to interview us and then took us out to lunch. In the afternoon Reuters sent a photographer who took a lot of pictures. On the morning of the 12th we were scheduled to hold a press conference aboard *Baraka A*.

On the 11th, we decided to treat ourselves to a night in a hotel to make use of the shower facilities and the phone. I needed to double-check that my three cousins were still planning to join us here on the 12th to help me sail the boat back to Gibraltar.

During the press conference the following day one of the French journalists asked us our opinion of the harbour. I knew that ten miles to the north, at the city of Mohamadeya, there was a beautiful harbour, very clean with a sand beach and all the facilities; even a club with a good restaurant and a swimming pool. If the reporter was expecting me to slam the old harbour, he was destined to be disappointed. The new harbour had facilities but the old harbour had character, and characters, our favourite one being Mohammed. From this place we had set sail for a trip around the world. To this place we returned after a successful voyage. This particular marina would always hold a special place in our hearts.

Sherry's Journal, September 14, Casablanca

Well, all the festivities are over. We were the first Egyptian and the first Saudi to sail around the world in a 31 foot boat. Reality hit me in the face. Jameel's dream was no longer a dream but a fact. It all ended so quickly.

I am sure Jameel felt the same. A sense of loss filled the air between us. Baraka A *was our home for almost two years. We went places together. We lived through miserable storms and enjoyed the sunny weather together.*

When it was time for me to pack my bags and say goodbye, my heart ached with love and sorrow that I had to leave the boat behind. Tears filled my eyes as I jumped to the dock. While I flew to Cairo, Jameel and his cousins would sail the boat to Gibraltar. This was the first time, since the circumnavigation began, that Baraka A *would leave the dock without me on board.*

I would not store the food or fill the water tanks, check the fuel, or make sure everything was clean and tidy.

I was not only leaving our boat behind, but a whole lifestyle. It wasn't new to me any more but familiar. It was a life I had learned to live and enjoy all the way around the world. Now, back on land, what was I supposed to do now? I had no idea.

As we say in Arabic, 'You have to taste the sour to appreciate the sweet!' That's what life at sea taught me. Being uncomfortable for days in a small boat, working hard, sleeping less, surviving for weeks at sea and then finally the reward – landing on a beautiful atoll. The fruits were plentiful and the surroundings so picturesque. The beauty around made all the hard work worthwhile.

Sailing around the world taught me so many things, simple things. I learned to appreciate a hot meal, a cold drink, an island appearing on the horizon after weeks at sea: just ordinary things that we take for granted on land.

I know I should be happy that all the months at sea are finally over. But I don't feel very happy. Going back to live on land will be very hard. How will I explain this to my friends and family. Will they ever understand? I don't understand myself. I just keep wondering, 'What am I going to do now?'

Epilogue

Sherry reluctantly conceded that she was ready to leave the cramped confines of a 31 foot boat, and head home to Cairo. But in another sense, she yearned to stay on board. How could it be possible that their adventure was truly over?

When Jameel explained that the return journey to Gibraltar would be an uphill slog, into the wind all the way and that the Mediterranean was likely to be in an ugly mood this late in the year, she reluctantly agreed that it made sense to leave this leg to Jameel and his cousins. And so she gave *Baraka A* a final cleaning and made sure the galley was well stocked and then packed her bags. Jameel called his cousins who climbed aboard the next plane to Casablanca.

On September 16, *Baraka A* once again slipped from her mooring at Casablanca Harbour and headed out into the open ocean. And just like the first time, Mohammed stood on the shore waving farewell.

Boisterous winds and a heavy, lumpy sea combined with head winds, made for a rocky, soggy ride. The three cousins, who were unaccustomed to the rolling and pitching, and who scoffed at the idea of taking some of Sherry's Stugeron, were soon hanging over the rail, if they managed to get there in time. Looking back, Jameel described this leg as 'one of his worst ever'. Not that his cousins weren't charming, friendly chaps. In fact, a part of him had been looking forward to some days at sea 'with the guys'. But, he hadn't counted on his new crew not knowing a thing about sailing – so unlike his usual first mate who knew what to do without being asked.

"They were always in the wrong place, blocking the companionway or sitting on the sheets. And the weather was fierce. The interior of the boat was a mess of clutter and gear – no one, except myself, ever put anything away. With me on the tiller almost full-time and with no Sherry aboard to organise the meals, we were reduced to grabbing what was handy."

Jameel soon decided that the safest plan with his inexperienced crew was to tack out into the ocean and then head for Vilamoura, Portugal, where they would wait for the weather to clear.

The port authorities at Vilamoura gave this scruffy bunch a less than enthusiastic welcome. Four Arab males must be up to something and they were ordered to stay on board and to depart the next day. Later that evening, while sneaking off to town, Jameel thought back to all the harbours he and Sherry had visited. Only rarely had they encountered problems. On the contrary, they had been welcomed with warmth and enthusiasm at anchorages all around the world. He remembered too that one of the purposes of the circumnavigation had been to dispel the notion that Arabs were terrorists and they'd been successful - up till now.

The missing ingredient had to be Sherry! At her insistence, the boat would have been spotless and the crew, if not immaculate, at least presentable before they entered the harbour. And the authorities would have been charmed by her offers of coffee and friendship and intrigued by the story of an Arab man and his wife sailing around the world in a 31 foot boat.

They left Vilamoura the following morning, and headed through the Strait of Gibraltar into the Mediterranean. As Jameel predicted, the weather was foul with wind squalls howling from the cliffs, whipping the icy slate coloured water into waves as steep as mountains. His cousins stayed below overcome with nausea. When Jameel announced that they would call it quits in Gibraltar and continue the journey the following spring, not one dissenting voice was heard.

Jameel returned to Gibraltar the following June - alone. To his joy and gratitude, his friend and mentor, Roy Mullender, had said yes to an invitation to sail *Baraka A* back to Jeddah. Both men were eager to pick up the threads of their friendship while they sailed across the Mediterranean and down the Red Sea. But again, that capricious mistress of the seas was calling the shots. As they waited for the weather to clear they recalled another time and place - Plymouth harbour - when the raging rain and wind had kept them tied to the pier, day after cold and grey and numbing day.

Not this time, they vowed. Two experienced skippers, both of whom had crossed oceans and survived every kind of inclement weather, surely could handle anything. As they edged away from the pier, a raging sea slugged at the hull like a prize fighter defending his title. Once away from the safety of the harbour, the full force of the storm hit them. Screeching wind, scudding spray, reefed sails flogging the wind under a blanket of charcoal clouds forced them back to the safety of the harbour. That was the same day that President George Bush, who was conducting high level talks aboard a military vessel anchored near Malta cried 'enough' and retired to his bunk, wracked with seasickness. Just like Sherry had done so many times. Jameel and Roy wondered if Mr Bush had ever heard of Stugeron.

And so Jameel and Roy continued to wait in Gibraltar for the storms to disperse. On this occasion, it was Jameel who found himself in a time squeeze. His new diving shop in Jeddah needed his attention. Reluctantly, he and Roy called it quits. Jameel would return at a later date and pick up his boat.

The 'later date' turned out to be the following spring when Jameel, with just one cousin in tow, arrived back in Gibraltar. At last, the weather was co-operative, a sure plus with an inexperienced crew. Jameel set a course for the north shore of Africa where he picked up a favourable current which gave him a 2-3 knot boost. After passing through the canal, he stopped briefly in Suez City to drop off one cousin and pick up another. He also picked up some diving gear from the apartment in Cairo. If the weather stayed friendly, perhaps he'd get a chance to explore the reefs which dot the Red Sea. That had been his plan the first time he sailed these waters on the Jeddah to Suez City leg. But, like many other best laid plans, they had ended up in the scuppers. Keeping the boat upright and staying alive was all he'd been able to manage.

This time the weather remained postcard perfect. Maybe this was a reward for all the miles he'd sailed or for all the storms he'd survived. Jameel and his cousin sailed and drifted and explored the splendour of the coral reefs where they dived and swam with the beautiful, exotic fish. A real holiday and a perfect end to the voyage of *Baraka A*.

Today, Jameel and Sherry divide their time between Cairo and Jeddah. The *Arab Circumnavigator Dive Centre* continues to serve the needs of diving enthusiasts and is a thriving business.

Baraka A is moored in Obhur Creek in Jeddah. Jameel still dreams of another voyage. He says that his happiest days were spent aboard his boat.

"We did the trip too quickly," he admits. "How I wish we'd been able to find a place we loved and just stay for a week or a month, or however long we wanted and watch the world go by. Perhaps next time."

Or maybe next time he'll do it single-handed, which is an idea he keeps coming back to. In that case, Sherry says that she will fly out to join him when he reaches those islands in the Pacific which stole her heart and made her realise that there really is heaven here on earth.